Q
C
I
S

Terol McCullar (T-MAC)

Q
C
I
S

Terol McCullar (T-MAC)

ARPress
45 Dan Road Suite 5
Canton MA 02021

Hotline:1(888) 821-0229
Fax:1(508) 545-7580

Ordering Information:
Quantity sales. Special discounts are available on quantity purchases by corporations, associations, and others. For details, contact the publisher at the address above.

Printed in the United States of America.

ISBN-13:	Softcover	979-8-89330-997-3
	eBook	979-8-89330-998-0
	Hardback	979-8-89330-999-7

Library of Congress Control Number: 2024902560

To Tricia, Angela, and a long list of great friends

Richard walked slowly through Central Garden, gathering empathy from the many plants and trees that graced the paths and brook that entwined this retreat. The solar-emission cells produced the ultimate environment for the flora to grow to perfection. All the silent sounds filled the garden with the beautiful colors of a prism. Soft brown soil, giving way to gently swirling blue water that caressed each rock in the brook, gave complement to the tree implanted in an island in the brook. Atop the arch of the bridge, Richard paused and leaned on the rail with his forearms. His eyes focused on the deep luster of an apple on the tree. His face rolled into abysmal thought that nurtured his soul. The silence was ripped apart by his cool blue eyes resounding the energy generated within his mind. The apple seemed to scream with pain.

CHAPTER 1

The President: Accusation

"Ladies and gentlemen, the president of the United States," Press Secretary January Yee announced and then stepped back. Pale anticipation filled the auditorium as Tsirch crossed to the podium.

"Thank you, Mr. Yee."

With a long earnest look at the gathering, the president took a slow deep breath and began, "Good evening."

A chorus of voices responded, "Good evening, Mr. President."

"Members of the press... The floor is yours."

The lack of an opening statement took everyone by surprise. The first to gather any construction of thought was a woman, who quickly stood and was recognized.

"Ms. Walker, I believe you have the floor to yourself."

Glancing to either side, she half-smiled. "Thank you, Mr. President. Is it true that you have asked Vice President Natás for his resignation?"

The reply was reserved with a touch of regret, "Yes."

Puzzled by his lack of elaboration, she pursued further, "Can you give us the reason for this action?"

The inevitable arrived in Tsirch. He started his oratory slowly but became increasingly deliberate as he continued, "Yes, I can. According to my sources, Vice President Natás has, for the past seven weeks, been involved in a highly complex operation that could possibly undermine or destroy the very government he represents. This was to have been accomplished by overtly disarming the military, thus making it subject to attack by at least a dozen adversaries. The vice president has had monthly personal contact with military and scientific leaders in these nations. This is a blatant effort to combine their forces, while compromising certain military and scientific operations." The president nodded to the next querent.

Matt Shay took the floor, "Matt Shay, *Chicago Tribune*. Mr. President, you spoke of 'disarming.' Would that be nuclear or sol-laser disarmament, and how was that to have been accomplished?"

"The disarmament was to have been neither nuclear nor sol-laser. It was to have been accomplished by compromising our biochemical developments."

Cal Thompson's brow dropped and, having been given the nod, sought further explanation, "Cal Thompson, *Daily Wire*, Mr. President. *What* biochemical developments?"

Tsirch had expected this question for months, but now was not the time to answer it.

"For reasons of national security, I'll have to answer that by saying only that the developments in question are important to our world-defense program."

Everyone knew the next question. Jenny McRea stood and asked it, "Jenny McRea, CBS, Mr. President. Would these 'developments' be associated with biochemical warfare developments, which would tread on Resolution 612?"

The president had to handle this very carefully. He countered quickly with his usual uncanny sense of presence, "I feel the question is unfair as stated, Jenny. While any defensive development can be considered as a potentially offensive instrument, I don't feel that these developments should be construed as such, in light of our decades of peace. The World Court Resolution 612 is a beacon that directs this nation's purposeful conviction of world peace." Tsirch's rhetoric was successful.

Luis Avilla pressed for a new tact, "Luis Avilla, *Modesto Bee*, Mr. President, you mentioned sources. Will you disclose your sources of this information?"

"Yes, I will reveal one source at this time."

The expected reply of "sources close to" or "our intelligence-gathering sources have uncovered" was not to be. Anticipation rippled ominously through the audience.

"I received much of my information from a highly respected world leader, President Browning of England."

CHAPTER 2

VP: Response (Maybe)

Richard placed his hands, thumbs, and fingers in deliberate combination on the print lock. The door slid open. As he passed down a slope to the living room, a sensor activated, and the room flooded with light. He stopped at a table hanging in the center of the room. He leaned down to the table and touched one of the many sensor buttons. Out of a hole in a small box, the end of a cigarette appeared. He put the lit cigarette to his mouth and drew a modest breath.

Easily he sat on the sofa and leaned back, gently swaying with the subtle motion of the liquid within. The thought growing in his eyes was interrupted by the soft beep of the video communicator (COM). He reached again to the center table and touched the video sender (VS) button off, then touched the video receiver (VR) button. Instantly a cube on the table came alive in 3-D. A man was sitting at a table, awaiting a reply to his call. Richard smiled at the figure in the cube. He touched another button.

"Hello, Paul, I hoped you'd be the first to call." Richard's tone was almost happy.

"Richard?"

"Yes?"

"Turn on your VS so I can see you!"

"Are you alone?"

"Yeah, I'm alone." Paul's agitation grew. "Come on!"

Richard reached for the console and thought about scanning Paul's house but passed over the security scan button and touched the VS button so his trustworthy friend could see him.

"How's that, Paul?" he stated as he touched the DS lock to prevent scanning.

"That's better," Paul said in a less-anxious manner. "Richard, you really enjoy your electronic fortress, don't you?" Richard only smiled. Paul peered into Richard's face for a moment, then continued. "Richard, you're incredible."

Richard shrugged his shoulders a little and quipped, "What else is new?" He crushed out the cigarette.

Paul shook his head. "Ah, come on, Richard. You've got to be falling apart inside, but there's not a trace of a fracture on the outside."

"Not true, Paul, both sides are stable."

"Sure, and the pope's a woman. You'd have to be insane not to be worried."

"Maybe so, but I'm not worried but rather deeply concerned that some of my work may have to be redone, and I'm running short of time." A brush of thought lowered Richard's brow. "Now that I think of it…" Richard paused for more thought. "There are two things that do cause somewhat more than concern." He stared pensively at Paul. "Paul, can I call you later?" he said, reaching for the console.

"Hold on, Richard," Paul said quickly. "We have to discuss your statement."

"Paul, I don't need to make a statement now!"

"Like hell you don't," Paul served. "You have to say something, or you and a lot of others may take longer steps on your already-shortened pier."

Richard returned his serve, "Well, Paul, what would YOU have me say?" Paul's volley was sent in earnest.

"How about the TRUTH?"

Richard's thoughts reflected his standing among his constituents and fellow politicians and has always been known to tell the truth, but reality has known him to tell the truth but not the WHOLE truth. Richard came to the net with his own volley.

"The TRUTH is, Paul, that I don't know the truth, and if it were known, probably no one could handle the truth. I am just now beginning to find that some things I thought were true may not be true. That, my friend, is the truth." It was a passing shot.

Paul lost his serve in confusion. "Richard, what the hell are you talking about? What may not be true?"

Richard knew Paul could handle the whole truth, but he wouldn't want to be responsible as its keeper. He served this time.

"Okay, Paul. You tell the press the truth as YOU know it."

Paul was given a chance to hit a winner but suddenly decided the game was over. His tone was desperate. "Richard, if I tell what I know...I mean, I wouldn't know where to start or even how to explain what I know without everyone going down in flames, even though in my mind, there has been no wrong done."

Richard leaned forward on the sofa, placed his forearms on his knees, and lightly clasped his hands. A knowing half-smile filled his face.

"Now you know where I'm at, Paul, and why I'm glad you're a friend that I can trust."

Paul gathered his composure again. "Richard, don't try to sweet talk me. I know where we stand."

But do you? Richard thought to himself. He wasn't sure HE knew.

"All right, Paul. You play press secretary for me and issue the standard 'categorical denial of the charges,' 'to the best of my rec-ollection,' or 'I haven't had time to assimilate the information,' and throw in a few 'no comments' and finish with a 'no further state-ments at this time' for me."

"Okay, Dickie." His spirit was returning. "I know you're not going to tell me anything now, but sooner or later—"

"Later, Paul," Richard interrupted. "Much later."

"Richard, let me know before the iceman cometh so I can catch the slow shuttle to Alpha Centauri A."

"Paul...thanks for understanding."

"Richard...I'm not sure I do."

Paul disappeared from the cube. Richard reached toward the table and, ignoring the communication waiting light flashing, placed his hand/digit combination on a print lock. A soft computer voice broke the silence.

"Voice recognition code?" it asked.

"Zero, two, nine, twenty," Richard said clearly.

"Code accepted. Voice recognition."

"Richard Natás."

"Recognized. Communication mode?"

"Digital," Richard replied.

"Run program," the computer stated.

Richard's fingers were busy on the computer keyboard. His eyes read the screen that effected no change of expression, and continued his work.

"End digital program," Richard said, as his fingers left the keyboard.

"Ending communication code?" the voice asked.

"Two, seventy, four, nine, Richard A. Natás." Richard paused a moment.

The light still flashing on the console caught his eye. He touched the VS off, the DS Lock, and the VR on. The cube again was activated. The figure shown was a woman in business attire. After admiring her for a few seconds, Richard touched a button and spoke.

"Ms. Walker, I'm beginning to understand how you are always one of the first journalists to get a story."

Obviously startled, but only momentarily, she cleared her throat and replied, "Oh! Mr. Vice President?"

"Yes, Ms. Walker?"

"I'm sorry, Mr. Vice President, but this is a first for me, to get through without going through the Auto-answer. Actually I didn't expect you to be in your office."

"Actually I'm not in my office. I'm at home."

"You're having your calls forwarded from your office to your home? Aren't you concerned that someone's call locator will record your number?"

"I preselected your call code to be forwarded here. Anyway with all the electronic wizardry available, it's not difficult to get ANY number, and…if you'll look in your directory, you'll find my home number has been placed there already."

She checked her directory, "I don't see it, Mr. Vice President."

"Look under your code name for me."

She was inundated by his request and, mumbling to herself, did as he asked.

"How did you know what my code name for you was?"

"I have my sources," he bantered.

"When did you put your number in my directory, and why?"

"Late last night, and because you'll probably be needing it?" he countered.

She digested that statement. "While I feel very honored, I don't understand—"

"Ms. Walker," he interrupted. "If you will permit me some latitude, I shall tell you the reason for having been selected, to what end, and…" He touched the DS Lock and VS buttons. "I want you to see me while I tell you."

She was surprised at his appearance on her video cube.

"Thank you, Mr. Vice President."

"Ms. Walker, I've read many of your bylines, interviews, and stories, and I've found that you are one of the few journalists who doesn't need to editorialize to make a story work. You seem to see the heart of an issue and present both sides without weighing subjective morality but with an eye more to truth and justice."

She cracked a half-smile. "Being a member of the Bar, I feel I should wave the flag."

Richard's returned half-smile slowly faded. He reached to the console and touched a few buttons.

"Ms. Walker, is your residence prepared for a level 3 security scan?" Total shock came upon her face. Richard saw her reaction and quickly continued, "There's no cause for alarm. This conversation will not approach level 3, but I like to have a wide margin for safety. So is it okay?"

She regained her composure. "Well, uh, of course."

"Thank you." Richard touched more buttons, then went to the keyboard of his computer and busied his fingers for a long moment.

He watched the display intently. As she watched him with interest, the words "Scramble COM Level 3" appeared on her cube, and then it suddenly went dark. She became curious, and momentarily her cube lit up again. Richard looked up from his display and spoke.

"Could you put your pet outdoors during the rest of our conversation? And as you do, could you close all inside and outside doors, windows, and turn on all viewers? When you put your pet out, could you step outside also, count to ten, and then you can come back in."

Puzzled, she proceeded to do as he had asked. During these activities, Richard continued to watch the display and answered prompts on the keyboard. She returned and sat down to a dark cube. She waited anxiously. Richard reappeared, but a message also appeared.

> Remove light emitters from: main bedroom ceiling; connecting bath on mirror; living room—right of fireplace; video communication room—lamp to your left; and all emitters in storage shelf in pantry. Place these in your disposal unit.

She stared at the words for a second, stood up, and did as directed. "Things are getting bizarre," she mumbled to herself as the last emitter was placed in the disposal unit. She engaged the disposal cycle that caused a hum that was interrupted by several jolts within the unit. She gave a second look at the unit and went back to the COM-room and sat down to yet another dark cube. It came back on. More words appeared. "Jesus Chr—" She sighed.

"Under the base of video cube, remove second right front screw with slot-head screw driver."

She got up, left the room, and returned with a screwdriver and removed the screw. She looked at the cube and read the message asking her to place the contents of her purse on the table. She picked up her purse off the floor and emptied it and spread the items out on the table.

"Hold up set of keys to the cube," the message prompted.

She held them up with a quizzical expression on her face.

"Remove rabbit's foot and dispose of it and the screw."

Chuckling, she removed the good-luck charm, went to the disposal, and returned.

There were no words on the cube, and she pretended disappointment.

"Thank you, Ms. Walker," Richard announced.

"Are you quite through?" she said with some disgust.

"Actually…" As he paused in his speech, she made a motion to rise but stopped her movement as his statement continued. "Yes and no. Your 4201 computer should not be used to process or store any sensitive information. When was the last time you sprayed for bugs?"

"Bugs, Mr.—you mean those items were bugged?" She became anxious.

"Someone wants to know more about you, Ms. Walker."

She squirmed in animated thought and stammered, "Well, who would…why would…how could…"

"Spoken like a true journalist," Richard quipped. "Don't be surprised, you probably purchased those items yourself," he added.

"Yes…except the rabbit's foot. It was given to me by…" She grew angry. "Well, that ss—you mean those bugs are planted in retail items and are bought by Jane Q. Conservative so they can be spied upon by who knows who?" She glared at Richard. "YOU know who, Mr. Vice President!" she demanded in subsiding anger.

"Really, Ms. Walker? That's an interesting theory that you should explore in the near future. It is possible that these items were replaced with replicas by someone you know or that you gave access to your house." The numbers 112019474261944 appeared on her cube. "By the way, these numbers appearing on your cube, if entered prior to and after a communication will make it less susceptible to listening devices, unless the WJC override code is implemented."

"Of course, the Justice Court can override almost everything, but why tell ME these things?" she queried as she wrote them down.

"My computer has cleared you, and even more to the point, I feel comfortable with you. So let me give you an overview of what I have in mind, and then we'll decide IF there will be or what will be the next step." Richard leaned back on the sofa to get more comfortable. She also relaxed her posture. "What I am about to relate to you is not exclusive information. In fact, it is common knowledge among many people. The interesting point is that no one person has all the information, and all the parties involved are withholding other key bits of information as their own little secret. Not to sound semiomniscient, but as far as I know, I alone am about to obtain all the information the others have as a collective whole. I will soon be put to task to collate this information in the sequence that will reveal certain truths or untruths. That which I choose to share with you, Ms. Walker, will be the truth, but probably not the whole truth."

She leaned back in her chair with a notebook in her hand.

She was wrestling with several questions in her mind. "Mr. Vice President, I'm not quite sure I understand where all this rhetoric is leading. I would think that if you wanted to report something to the people, you would utilize your press secretary.

"If you'll give me some latitude, counselor, I shall apprise you of the direction and nature of my oratory and any possible promulgation."

"You have my attention. I'll just be a good little journalist and take notes," she said in jestful condescension while waving her notebook. Richard got up and began to walk toward the bar.

"Au contraire, I wish exchange, reaction, and interaction with you," he retorted with deliberate gestures. He poured himself a glass of iced tea. She started to speak, but she was cut off.

"Would you like me to wait while you get yourself something?" he asked, holding up his glass. She shook her head and started to speak, and again he spoke first, "Walker!" He paused as he came back and stood at the end of the sofa. "Have you ever taken a walk in the forest?

She was surprised at the question. She hesitated her answer. "Yes."

"How do you feel about the forest?"

"It's beautiful, relaxing, peaceful—"

"Now before you ever walked in the forest, how did you feel about it?"

She was puzzled. "I didn't have a feeling for it, I only had impressions from what I'd read, seen in video, or had been told about it."

"How did your impressions compare to your actual presence in the forest?"

"There was no real comparison. My prior impressions of the forest didn't do it justice. I guess, you had to be there."

"If you were to have written about the forest prior to your visit there, could you have done it justice?"

"First of all, I wouldn't have written about something that I didn't know about, but to answer your question, no, I couldn't have done it justice."

"And if you had lived there?"

"I would have had an in-depth story about an intimate relationship with my environment."

"And that would be the better story?"

"The best possible story," she affirmed.

"Perhaps," he said, walking back to the sofa. He sat as he continued, "But you may be so caught up in the real inside story that you might fail to establish a rapport with those who have never walked in the forest. You might not relate the excitement, the anticipation, the anxiety of that first walk."

She added in a knowing voice, "So you want me to write about my first walk."

"More than that, Walker, I want you to write about each step so that even those who have taken those steps before can feel them again." He leaned up on the sofa and grew serious in his face and his voice softly earnest. "Your first walk, yes, but if we're not careful… we may not get the chance to take another." She felt fear within from this ominous statement, but his voice seemed to ease her fear, as though he was in control.

"Mr. Vice President," she said, rising, "I'd like to write this story." She walked around behind the chair and continued, "But as an officer of the court, IF I found a conflict of interest, that would take priority over my being a journalist."

Richard smiled and eased back on his sofa.

"I'm aware of your dual professionalism, that's another reason I selected you. In your desk drawer, you will find a modest retainer as my legal counsel. You merely have to negotiate the draft to accept the position. Thus any conflict of interest will be nullified, as anything I tell you will be privileged communication. However, Ms. Walker, I want to make this clear. IF you discover anything actionable, you may pursue a legal course of action."

"Do I have your word on that?"

Richard smiled, almost to a grin, and leaned toward the cube. "Trust me."

It was her turn to grin. "The first time I heard that was at a midnight picnic for two on a beach under soft moonlight."

"I trust, Ms. Walker, that was not the last time you heard those words."

She reflected for a moment. Richard watched her eyes intently.

Returning to reality, she retorted, "No, but it was the last time I believed them."

"Surely." He smiled. Richard settled back in his chair. "I would like to meet with you, after you've had time to consider my offer, okay?"

"Sure, I'd like that."

"Good." He busied himself with the keyboard, looking at the display. "How about Thursday, after 8:30 a.m. for breakfast? Will you be available?"

"If I'm not, I will be."

"Good, then I'll see you here."

"There, at your residence?" She was surprised.

"Of course!"

"Yes…of course," she repeated, as she became somewhat numb.

"Until then, Ms. Walker."

"Until then, Mr. Vice President." The cubes were again in darkness.

CHAPTER 3

Sal v. 'Gemo

Among his many other talents, Sal was probably the foremost biochemist in the world. He had been known to study at twenty-two different world-renowned institutions of learning, and probably more. It was hard to tell exactly how many, as he always used a different name to maintain his anonymity. The curious thing was that he had never bothered to graduate or apply for any degrees, though he had forty-two honorary degrees bestowed upon him. This eccentricity compliments his dislike for being called "Doctor" Uschin. He also had the distinction of having held more than a hundred jobs since he reappeared fifteen years ago, much in the style of his mentor Dr. 'Gemo. Sal's work for the moment was focused on certain biochemical reactions and combinations that would be a challenge for even the legendary Dr. 'Gemo to comprehend. Sal had studied with 'Gemo in New York and was probably the last one to see him before 'Gemo disappeared. Some say 'Gemo is still alive. That opinion is due to some miraculous breakthroughs, almost overnight, in biochemistry, genetics, and physics, occurring in various parts of the world thought to have been 'Gemo's work. Still, it wasn't the first time 'Gemo had disappeared. A child prodigy at six, he disliked the structure in his life. At the age of thirteen, he disappeared. On New Year's Eve, seven years later, he knocked on the door of the Oval Office and asked the president if he could use his VC to call his parents. No one yet knows how he slipped through security. He rarely gave specifics of his activities during his periods of absence.

Others likened 'Gemo's disappearance to that of President Marsh in the late '30s, who failed to show up at his successor's inauguration. He had breakfast with his family and left for his morning walk, and that was the last time he was seen. He served his two terms, wholeheartedly endorsed his capable vice president, and vanished. Since then he has been the victim of many a punch line to jokes, but history shows he was effective and popular.

Sal was well versed in most every subject and enjoyed exchanging ideas and asking questions. One important trait of Sal's is that he listens to what the person says. Some say he can look into your eyes and see you form the words. This, of course, he says, is ridiculous.

*****

Lights flashed at both ends of the lab, and a soft tone sounded twice. Sal walked toward one of the lights and slapped lightly at a sensor.

"If you're not Richard, Pete, or Johnny, you've got the wrong number," Sal quipped as he continued working.

"Sal, I'll never know how you do it." The voice was decidedly feminine.

"It's simple, Johnny, they're the only names I can remember, and screening calling codes helps. Besides, you are the only ones that get hungry when I do. And…yes. I'd love to have a bite with you."

"Great," she said. "Two o'clock, Makos."

"Yeah, yeah," he said, acting annoyed without breaking his routine. "Oh, and, Johnny…wear that see-through thing… I need the diversion. 'All work and no play…'"

"Well, I'll see if I have something NOT to wear for you. *Bye…*" she finished with a tease.

Sal took three test tubes from the centrifuge. "Damn!" he muttered, as he looked at one tube. He looked at the other two and had no reaction. He placed the one in the auto disposal, and the other two he placed in the cool-vac chamber. He set the displays to -100°C and 24 ATM. He walked over to a glass door and pushed a button. He waited for the sound of pressurization to stop. He opened the door, stepped in, and closed the door. He pushed another button, and the room depressurized. When it stopped, he opened the door, stepped out, and closed the door. He carefully took off his positive-pressure bio-suit. He grabbed his coat and went to a chart on the wall and picked up an odd-sized pencil. He entered some notations on the chart. He turned and stepped over to another chamber. He peered in through a glass door and said to himself, "Getting close, Richard, getting close."

CHAPTER 4

Johnny and Sal

Congresswoman Johnny Walsh, 91-55-86, all that and brains too! She left her mark on the modeling world and on many unknown hearts. She somehow slipped through those years with only a few scars on her own heart. She always knew who she was and who she could be, and that was anything she wanted, she knew all the right people. She was a throwback from her grandmother's era yet touched with the women's lib movement of the 1970s of her great-great-grandmother. It seems that in their ongoing fight for equality, they won more than they expected. The by-product of equality had a confusing effect on both male and female sexuality. Women complained about being treated as sex objects and not as equals.

When major advancements in their causes were made, sexuality became less a factor in the business and domestic world. Sexuality was placed properly as being a special and personal expression. As a result, expression of sexuality became more difficult for the many that didn't understand the rules, rules that were never put in writing. Those who were still being treated as sex objects became even more ashamed to speak out because they thought it was their own fault. Grandma Walsh changed all of that and took sexuality "out of the closet" with her now-famous quote: "Sexuality should not be used or abused it should be expressed." In her own way, Johnny restated that slogan by climbing to the top of the world of glamour and walking away for a career in high finance and politics.

To look at Washington, it hadn't changed much in the last one hundred years, except for building and land restructuring and modifications made by the Department of Energy and Resources Conservation. The ERC, much of its importance now gone due to energy production advances, is still added to the budget each year with a $500-million grant, over the efforts of the People's Representation Association to delete it.

Under the Silicrete, concrete, asphalt, steel, and neosteel that supports this political capital is a modest network of subtransportation. Some of the system utilized refitted tracks and rails of earlier subways. The majority of the system was built to accommodate state-of-the-art low friction, energy efficient, solar/chemical powered air-cushioned cars. The SAC System, an acronym of SOL-AIR-CHEM, is much safer than the atomic-waste-powered system it replaced. With all the great technological advances, the wheel is still the greatest discovery in transportation, except for walking.

Johnny walked up the SAC stairway to the street above. With only ten blocks to Makos, she hadn't even thought of hailing a cab; walking was wonderful for someone who couldn't twenty years ago. As Sal was paying his driver, he saw Johnny, smiling as she approached from around the corner. He wrapped his arms around her, and they held each other longer than a hello, and the kiss also said more.

"Sal, I'm so happy to see you," she said exuberantly.

"No happier than I am to see you," he said with a big smile. Arm in arm, they bounced through the doorway into the restaurant. At the dining room entrance, the maître d' noticed his guests.

"Ms. Walsh...Doctor, uh—" He stopped in midsentence, then continued with a smirk on his face. "Sal, forgiven?" he begged.

Sal smiled and nodded.

The host clasped his hands and, with a smile, said, "It's wonderful to see you both."

"Jack, you know this is our favorite institution, and you are our favorite keeper!" Sal quipped.

Pretending to act gracious, Jack answered, "Sal, you're always so kind."

He led them to a table, seated them, and waved his hand to summon a waiter.

"Again, Ms. Walsh, it is nice to see you BOTH."

His head ticked to indicate Sal also.

"Enjoy your meal."

As Jack started to leave, Sal touched his elbow to stop him.

"Do you have female crabs, today?"

"I beg your pardon?" Jack said, acting appalled and smiling.

"Your female crabs…how are they?"

Jack smiled for an instant, then said with a straight face, "They'll do in a pinch." He left.

"Sal, you're terrible," Johnny said, laughing.

"Yeah, I know, but let me show you how terrible." He started to reach for her across the table.

She held her hands up to stop him and said softly, "I remember it well."

He smiled and paused in thought. He said dramatically, "Yeah, so do I."

Sal was enjoyably gazing at her dress that let his imagination run all over it.

His thoughts were broken by the waiter's voice.

"Cocktails?"

Johnny held up her hand and passed.

Sal said, "Thank you, no. We would like to order now."

"Yes, sir, of course, and what would you have?"

"Two, uh…" He looked at Johnny, holding her breath with a soft grimace. "Crabs," he finished. She released her breath in relief.

The waiter nodded. "Two crab dinners, and may I suggest a Rougeux '89 with your meal?"

Sal suggested, "How about your best rosé?"

The waiter slightly lifted one eyebrow.

"Of course. Beverage now, sir?" he added.

"Hot tea?" he asked, looking to Johnny for approval and getting it.

"Yes, two," Sal added,

The waiter said, "Thank you, sir," and addressing Johnny, "Madam." He left.

"I'm really glad you could make it," she said, grabbing his hand.

"So am I," he said.

"But you've never left a project before to socialize."

"I got a couple of major breaks. And I have some cultures in cooldown, and that takes a couple of hours. Besides, I've began to reorganize my priorities in the last few weeks." He became more serious.

She began to offer her thoughts, "I trust your insight and ability, but the timing of this restructuring, that causes some concern. This project, your work, it means so much to so many. Richard has the highest regard—"

"Whoa! Hold it. Hold it. The new priorities are a result of my work. I realize the importance of the project. But I am not the only one on the project nor am I the only one capable of doing the job." Sal's tone was calm and deliberate. "A number of qualified researchers, within shouting distance of this establishment, would be glad to be a part of this."

"You forgot to add some things," she interjected. "You were selected not only because of your ability but also because of your character and the trust that it begets. Qualities, all of which, I personally perceive as unsurpassed," she ended with a purr in her voice.

"Well, not to worry. The new priorities won't go into full effect until the project is finished or it's too late."

He paused in thought. "And in the latter case, my priorities wouldn't matter." He became lighter in spirit. "So I decided to ease into the change, today, now."

The waiter brought their tea and left.

"Okay, Johnny. Why did you drag me here? If you wanted my body we could have—"

She grabbed his hand.

"First things first."

She took a sip of tea. Sal took the cue.

"I'm meeting with a few diplomats and scientists, and I want to be up to date. I don't want to cross any wires. Their sources may know more than I do. I want to know what I can and can't say."

Sal settled back in his chair. "First of all, if their sources are accurate and up to date, they will at least know the general status on a daily basis."

"You have a leak?" she urged.

He smiled. "More like a fountain of knowledge."

She was curious, and he knew it.

He continued, "Lucas."

"Lucas!" she said in total shock.

Sal smiled and shook his head. "No, now it's not really what you think."

"I hope not. Lucas is Richard's right hand."

"That's exactly why Richard chose Lucas to keep Ren Lang abreast of everything he is doing."

Sal took another sip.

She sat in thought for a moment. "Actually I guess there's no reason for Ren Lang not to know what's going on. He's the one who sees all this as some nefarious scheme."

Sal silently nodded and said, "It's a shame that political differences have come between them. They actually are good friends."

"Tsirch seems to have developed a jealousy of the public's continued support and favor of Richard," she noted, sipping from her cup.

Sal took his turn, "Actually Richard's charisma is a point of Tsirch's admiration for Richard, not jealousy. I honestly feel that Tsirch is getting caught up in what he sees a president should be, and working toward that, not being the person he is and that the people elected."

"I can understand that," she said. "He hasn't let the power of the position go to his head, but rather the position itself is sapping his identity.

"That, my dear Johnny, was a very apt summation. God, you're intelligent." Sal smiled and cocked his head in admiration.

"Save the bullshit for later," she countered his thinly veiled humor and continued, "So now, give me some more intelligence." Sal didn't follow. She noticed and feigned aggravation. "The research?"

"Oh, the research."

The waiter came with their serving cart. He placed their meal on the table in a precise manner. He showed the bottle of wine to Johnny, then to Sal. Both gave a token nod. He then poured a sample into both glasses.

Johnny noticed the waiter was waiting.

"Oh, I'm sure it's excellent. Thank you," she said to the waiter.

He replied, "Of course. Thank you." And he left.

Johnny perused the food. "Looks good. Food will always be better than supplements."

She noticed there was no answer from Sal. She looked up to see him in thought.

"Sal...the food," she drew him back.

"Yes, it looks real good. Sorry, just drifted a moment. Anyway now as to your intelligence." Sal picked up his napkin.

"*Yes?*" she catted, her chin leaning on her palm, anticipating a need to retaliate. Sal noticed she was ready for any foray.

He smiled in thought. The temptation passed.

"Actually we are in a unique, if not precarious, circumstance."

"How so?" Johnny began to set up her meal.

"Running tests, trying not to find something. I'm sure you understand what we have to do. We have to duplicate a biochemical substance, a composition of which we can only guess."

Johnny began to eat.

Sal continued, getting excited, "Then we must combine it with every culture combination imaginable to find it's mutation characteristics. Create something to neutralize it, if possible, and then search the Earth and moon to find it. Do you realize..." He finally looked at Johnny. She paused midbite and looked at him understandingly, reached out, and placed her hand on his.

"I'm doing it again." He sighed.

"Sal, it's not a sin to be involved in your work."

"How about obsessed."

"Dedicated," she countered.

"Semantics. Not as bad as I used to be." He began to eat.

"Sal, how are the others holding up? It's been three months."

"Well, two six-hour shifts, that ends up twelve hours straight. Three people per shift, except for Susan. She's there when I'm there, and that's most of the time."

He paused in thought. "You know, I'm lucky to have her on this project. For that matter, I'm lucky to have found all of them. They're all superqualified, dedicated, and trustworthy."

"Having been your students didn't hurt," she added.

"Only three! The others came from Susan, Makiev, and Richard."

"Ah…the plot thickens," she said dramatically.

"Enough of pleasure, now let's get down to business. After dinner, I'll take an extra half hour." He looked at his watch and continued, "Then how about you and I—"

She retorted, "Only a half hour! You could never change that much and…" she said softly, reaching for his hand. "I hope you don't."

As they left the dining room, Sal approached Jack and leaned to his ear, as he pretended choking, he said, "Your crabs go down sideways."

He leaned away, looked around, leaned back, pinched Jack in the ribs, and said, "I still love you."

Jack, in his own pretense, stuck his nose in the air and said, "Trollop!"

Johnny and Sal bounced out arm in arm, laughing.

Secrets?

Tsirch leaned back in his swivel chair, his brows sagged in thought. He looked out over the city that had been his home for more than three years as the president. They had been good years, productive and meaningful years, that any president would be afraid to dream about, lest he awakened to find it was indeed only a dream. Now Tsirch had to deal with a reality he would rather be a dream. The COM light broke his thought. He touched a pad.

"Yes, Philip."

"Sir, I have Paul Le Cross and President Browning calling."

"Ask Paul if I can return his call, then put Browning through Code 1."

"Yes, sir."

Tsirch gathered some papers on his desk, placed them in a pile in front of him, and turned to read the display on his desk. The call light flashed, and Tsirch touched the COM on, and the cube lit up. Seeing Browning was alone, Tsirch engaged the VS.

"Mr. Browning. Good to see you," he stated.

"Ah, Mr. Ren Lang. It's good to see you also. Your statement this afternoon was also rather eye-opening." His accent was typical English.

"Much to your credit, Mr. President," Tsirch returned.

"Had I known it was to be so revealing, I would have prepared a complimentary statement."

"You're referring to my disclosure of you as a source?"

"The disclosure was secondary. My surprise was that the conference was so sudden."

The COM viewer followed Tsirch as he rose and went to the wet bar.

"Nevertheless, I must apologize for not notifying you of the content. Although I did preselect what I could say, I didn't know what questions would be asked."

"Yes, it could have gotten a bit sticky."

"I did try to reach you just before I went on, but your wife said you were in transit," Tsirch added.

"Vicki told me you rang, but I only had time to sit with a spot of tea and catch your performance on the viddy."

Tsirch poured a finger of red wine. "Yet, Carl, I do apologize."

"Not necessary, Tsirch. I understand the situation."

He returned to his desk. "Carl, do you have any more information?"

Carl leaned on his desk. "Only a tad. It seems that Mark Narkiewicz has been recruited by Richard—"

"Narkiewicz," Tsirch interrupted. "Another biochemical genius?"

"Genius…he prefers to be referred to as inspired, but he's definitely not a biochemist."

Tsirch paused in thought. "Narkiewicz…Oh yes, a military-tactics expert."

Carl was smiling. "Right…and wrong, ole boy. His work encompasses communications."

"Communications…" Tsirch paused again. "Bugging? Surveillance?"

"Nothing so nefarious. His studies have been almost exclusively in space communications."

Tsirch was puzzled. "What new venture is Richard into now?"

"I'm afraid it's not new. He was doing research for Richard even before the biochemical push."

Tsirch was silent. He was searching his mind for something to fear or a connection somewhere. He needed to know more. "What did he have to say?"

"Actually he isn't my source. It's his brother, Edward."

The connection flashed in Tsirch's mind. "Colonel Edward Narkiewicz. My recall hasn't failed me. He's the military tactical containment expert under Admiral Scott during the Lunar Fall."

"Yes, he did the work. Scott took the credit."

"Now I see, Richard is trying to get to Edward through Mark. Doesn't Edward work with your scientists?"

Carl nodded. "Going on fifteen years, with top security clearance. He rarely sees his brother. I only found out in a passing conversation when Edward used my cube to call home. His father had had an accident, and he found that Mark had called from Berlin. Mark was with Peter Simmons, Richard's left hand."

The mental connection was broken.

"Could Edward give you anything else?" Tsirch interrupted himself quickly. "Wait...how is their father?"

"Oh, his injuries were minor."

"Good. I'm glad."

Carl settled back into his chair.

"I made casual inquiries, but it's a dead end. He barely knows who Peter Simmons is."

"It may be worth watching," Tsirch said. "Blood is yet thicker than water."

"It probably isn't necessary, but I am monitoring the situation as Edward is a storehouse of military knowledge."

"If you need any help, Carl, let me know."

"Will do. I'll ring you next week."

"Good, Carl, thank you. Kiss Vicki and the children for Trish and me."

"Righto, Tsirch."

The cube went blank. Tsirch touched on the intercom.

"Philip, did Paul leave a number?"

"Yes, and he said to get back to him when you were finished."

"Give me about five minutes, okay?"

"Yes, sir."

Tsirch sipped more wine, turned to the display, and began to feed information into it. He read carefully and fed more information into it and read again. He leaned back in his chair in deep thought. There had to be a connection. Anything Richard did had an end in view. The information related that Narkiewicz's work had involved Maser, Laser, Pulsar, SOL Laser, and Multi-Modal/Directional Signal research. The latter was his latest brainchild. It also showed a growing interest in time relativity and theory. Tsirch could only guess that the research he was doing for Richard had to do with MMD signal and time research. But how that was related to biochemical research was what he needed to know.

He buzzed Philip. "Philip. Get a hold of Sol-Chem and have them get me an update on MMD signal research and any relationship to time relativity and theory and the communications field, okay?"

"Yes, sir. Paul Le Cross is on the line," he added.

"Thank you, Philip." Tsirch engaged the COM.

Paul appeared on the cube.

"Paul, sorry about the wait."

"That's all right, Mr. President. At this point, its par for the course."

"Richard keeping you guessing?" Tsirch said, rising.

"Me and everyone else."

Tsirch secretly agreed. "Well, Paul, which questions can I answer for you?"

"One that wasn't asked today, one that your press secretary didn't have an answer for."

"What is that, Paul?"

"How will this affect the primary elections? April is only two weeks away."

"Leave it to you to ask the hard ones."

He paused and swirled the wine in his glass.

"The obvious answer would be that since I've asked for Richard's resignation, I would not endorse him for the VP spot. The question seems moot to me." Tsirch was confident and controlled.

"I would have thought so, too, Mr. President, but we may be thinking in suppositions, of which there are many." Paul had a matter-of-fact tone.

"Oh?" he said cautiously.

"Suppose he doesn't comply with your request?" Paul countered.

Tsirch stated, "He has yet to answer the allegations. And there's the possibility of impeachment."

"It takes more to impeach and remove than to ask for a resignation," Paul said and added, "It could get messy in either case."

Tsirch stated, "True, but necessary if my information is as damaging as it seems."

"That may be another supposition," Paul added.

Tsirch was becoming anxious, but he didn't show it.

"Paul, are you telling me that is his official position?"

It wasn't often anyone held the cards against the president, and Paul was going to play them for all they're worth, yet not at Richard's expense.

"He hasn't given me any position."

Tsirch breathed easier, momentarily.

"But, Mr. President, he has the characteristic of standing up to anyone and letting the chips fall where they may," Paul stated.

Tsirch again was in secret agreement.

Paul continued, "You, sir, as well as anyone, are aware that he doesn't conform to political structure. He didn't even ask for the vice presidency his first term, and you were, shall we say, 'obligated by popular choice' to make him your running mate. It's a possibility that if he does resign, he could run against you. And if you fail to get him removed…well, you see the possibilities."

Tsirch had already run these scenarios before he'd decided to ask for Richard's resignation publicly. Richard refused Tsirch's requests to resign on his own. Having these thoughts reappear created much anxiety for Tsirch, but he was at his best under pressure. His decision had been made—let the chips fall where they may.

"I appreciate your concern, Paul, but I've had no choice."

"Perhaps not."

Tsirch moved on. "Has Richard made any statement as to his reaction or intentions?"

"Actually he wasn't concerned about your statement, which worries me but doesn't surprise me."

"Nor I. Well, Paul. When he does decide something, let me or Marilyn know."

"Yes, Mr. President, I'll give you more notice than you did me." Paul smiled.

Tsirch returned the smile. "Thank you, Paul. Good evening."

"Good evening, Mr. President."

As Paul disappeared from the cube, Tsirch buzzed Philip.

"Yes, sir," Philip stated.

"I'm calling it a night, Philip. I want to thank you for staying to wind things up."

"No problem, sir. I want to do the best I can."

"Thank you, anyway. Oh, and on my morning calendar, I need to fit Marilyn in."

"Sir, the Secretary of State is already scheduled for 8:00 a.m. to 8:30 a.m."

"Get her another hour, she'll need it. Say, 7:00 a.m.?"

"Yes, sir. I'll call her. Good night, sir."

"Good night, Philip."

CHAPTER 6

Operation Haystack

Lucas, in deep thought, looked out over the land and ocean. Whatever he was searching for could be anywhere in the air, water, or on the land. One good thing was that the compound didn't seem to spread easily on soil; air and water were a different story. Trusted personnel with sophisticated equipment were taking air samples on all major airlines without their knowledge. Water samples were being taken in the same way with government authorization under a variety of covers. Being the coordinator of Operation Haystack kept Lucas on the go a great deal.

London, Jakarta, Sydney, Barcelona, Bermuda, Martinique, Hawaii, Galápagos Islands, a travel agency listing perhaps, but they were all on Lucas's route. His enjoyment of these places lasted long enough to hang his hat and catch the next flight. The attendant's voice disrupted the soft music.

"Ladies and gentlemen, please fasten your restraints as we are beginning our descent. Secure all privacy tents, please."

The flight over Africa became more interesting each time. The widening of the Afcon Highways was bringing progress to rebuild and smooth out the scars left by the African Wars, much of which nature had covered with vegetation. The roads that stretched from Cairo to Cape Town and from the Atlantic to the Red Sea were a product of the *burning* of the Congo. The transport glided to the earth and came to rest.

"You may disembark when your release light is turned on." The voice seemed to beg for compliance. We hope you enjoy your stay in Cape Town. Thank you for flying Tri-Africa."

Lucas went to the security area to pick up his containers and then proceeded to retrieve his luggage. At the luggage area, a man approached him.

"Mr. Makiev?" the man asked, extending his hand.

"Yes." Lucas took his hand with a friendly smile.

"I'm Umzintho Lee, the South African collector. Call me Lee if you like."

"Yes, I recognize you from your module." Lucas held out a hand. Lee shook it.

"May I help you with your luggage, Mr. Makiev?"

"Thanks, Lee. And it's Lucas, please."

Lee nodded and smiled. "Of course, Lucas. Please." His smile turned to a grin. Lucas started to correct Lee but stopped when he saw the devilish grin. He carted the luggage to Lee's vehicle and loaded it.

As they got in, Lucas scanned the vehicle, noting the tires.

"Is this a Lora model?" Lucas asked as they began to drive.

"Actually it's an Image-Mold I've had since '82. I put in the solar power-train from a Lora, along with the fabric tires. I prefer the traditional styling. The new ones all look the same to me."

"You had this molded in '82? You should have been a designer. This looks like the next year's Lora model I saw at the factory."

"Well, if they get too close to my patent, they'll here from my solicitor." Lee turned to smile at Lucas. Lucas smiled back.

"By the way, Lucas, I have a surprise for you in your room."

"A good surprise, I hope. Is it animal, vegetable, or biochemical?"

"Possibly a little of each, but it talks and it will make you feel real good?"

"I'm sorry, Lee, but I'm a married man, and I'm also tired."

"I said the same thing to my other wife last night." Lee laughed. Lucas chuckled somewhat.

"The spark went out of your marriage, huh?"

"No, I just added to it."

"How's that?" Lucas questioned.

"I have two wives." He laughed.

"Two? I can't handle one very well."

"Yes, but the story gets better. My second wife wants another husband."

Lucas shook his head. "It's too complicated for me. How do you cope with two wives?"

"I'm not sure I do. This *new morality* is not for everyone."

"That's for sure." Lucas paused. "Hey, Lee. What if…your first wife wants another husband? And your second wife's second husband wants another wife and—"

"Hold it. Hold it right there," Lee said, laughing.

Lucas continued, "Would you have the rights to one another's significant other and if—"

Lee took his hands off the wheel and put them over his ears, laughing. "Stop! Stop! No more!"

They both laughed as they drove.

When they reached the hotel, they were still laughing. They unloaded the luggage onto a carrier. They shook hands.

"My samples are in your room, along with…uh, your key is in there too. If it's locked, just knock. Your surprise will answer."

Lucas's tone was one of dread.

"Lee, I can't—"

"Lucas. Would I steer you wrong?"

Lucas mustered a banter, "You, a man with two wives? Yes, you would." He continued, "This…lady, how do I get rid of her?"

"You're a man of the world. You give a lady what she wants."

"Oh, Lee, I don't want…" He stopped. "How MUCH did you offer her?" he said in disgust.

Lee opened his door. "You'll be looking at about two hundred pounds." Lee got in the car, closed the door, and put down his window.

Lucas was shocked. "Two-hun-dred pounds? My god, Lee, I don't—"

"Not to worry, mate, a man of your wiles probably won't have to pay." The vehicle began to move quickly.

"But, Lee—" Lee was gone.

Lucas shook his head as he walked toward the lobby.

"Which room, sir?" The carrier inquired?

"Room 333," Lucas replied and paused. "Oh…uh!"

"Yes, sir?" the carrier said as he wheeled the luggage toward the elevator.

"Oh, nothing?" How could he get out of this gracefully?

They entered the elevator, and it went to the third floor. Lucas was in thought the whole time. They left the elevator and walked down the hall. As they got to the door, Lucas stopped the carrier, handed him his tip, and said, "This will be fine, thank you. You can leave them here."

"Here, sir…in the hallway?"

"Yes, I want to surprise my guest."

The carrier merely lifted his eyebrows, nodded, and complied with the request. Lucas stood at the door in thought. He had never cheated on his wife, although he'd had uncounted opportunities and even a few offers. He was curious, though, as to what a £200-a-night-or-hour lady looked like or could do that was worth it. He grabbed the handle, paused, and took a breath. The door was unlocked, and he pushed it open. His face showed a mixture of emotions: surprise, relief, joy, and a knowing smile. A figure reclining on the bed looked up at him.

"That goddamn Lee!" Lucas said loudly.

"Hey, Lucas!" Mark Narkiewicz rolled off the bed, stood up, and grabbed Lucas by the shoulders and shook him excitedly.

Lucas smiled, gritted his teeth, and said, "Mark…Do you know what that damn Lee did to me?"

"What'd he do?"

"He led me to believe that he had a £200-a-night hooker waiting for me up here."

"A what?" Mark shrugged his shoulders. "I may be two hundred pounds but categorically deny any reference to being of easy virtue, unless the price is much higher."

"Oh…I'll get him! Help me get my bags, will you?"

"Sure, Lucas."

As they brought the bags into the room, they continued to talk.

"Mark I'm surprised to see you. I thought you were in Berlin with Peter."

"I was, but I took the red-eye to Cairo and the morning flight here. I had to make some signal verifications and realign some receiving dishes." Mark sat down.

"You getting anywhere?" Lucas took off his coat.

"I don't really know, but at this point, it's extremely interesting. We're trying to filter some signals that may mean something. Tell you what, grab a beer or something, get comfortable, and we'll trade secrets."

"That's a deal, but first I'm going to get comfortable."

"Good idea, Lucas. Wash the travel off and cleanse your soul."

"You don't have that much soap," Lucas said with a grin. Lucas grabbed one of his suitcases and pointed toward a door.

Mark nodded and said, "Bathroom."

Lucas opened the door, and a light automatically came on. Lucas closed the door behind him.

*****

In the lobby of the hotel, a man was talking to the desk clerk. He nodded to the clerk and started toward the entrance. As he stepped outside, he looked around the area apparently to see if anyone was watching him. He tapped a device in his ear and spoke.

"Eighty-eight." He paused, then spoke again, "Hotel Afrik. Ten-eight. F-two, out."

*****

Mark was watching the TV cube when he heard the door to the bathroom open.

"I take it the bed next to the window is mine, since I saw your personal pillow on the other bed," Lucas said.

"It's hard to sleep without it," Mark said.

"I brought mine too. We still do a lot of things the same way."

Mark smiled and said reflectively, "Good habits and good memories."

Lucas walked to the cooler, opened it, and took out a soft drink. "You want something, Mark?"

"Yeah, give me one of those."

Lucas took another drink from the cooler, closed it, walked over to Mark, and handed him the drink.

"It's a relief to be able to talk to someone without having to guard what you say. I trust your room is secure."

"C-6 antibug blockers," Mark replied as he switched the TV cube off.

"Good, then I won't have to check my luggage. This antibug stuff is a pain in the ass."

"It's not as if we are subverting any government actions. We just have to guard against any misinformation," Mark explained.

"Nevertheless, I almost feel like a criminal at times."

Lucas sat down on the arm of the sofa.

"Well, who goes first?" Mark said.

"You started, so you can finish," Lucas stated.

"Okay, I'll put you to sleep," Mark said, laughing. Lucas smiled. Mark continued, "I don't know how much you know, so I'll start at the beginning."

*****

Outside the hotel, a Club-Coach was parked. The man inside was sitting in the back and listening on earphones. He touched a few buttons on a console and spoke, "This is Fuller. I am getting no conversation. Either the device was discovered, or they are using a blocker." He listened for a response.

"Mark Narkiewicz and Lucas Makiev." He listened again. "Negative. Not Edward, Mark." He waited. "I'll wait to see if the device is missed." He paused. "Right, I'll call tomorrow from wherever he goes."

*****

Inside the hotel, Mark continued his story, "And then Cory James, the director at the Johannesburg Communication Center, called me yesterday while I was meeting Peter in Berlin. He was having problems filtering out some signals that were apparently being transmitted on the same frequency."

"It sounds like a job for a sixth generation processor to me."

"Yeah, I thought so too. I brought a modular A-6 keyboard, type-D sensor display, and an L-8 multirecorder."

"And your Boy Scout knife," Lucas added. "You came well prepared."

"Loaded for bear, in every sense, but I didn't get one shot off."

"Struck out, huh?" Lucas said.

"No, actually there were so many, I didn't know which one was the real bear," Mark explained.

"I'm all ears, Goldilocks, go ahead," Lucas bantered.

"When I arrived, Cory and his assistant, Jo, had all the data recorded and broken down by type, magnitude, carrier strength, origin—a complete profile."

"They seem like very efficient and capable scientists, and if you'll forgive me for asking, why would they need you?"

"Well, Lucas, I asked them the very same question. They said that their interpretations of the signals were the problem. I still didn't understand their need for me, but they assured me that I would 'see the light' when I had heard the recordings of the old signals and compared them with the current signals. They added that the analyses and interpretations of the computer would be secondary to my opinion. And that's what intrigued me."

Mark stood and walked to the cooler.

"You want a glass and some ice?"

"Yeah, sure, but I'm about through with this one. I'll get another." Lucas got up and joined Mark.

"Here are some cookies too," Mark said as he reached into the cooler and took them out. They fixed their drinks and opened the cookies as Mark continued.

"They were really concerned about verifying the authenticity and accuracy of their data, but their real excitement was in the interpretation of their data. They insisted I go over the data completely on my own without their bias."

They sat down again.

"I was curious enough before I left that I obtained some communications data from the Swiss lab, for third-party comparison." Mark took an earnest pause.

"I've reviewed their data and"—Mark was becoming somewhat excited—"compared that with the Swiss data. I analyzed the current signals and sent ALL of the data to Tokyo and Hat Creek for yet another analysis. Now if…the data interpretations are as I expect… I think humankind should take a deep breath."

Lucas had known Mark since college, and he knew Mark was not given to drawing unqualified conclusions. He was becoming as excited as Mark.

"Intelligent signals from space? Life in another system?"

"More than that, Lucas, possibly life in several systems."

Lucas took a long look at Mark. "That's amazing, Mark." There was a short pause. "Have you told Richard?"

"Yes, I did, and I'll tell you what I told him. I have between fifteen to twenty years of back data to go over, some not on computer media, in order to substantiate any type of opinion or conclusion."

"How long until you get corroboration?" Lucas urged.

"To anyone not in our circle, I'd say six months. Otherwise I'd say six weeks. But between you and me, I'm shooting for a week after I get the Tokyo report from Onizuka."

"That's great!" Lucas howled.

Mark paused in thought. Lucas noted his change.

"Something else, Mark!" Lucas asked.

"Just waxing introspectively. After the dust settled, I sent my report to Hat Creek. I've had a chance to ponder the reality or unreality of the possible effects of such a discovery."

"I'm listening," Lucas said sincerely.

"These are only conjectures, ifs, it follows that, and it could be, you understand? So we'll take that as a basis."

Lucas was becoming anxious.

Mark stood up.

"Suppose these signals are on the same frequency, which I think they are. They do repeat in a pattern, a deliberate intelligent pattern. That alone would indicate intelligent life other than our own."

Lucas pursed his lips in agreement.

"Suppose that they are of the same type, carrier strength, and are from the same source—more evidence. Suppose they are from different sources. That would indicate life on several planets. You follow?"

Lucas nodded.

"And if the same pattern is coming from different sources, that would be more incredible. Of course, the signals could be reflecting from a single source or even our own signals 'bouncing' back, those possibilities are being checked now."

Lucas interrupted, "Mark, I think the possibilities are incredible, but I get the feeling that you are thinking in more than possibilities."

Lucas looked into Mark's face analytically. "More than that, it goes much deeper than you're saying."

Mark took a few slow steps away and stopped at the window and looked out. He spoke with gravity, "Yeah, I think we've finally got the brass ring on this trip around."

Lucas's face was pulled in thought. He spoke, "Okay, back to tangible thoughts. I assume you've checked out Dr. James and his wife."

"I have the standard class-H security report, and Richard sent me his file on them. I also know them personally. I realized the possibility of a fraudulent claim here. After all, some people look for glory and its benefits."

"What did the reports tell you?" Lucas asked.

"They appear to be legit, eminently qualified, experienced, dedicated scientists. For myself, I feel they are respectable honest people. And their insistence that I gather separate data of my own lend more support to their credibility." Mark began to walk slowly around the room, almost pacing. He continued to vocalize his thoughts, "I don't see any glory chasers here. These two are on the brink of a discovery that millions of scientists and untold billions of lay persons have dreamed about since the dawn of man. Many of those people would have given anything—perhaps their life—to have proof of intelligent life other than ours."

Mark took a breath and continued, "And…they have chosen ME to be a part of it by verifying such a discovery. Quite an honor."

Lucas added his thoughts, "I don't mean to cast pebbles in your pool, but they could be using your greed to help color the facts to help support their discovery."

"Lucas, you've always been brutally honest with me, but I've run that scenario myself in my own mind. I could, or anyone could, want something badly enough and see only what they want to see. But this is far too important for that to be an issue. I'm dealing with facts, and facts existing at a certain time are true and alterable only by time. The interpretations of facts, however, are subject to review and change."

Lucas smiled. "A philosopher inside every scientist."

"Perhaps. But I seek an accurate and verifiable interpretation of the facts. To that, I will add this—greed has its price, but a man's' intrinsic desire of purpose has no materialistic value. Truth belongs to everyone, but not everyone can accept or cope with the truth," Mark finished pompously. He smiled at Lucas.

Lucas dropped his brow. "That one, I'll have to give some thought."

Mark walked over to Lucas and stood in front of him. "I did something, Lucas," Mark said with concern. "Something that, if I'm in error, I hope I can explain to Cory and Jo, his assistant, so they'll understand."

Lucas stood up to Mark. "What, Mark?"

"I'm testing their sense of purpose. Richard suggested I do it."

"Do what?"

"Before I left the JC Center, I left an envelope with a note for Cory and Jo. I made them an offer. If they would walk away from the project, they each would receive $10 million, tax free."

Lucas looked at Mark incredulously. "And do you think any sane person wouldn't accept that offer? Even if their findings proved out, they wouldn't even get one tenth of that amount in publicity or residuals for the rest of their lives."

Lucas walked to the window and turned to Mark, who followed his movement.

"But there's more, Lucas. The real test is that they would still get credit for the discovery, IF it goes public. They just wouldn't be involved in any subsequent developments."

Lucas was surprised.

"Okay. They get the money and the credit, but the hook is that if the project is buried, they may never know for sure if there is intelligent life elsewhere?" Mark nodded.

Lucas turned toward and looked out the window into the stars.

"What price glory. What price knowledge."

"Exactly, my friend. Exactly," Mark acknowledged.

"This must be extremely important to Richard," Lucas said, walking back to Mark.

"The importance is to humanity, not to any one person," Mark replied. "As true as that is, it would appear to someone that doesn't understand Richard, that he wants to control this information for his own gain."

"That's why Richard formed his own committee comprised of representatives from each political, religious, geographic, ethnic, and scientific faction."

"Yes, but his Common Interest Committee hasn't had much support since he formed it seven years ago," Lucas noted.

"However, it has been there for those who chose to join and use it. And I have a feeling that its membership will become very active very soon, since that is where all of Richard's information is delivered."

Mark walked to the sofa and sat down. "It's sad and ironic, that man searches all his life to discover other intelligent life and reaches his goal just as he is on the verge of extinguishing his own."

Lucas walked over and sat down also. "Another philosopher in the room."

Mark smiled. "I guess that's a good cue for you to tell your part of the story."

Lucas went over to the cooler and opened it. "Okay, but first. Are you hungry?"

"You know, I forgot about eating," Mark said. "Yeah, sure, I could eat." Lucas closed the cooler.

"Good, what do you want?" Lucas said, as he engaged the device on a table.

"Front desk," a voice prompted.

"We would like to order dinner for two, in-room, please," Lucas said.

"Yes, and what will you have?" the voice asked.

"I'll have the special," Mark said.

Lucas paused and shrugged his shoulders. "Make that two specials."

"Will there be anything else?" the voice again asked.

Lucas looked at Mark, who shook his head. "No, thank you. That will be fine."

"Thank you, sir. Two specials. They will be prepared and sent up shortly," the voice stated.

"Thank you," Lucas said. He disengaged the console.

"What is the special?" Lucas asked.

"It's an esoteric food," Mark said earnestly.

"Esoteric food?" Lucas said suspiciously. "Can you expand on your statement, please?"

Mark continued in earnest, "An esoteric food is one that requires a certain acumen of taste to fully comprehend and enjoy its ribald flavor."

Lucas became deliberately articulate, "I don't think I like where this explanation is headed. Okay, cut the bull and tell me what the 'special' is exactly."

"Actually it's difficult to define without being crass."

"Mark!" Lucas urged.

"You were close when you spoke of the bovine genre," As Mark continued, his speech was altered to a Midwestern drawl.

"It's something my Great-Gran-Pa use 'ta call mountain oysters."

Lucas's face and nose twisted in disgust as he reached for the communication console.

"I'm not eating that part of the bull."

Mark began laughing uncontrollably, holding up his hand to stop Lucas from engaging the console.

"No, no, Lucas. I'm just kidding. The special is fresh cod."

Lucas shook his head and smiled. "Mark, it better be fish, or you'll have 'bull balls' coming out of every body cavity."

"The look on your face is worth getting stuffed over," Mark said as he continued laughing.

"You ass. Now I owe you and Lee," Lucas said as he laughed. He went back to the cooler and opened it.

"You want another?" Mark nodded.

He took two drinks out, closed the cooler, and walked over to Mark.

"What's happening on your end?" Mark said.

Lucas took a breath before he began. "You know, the basics," he said as he handed Mark a drink.

"Yes, but how's Sal's research coming along?"

"The bottom line is only time will tell. He, or I, should say, they are busting their asses to stop a death organism they are not sure where or what it is."

"No breakthroughs at all?"

"That depends on what you call a breakthrough. They've created some five hundred organisms that have some of the characteristics of what they may be looking for. They narrowed it down to about thirteen organisms that theoretically, if synthesized properly and in the proper environment, could alter cell division of life organisms. That, in effect, would destroy life as we know it now."

"And the antiorganisms to neutralize those effects, have they been developed?" Mark asked.

"SOME neutralizing agents that have been developed are effective individually on a few of the organisms, but none are an antiorganism for ALL of them. The only thing that will destroy them ALL is fire…not very practical but effective." Lucas walked aimlessly.

"How's your collecting going, Lucas?"

"Hell, I don't really know. Five hundred samples and growing. Five hundred cities, lakes, rivers, seas, and oceans and growing."

Mark smiled wryly and said, "Five hundred women and growing?"

Lucas shook his head and laughed. "*Et tu*, Marcus? I'll get back at Lee for that trick."

A light flashed above the door. "That's our dinner," Mark said.

Lucas went to the door, glanced at the view screen, and opened the door. The waiter rolled a dinner cart into the room.

The waiter started to uncover the meal, but Lucas slapped some money in his hand and said, "If it's not what I ordered, I don't need a witness to a murder."

"I beg your pardon, sir?" The waiter was puzzled.

Lucas smiled. "We'll take it from here, thank you."

"Of course, sir. Thank you." The waiter left.

Mark walked toward the bathroom. "I'll just duck in here for a moment."

"Mark!" Lucas said sternly.

Mark stopped and smiled.

Lucas took the covers off the plates and looked intently for a moment.

"Okay. You can go," he said, nodding.

"Why, Lucas. You act as if you don't trust me. I'm very hurt."

"Yeah, and you would have been more hurt if this had been something else."

They laughed as they both headed toward the sink and washed their hands. After they finished, they took the plates off the serving cart and placed them on a small dining table. Mark retrieved their beverages.

Lucas took the first bite. He nodded appreciatively. "This is good."

"Yeah, they do have good food here," Mark said while his voice audibly trailed off.

Lucas smiled at Mark, having noticed his introspection. "Hey, Mark, a gold nugget for your thoughts."

Mark came around slowly. "I get this eerie feeling when I think of what Richard told me when he first approached me to help him, weeks before he had cause to begin his projects. He asked me how I would feel if intelligence was found elsewhere in the universe, not whether I would be excited or welcome it but how I would handle it. He didn't want me to answer to him but to answer to myself. He wanted to know what I felt what the impact on mankind would be, specifically religion."

Mark paused and took a bite. "I've thought about it from time to time," he began again as he chewed. "But a strange almost-supernatural feeling comes over me when I think of what he said, it seemed to compel me to want to help."

He paused again. "As he spoke, I was almost mesmerized by his conviction." He dabbed his mouth and hands with his napkin, reached into his shirt pocket, and pulled out a folded paper and unfolded it. "I reprinted this from my personal recorder."

He began to read:

> *Man stands in his own way in his search for the ultimate goal, knowledge. I believe in man's self-efficacy, not in fate. I need you and others to help me in my search for the survival of man. I've had no visions or dreams. I've heard no omnipotent voices. Nothing but my "self" compels me. I feel changes coming; one positive, one negative, but not an evil negative. I need your help and others in identifying these anomalies.*

Lucas came out of thought. "That seems prophetic, but if we are indeed looking for knowledge that may result in a positive and negative change, then which of us is in pursuit of the positive change and which the negative?"

Mark made his addition, "I've pondered this for a while, and I believe that whichever we are in search of, the knowledge obtained can effect either a positive or negative change depending on who has the knowledge." Mark took a bite of food.

Lucas took a long moment, trying to follow Mark's statement. He collected his response carefully, "Whatever we find belongs to everyone."

Mark finished chewing and took a couple of drinks to clear the way to speak with effect.

"Yes, but then what?" he questioned Lucas.

"What?" Lucas was puzzled.

Mark spoke in earnest, "We give to all humanity, this...knowledge, this fruit of our endeavors, the positive and the negative." Mark began to speak introspectively, "The positive result of our quests would be the saving of lives and the discovery of alien intelligence. But which negative would be the most detrimental to mankind—losing lives...or losing faith?"

*****

As the dawn broke in Cape Town, Mark and Lucas were standing in front of the hotel.

"Well, Lucas...I'll see you in London, maybe, or at least in Washington next week."

"By the time I get to Washington, I'll have permanent jet lag, and I won't even know what year it is." A car pulled up to them.

"Here's your car, Lucas...got all your samples?"

"Yeah, less one *bug*." Lucas put his luggage in the car and took Mark's hand and continued to speak.

"You tell Lee, when you see him, that I owe him one."

Mark smiled. "Yeah, I'll tell him."

Lucas got in the car and looked at Mark. "Kiss the wife for me."

"Will do."

*****

Watching the car drive off was the man in the Club-Coach that had been parked outside the hotel all night. He started it up and followed the car. Mark noticed the vehicle as it drove away. He smiled a knowing smile and shook his head in disbelief.

He spoke to himself aloud, "Should'a at least invited the poor guy up for coffee."

*****

The airport was busy with tourist trade. If Lucas hadn't had diplomatic preference, he would have spent half of his life, as of late, on airport lobbies or waiting rooms. Loss of time was something neither he nor Richard could afford. Both he and his luggage went directly to the shuttle. This time his diplomatic ties helped his cause more than he knew.

A man pulling a cart stopped and left it and followed Lucas's luggage to the check-in shuttle. An officer approached the man.

"English?" the officer inquired of the man.

"Yes."

"You'll have to enter through the security scan," the officer said.

"I'm not taking a flight. I'm looking for my associate." He pulled out an identification folder and offered it to the officer.

"Agent Fuller, CIA," the officer said, looking at the folder.

"Okay, but stay in the staging area. If you cross into the blue area from this way, you'll set off an alarm."

As the officer spoke, Fuller noticed the luggage was getting closer to the blue area. Fuller nodded, distracted by the officer, turned, and anxiously walked toward the carrier. He reached out furtively to plant the device.

The officer tapped him on the shoulder, interrupting him. "Mr. Fuller!"

Fuller turned calmly. "Yes?"

"Your identification, sir." He offered the folder.

"Oh, thank you." Fuller took it, and as the officer turned away, Fuller, without looking, reached once again to place the device. The carrier was gone. He cursed to himself as he saw the luggage traveling well into the blue area.

Fuller walked back to his cart and sat down. He touched his finger on a device in his ear.

"Fuller, here...no bug. Destination, Martinique."

He listened intently. "Got it. New assignment, Narkiewicz."

CHAPTER 7

Thick as Thieves

Richard stood looking at his face in the mirror. A couple of neat strokes with the razor, and he was satisfied. He washed off his face, dried it, and went into his bedroom. He began dressing, leaving off his coat and tie. When he finished, he went to the kitchen. He finished brewing some coffee and tea. He was buttering some toast when the door chime/light interrupted his routine. He went through the living room, reception room, and into the hall to the door. He looked at his watch. *Ten to seven.* He opened the door.

"Good morning, Peter. Glad you're early."

"I knew you wouldn't mind." Peter came in, took off his coat and hat, and hung them in the guest closet.

"You just get in?"

"Yes, I came straight from the airport. Julia went on to her place." They walked toward the living room.

"It's still Julia, huh? Must be going on five years. Are you two serious?" Richard smiled.

"It's only puppy love," Peter said, smiling.

As they walked into the room, Richard motioned Peter toward the sofa.

"Have a seat, Pete, I'll get us something to drink and eat," Richard said in rhyme.

Peter shook his head, smiled, and said, "A poet now?"

He set his case down on the table. He looked around the room and sat down. He heard Richard singing from the other room. Momentarily Richard came in to the room pushing a serving cart.

"At your service. What is your pleasure?" Richard said smugly.

"Coffee, please," Peter said politely.

Richard ignored Peter and took his tea off the cart and began fixing it. He looked at Peter, who was sitting in wait. Richard paused and gestured with his hands to Peter.

"What do you want?" finally he said. "Well...there it is. Your arm isn't broken. Pour it yourself." Richard laughed.

Peter shook his head and played indignant. "You just can't get good help nowadays." He poured his coffee.

"You should get yourself a helper to do this for you, or better yet a wife."

"I have a *helper*. This isn't what a wife is for...and...I can do this myself. Besides, I can't find anyone that will put up with me."

"How about Marcia, Aileen, Bev, Trish, Jill?"

Richard smiled as he interrupted, "You know they were, for the most part, relationships wished for by the media."

"Yes, and they knew it. But any one of them would give anything for a night on the dark side of the moon with you."

"Right now I could use nights that last seven days."

Peter leaned back. "So could we all."

They sat for a moment, drinking and thinking.

Peter spoke, "I heard the president's statement yesterday. It's unfortunate that he doesn't believe what we've told him."

He continued, "He believes his political and military advisors... and Browning. But Carl knows the facts and our intentions. Surely he can support the cause."

Richard finished a swallow, "Carl, like the president, believes that military strength is the answer to continued world peace. Thus to maintain a balance of military power, they must not only keep abreast with new technology but also try to keep a step ahead."

Peter was chewing a bite of toast. "Richard, how can they ignore that going ahead aimlessly with biochemical developments without safeguards can cause irreversible environmental damage and threaten the existence of man?"

"Ren Lang gave me a month to prove my concerns, and when I ran out of time, he called his plan into action. I chose not to resign as he had expected, and doing so forced his hand."

"But we haven't analyzed all the samples yet."

"True, but he said he'd forego any further action until we had retraced Dr. 'Gemo's travels and had a chance to go over his notes."

"Whose notes?"

"'Gemo's notes."

Peter was shocked.

"Ren Lang had 'Gemo's notes, and he kept them from us all this time? That son of—"

"No, no, Peter," Richard interrupted. "'Gemo's notes were discovered on the moon only this morning." Peter calmed down as Richard continued, "A uranium expedition was taking samples near the Reinhold crater and found a safety container with the notes in it. It seems that when 'Gemo's lab exploded, it blew the container about thirty miles to the northeast. 'Gemo thought that his notes had been destroyed, but he probably forgot that he had placed the notes in the container before he left for the Aitken basin."

Peter was overjoyed. "Where are they?"

"They're being placed on a special shuttle, and they should be here in a matter of hours. I want Sal to authenticate them. We'll need copies of them and so will Ren Lang."

"Okay." Peter took a slow breath. "What a stroke of luck."

"Luck? Perhaps. But if they hadn't been following 'Gemo's geologic analysis maps, they wouldn't have been in that area for another two or three years."

Peter paused in thought. "You know, it sounds a little prophetic, but in one way or another, everything seems to come back to 'Gemo."

Richard spoke softly, "More than you know."

Peter broke his thought. "What? What'd you say?"

"I said tell me what you know. Bring me up to date. Give me your report."

"Oh. Sure."

He opened his briefcase sitting on the table and reached inside.

"Mark and Lucas called me last night from Cape Town. Here's their chip. Here's Sal's and...here's Johnny's."

"Mark met Lucas in Cape Town? I hoped they would get together. Those two are as close as brothers."

Peter nodded. "Maybe we all can cultivate our friendships when this...crisis is over."

Richard paused, raising his cup to toast. "I'll drink to that."

Peter mirrored with his cup.

Richard poured more tea in his cup. "Oh, uh, Peter. The notes... until they are authenticated, are classified. Oh...and you have the pleasure of telling Sal the good news."

"Sal doesn't know yet?" Peter was surprised.

"I tried to reach him, but I couldn't get an answer at home or at the lab. I've had him on search-call since," Richard added.

"He's probably at the lab and deep into his work," Peter said.

Richard nodded. "That sounds like Sal. But..." Richard had a pensive smile.

"But what?" Peter said.

"Oh, just a thought."

"What?" Peter prodded.

"It's nothing?" Richard stood up, and Peter moved slightly with the motion of the liquid in the couch.

Peter pushed on the couch with his hand. "Say, Richard. I still like this sofa. I'll have to get me one of these." He tried to bounce on it, but his efforts resulted only in a very slight motion.

"You have a bed like this too?"

Richard walked into the kitchen. "Two of the bedrooms have Bio-beds, and the other two have regular beds. The Bio-sofa also converts to a bed."

"You hustler you." Peter grinned.

Richard laughed. "This isn't the twentieth century. I have them for comfort, as do a third of the population. And if I recall correctly, your mother included."

"All right. Just wanted to get a dig in." Peter laughed.

"Want some breakfast?" Richard asked.

Peter stood up and walked toward the kitchen. "Yeah, hot cereal," he added quickly, smiling. "And don't bother for me, I'll fix it myself."

The two busied themselves in their preparations. The front-door tone interrupted them. Richard looked at his watch.

"That must be Paul."

Richard went to the door and opened it.

"Good morning, Paul," he said, extending his hand.

"Richard," Paul responded and shook the offered hand. He stepped in. Richard closed the door.

"Peter's here. You want to have breakfast with us?" Richard asked.

Paul put his coat and hat in the closet. "Yes, I will. Thanks."

Paul followed Richard to the kitchen and dropped off his briefcase in the living room reroute. When he got to the kitchen, Paul put his hand on Peter's shoulder as he stood at the range and quipped. "Ah, Peter the domestic, I presume!"

Peter turned to Paul and shook his hand. Acting disgruntled, Peter stated, "Can you believe this? A guy gets elected vice president and with all the benefits that go with it, won't even get a cook." Paul looked over Peter's shoulder.

"Uh...I'll have some of that...if you don't burn it."

Peter turned back to the range. Richard left the kitchen.

"Well, Peter. The VP doesn't get the same benefits the president does. Richard has to cut corners to pay for other things he thinks are more important, like our services, among his other aids."

"How about the Powers and Compensation Act? I thought it took care of the needs of the vice president," Peter stated.

"It did increase his salary and administrative allowances, and gave him an aircraft to use, but much of the extra travel and expenses are covered when incurred under presidential request or directive. As we know, the past few years have seen fewer of such requests."

Paul paused. "The compensations given in that act are practically offset by the increases in the duties and responsibilities given in the same act."

Richard came back into the kitchen, took a plate, and began to fill it. Paul took some bowls out of the cupboard and turned to Richard. "Richard, can't you use the Powers and Comp Act to put some pressure on Ren Lang?"

Richard inquired, "What...to get me a housekeeper? That's overkill, don't you think, Paul?"

Paul shook his head; both he and Peter snickered.

"No, Richard," Paul said. "To force him to make his information available to you." Paul and Peter spooned their cereal into their bowls.

Richard gave a gesture that said *maybe*, and said, "I'm ready to eat." He took his plate and walked into the dining room. The two seekers followed. They all sat down at one end of a large table.

"Richard," Paul urged.

Richard took a bite, chewed his food, and thought. "I've thought about that..." He paused in thought, still eating. "And came up with a few answers. It would be hard to prove...and only would serve, if successful, to delay any action against me. And it could be perceived as a smoke screen. Besides, he has no information I need. Ultimately it would be a waste of time and energy that could be better utilized."

"Perhaps, but I'd like something to stick in his face," Paul said, making a jab with his knife into the butter on the table.

"We do have, Paul—the Truth," Richard tendered.

Paul looked disgruntled. "The *Truth*. Here we go again." Paul started to take a bite but stopped, and began. "What is the *Truth?* You've given top-secret research information to foreign agencies, friendly and not. You've supported the removal of military installations on the moon and those on Earth and solar orbit. You've encouraged the regulation of biochemical developments of military importance." Paul stopped for a breath. "On paper and unanswered, Richard, these *Truths* can get you a vacation to Mercury, all expenses paid."

Peter and Richard were listening but still eating. "And to top it off," Paul continued, "the primary elections are coming up."

Richard finally spoke. "Peter can give you some answers to some of your problems and some happy news."

"That I can use. What do you have, Peter?" Paul asked.

Peter looked at Paul's bowl and said, "Your cereal is getting cold."

Paul sneered and began to eat. Richard stood and picked up some empty dishes off the table and started toward the kitchen.

Peter smiled and offered, "If you'd get a housekeeper you wouldn't have to—"

Richard interrupted Peter, "I wouldn't have to do these menial chores, but I would have to watch what I say and do. I have a house-keeper on call. In fact, she should be here shortly to tidy up. I call her when I need her." Richard continued, "Paul, do you have anything for me?"

"Uh…yes," Paul said. "In my case, module number 6."

Richard went to the living room and took the module out of Paul's case and picked the other modules off the table. He stepped over to the wall safe, placed his hand on the print lock, and entered some numbers into the keypad. He opened the safe and placed the modules inside and took out a small book and put it in his pocket and closed the safe.

Richard spoke loudly, "Hey. When you two get through, come in here. We've got to get started."

Paul looked at Peter and said, "Good. I have a lot of unanswered questions."

Peter countered, "He has the answers, but they may not be the ones you want."

"I know that only too well," Paul said as he finished.

They both got up and walked to the living room. When they arrived, Richard was typing on the computer on the table.

Richard began, "First of all, get your drink, get comfortable, and if you will, both of you, read the display. This will answer most of your questions and bring you up to speed."

Richard stood and walked to the bar and fixed a glass of iced tea. Peter and Paul stepped to the bar and prepared their beverages and sat down in front of the screen. They read the display, advancing the print as needed.

The door tone sounded. Richard went to answer the summons. He paused, looked at his watch, and engaged the outside viewer. A woman—thirtyish—was on the screen. He turned off the viewer and opened the door.

"Good morning, Shari."

"Good morning, Mr. Vice President." She spoke cautiously as she continued, "How are you today? Did you sleep well?

Richard smiled. "Shari, please. You don't have to walk on eggs around me."

"I know, sir," she said as she took her coat off. She opened the closet and hung her coat next to the other coats.

She continued, "But after the president's speech, I—"

Richard interrupted, clasping her hands in his, "Shari. I'm not concerned with the president's statement. My concern is with the people."

His statement was genuine. He released her hands.

"Mr. Vice President. I'm concerned for you."

"Thank you, Shari. You can help."

He sat down on a settee and offered her a place beside him. She accepted. She was puzzled.

"You want my help? How can I help?" she asked.

"You can help by telling the people of my concern."

"You want ME to tell the people?" she questioned.

"I know that you have been swarmed with calls from the media and friends. They want any information they can get." His tone was gentle.

"Yes, but I haven't said anything, but how—" She was interrupted softly.

"Shari. Whatever you have said or will say, I trust, will be the truth. That is all I ask. You can do a great service to all of us by relating to the people that my concern is for the people and the truth."

He paused. "I have no desire to hide any information about my activities related to my job."

"But the questions they ask, some are about your personal life," she offered.

"Unfortunately my position and my private life are entwined. I only hope that those who know my character find that I have no inconsistencies in either. I feel that one's past deeds is an indicator of one's character."

He paused. "What YOU say is important. People seem to lend more credibility when they get information from an 'unofficial' source. So…the only thing that may damage me is the fact that I sometimes wear my socks for more than two days in a row."

He smiled. "Can you help me?"

Shari became somewhat empowered. "Of course, Mr. Vice President."

"Thank you," he said, clasping her hands in his and smiling.

She returned the smile. "Where should I start?" she asked.

"Since I have company, start in the bedrooms and then the kitchen, please."

"Of course," she said and quickly left.

When Richard came into the living room, Paul and Peter were listening with headsets to the information being displayed on the screen.

Paul became excited. "'Gemo's notes? What notes?" He looked at Richard.

Peter explained, "Apparently 'Gemo's notes weren't destroyed in the explosion at his moon lab. They were discovered some thirty miles away in a safety container."

"Where are they?" Paul asked.

"A shuttle is bringing them back in a few hours," Richard added.

"Thank God those notes weren't destroyed!" Paul exclaimed.

Richard thought and said, "I'll give credit where credit is due."

CHAPTER 8

Who's Doing What?

Tsirch sat at his desk reading the screen display concerning new research in the communications field. He was looking for any connection to any of Richard's entourage of assistants. He buzzed Philip Murray.

"Philip, is Marilyn here yet?"

"No, sir. Would you like me to—" Philip stopped as Marilyn opened the door. "Sir, she just walked in."

"Good, have her come in."

"Yes, sir." Philip looked at Marilyn Richter.

She nodded and said, "Good morning, Philip."

"Good morning," Philip returned.

Having heard the conversation, she went past Philip's desk and into the Oval Office.

"Oh and, Philip," Tsirch continued. "I'm switching your monitor to access channel B, see if you can find any connection between this research and Richard."

"Very well, sir. I'll try," Philip replied.

"Thanks, Phil, and code 2 my calls."

"Will do, sir."

Tsirch got up as Marilyn came in. He walked over to the wet bar. She put her briefcase down.

"Good morning, Mr. President."

"Good morning, Marilyn. I have your special tea, and it's almost ready."

"Thanks, Tsirch, uh...Mr. President, I need it. My protocol slipped."

"You know what I think about protocol and friends."

"Thank you." She went to check her tea. "What was that about research and Richard?"

Tsirch filled his cup with coffee.

"It's about some communications research that Mark Narkiewicz, one of Richard's protégées, is working on. I can't find any connection between that and the biochemical research."

"Maybe there isn't any direct bearing of one on the other?" she said, pouring her tea.

"We have to assume that everything Richard does is interlocked somehow." He sat down at his desk and glanced at the information Philip was reading on the screen.

"I've never really thought of Richard as the nefarious type. He just tells you only what he wants to tell you and nothing more," she offered as she sat on a soft chair in front of Tsirch and placed the cup on a table.

Tsirch leaned on his desk.

"I feel that specific defense mechanism is the only thing that keeps his reputation for being truthful intact."

Marilyn reached for her briefcase. "I'd say that most of us have some measure of that trait in us. It's just that Richard has more than his share."

Tsirch turned toward the screen, paused, and entered some information on the keyboard. Marilyn took out some COM chips and folders and placed them on his desk. Tsirch turned to her.

"I trust you've contacted him since I called you this morning."

"Yes, I spoke to him briefly. I relayed your agreement to his request about 'Gemo's notes." She reached for her cup.

"I'd guess he was more than pleased," he said.

"Yes, he was going to call you himself to thank you, but I told him that it really wasn't necessary as it was in the world's best interest for Sal to authenticate the notes, and that it was the obvious course to take." She spoke as if she was reading from a press release.

A smile came to his face. She noticed the smile.

"What?" she said.

His tone became lighter. "You always give such noncommittal statements. You should be in politics."

"I am and I've never even run for office," she countered. She sipped her tea.

He leaned back in his chair and grabbed his cup. "Okay. I'm ready. Fire away. What does your little red folder say today?" he bantered.

The folder was already open.

"You know Carl's response to your statement. The cabinet supports you publicly, of course, but there is some split sentiment over the issue. In a straw poll of the Senate, you have all but 10 votes. The house is non-committal until you ask for a COM poll, but sources say that 348 are leaning toward Richard." She paused to sip her tea.

Tsirch's expression changed little until the figures for the house were revealed. Yet he said nothing.

She continued, "The governor's poll has your stand at forty-nine out of fifty-two. The World Justice Court is still in caucus. Their aides report unusual figures that need verification when the WJC adjourns. You are aware that last night's unofficial COM poll was inconclusive, since 83 percent of the viewers were undecided, and 11 percent were in support of Richard until proof is provided. Charea Dixon will call the Peoples Caucus to a special session after she meets with you and Richard. "

She paused to look at some papers.

"And finally, I polled the four winos on the capitol's steps, and three of them would vote your way for a bottle of champagne… I think two of them were congressmen." She smiled and half-laughed.

Tsirch smiled. "How about the fourth wino?"

She replied, "The fourth was a woman who already had a bottle. But she did say that she'd see it my way if I'd see it her way. When she grabbed my behind, I quickly left."

Tsirch chuckled, stretching a bit. "Another *TAIL* from Mary's travels."

She drank from her cup and turned a page.

Tsirch looked momentarily at the monitor, then stood up and walked aimlessly in thought while drinking his coffee. He finally spoke. "So…it came down to proof." He continued walking.

She looked up at him and asked, "By any chance have, have you heard from Richard?"

He replied, "I had scheduled a meeting with him tonight, but with the discovery of 'Gemo's notes, he said he'd prefer to wait until he had a chance to look them over. That was this morning. I'd still like to talk to him sometime today."

She raised the corner of her mouth. "Good luck."

"Yeah," he said. He paused his walk at his desk and looked out the window. "How's the UN stack up?"

"As expected, a vote of confidence by the General Assembly." She glanced at some notes.

"The Committee to Re-elect is frantically trying to pull in their markers. You really stopped the campaign cold and, at the same time, made a lot of them happy."

He looked at her and put his cup down. "Well, you can't say I didn't give any warning. Having a president and vice president from different parties was suspect from the beginning."

She took another sip from her cup. "Yes, you did express your apprehensions, but the people felt Richard's nonpolitical ideology would pair well with you."

He continued his matter-of-fact tone, "Well, the people may have second thoughts if Richard doesn't answer my accusations to their satisfaction."

She sighed. "Yes, but WHEN will he answer?"

He turned toward her. "More importantly…what will be his answer?"

A light on the monitor began flashing. Marilyn noticed it and nodded to Tsirch, drawing his attention to it.

He went to his desk and sat down. He read the words on the screen with interest.

He buzzed Philip.

"Yes, Mr. President," came his voice.

"See if you can get Silver for me."

"Yes, Mr. President."

Tsirch turned to Marilyn.

"What do you know about Multi-Modal-Directional Communications?"

She paused in thought. Tsirch picked up his cup and went to the bar for a refill.

She started slowly, half-talking to herself, "MMD Communication. Narkiewicz...Mark and Edward are brothers. Mark is in communications. Edward has vast military savvy."

"Go on," he implored.

"That's about it."

His face lost hope.

"Except," she rallied, "that Mark advanced some research concerning the use of holography to confuse tracking and sensor devices used in weaponry."

His brows sagged, and his eyes lit up at her words.

"How in hell did you ever come up with that information?"

She shrugged her shoulders.

"I've been interested in photography for years, and holography has been melded into it for years. Just as it's the basis for our video cubes."

He smiled. "And I thought you were just another pretty face."

She retorted, "I could live with that if I wasn't so brilliant."

The inter-COM sounded. Tsirch answered, "Yes, Philip."

"The CIA director is on the line, sir."

"Thank you, Philip, good timing."

Tsirch engaged the video cube. A figure appeared.

"Ah, Silver. How are you this morning?" he said lightly."

"Fine, sir. I hope you are well also," Silver asked.

Tsirch replied, "Yes, thank you." He paused. "Silver, I want to ask what information you could get me on MMD Communications. And additionally, I'd like an update on Richard's associates, in particular Mark Narkiewicz."

"Narkiewicz..." Silver touched the screen in front of him and spread paper images across it. "As a matter of fact, I have a report concerning him in front of me. He was in Johannesburg at the

JC Center. My agent, Fuller, followed Makiev to Cape Town and Narkiewicz met Makiev there. I assigned Fuller to stay on Narkiewicz and had Agent Jackson pick up Makiev in Martinique."

"Very good," Tsirch said. "Marilyn just informed me that Narkiewicz worked on some holography research that could be used militarily." Tsirch drank from his cup.

"Very good, Marilyn. If you want a GOOD job, come see me," Sliver taunted.

"What, and take a step down?" she returned.

"Ouch, guess that makes us even," he replied.

Tsirch interceded, "Okay, you two. Silver, can you send me that report?"

"Yes, Mr. President," he said gracefully."

"Okay, thanks," Tsirch said.

"Good day, Mr. President." Silver vanished from the cube.

Marilyn stood up and went to get a refill.

"I don't exactly see a negative side to Narkiewicz's connection to Richard. Mark is an advocate of peace and would not condone or be a part of any activities against the US, or any other country for that matter."

Tsirch nodded. "That may very well be true. But he may not know the intended use of his knowledge. Richard has a way of getting answers without asking a question."

CHAPTER 9

Down to Earth

At one hundred miles, no one could deny the beauty and excitement the sight below instilled in everyone who had taken to space travel. The commander, a veteran of perhaps scores of flights, was yet dazzled by the brilliant blue and white swirls and subtle shades of brown, red, yellow, and green of his birthplace, Earth.

The voice from the COM brought him back to reality.

"Shuttle Flight 6, this is Houston Control. Do you copy? Over."

The pilot answered, "Roger, Houston Control, this is Shuttle Flight 6, Lieutenant Colonel Davis. Copy 4×4."

Davis scanned her panel screen.

"Roger, Shuttle Flight 6. I have Washington National Control standing by. Over."

"Roger, Houston, Shuttle Flight 6, ready. I repeat, ready for Washington National Control. Over."

"Roger, Shuttle Fight 6. Stand by. Washington National Control, this is Houston Control. Ready to release control of Shuttle Flight 6 to you. Over."

"Houston Control, this is Washington National Control. Will accept control of Flight 6 on your go. Over."

"Roger, Washington National. Houston releasing control of Flight 6 in five...mark...five...four...three...two...one...Go. Over."

"Roger. Shuttle Flight 6, this is Washington National Control. I have you on glide-approach lock. Over."

"Roger, Washington National. This is Shuttle Flight 6. Have glide-approach lock on screen. Over."

'Roger, Flight 6. Ready for your release on your go."

"Roger, Washington. Shuttle Flight 6, releasing lock in five, mark...five...four...three...two...one...Go."

The COM was silent for several seconds.

"Shuttle Flight 6, this is Washington National, I have computer control glide. Welcome home, Davis. Over."

"Roger. Thanks, Walters. It's good to be home. Over."

"Security will meet you on the tarmac. Dr. Uschin will receive Dr. 'Gemo's container. Over."

Commander Yost entered the conversation, "Hey, Walters, this is Yost. Could you have Dr. Kamazov and a rep from National Security Administration meet me at the tank? Over."

"Sure, Yost. Sounds important. Over."

"It could be."

Davis interjected, "Washington, you have complete computer control. Over."

"Roger, Flight 6. All systems go. Over."

*****

The shuttle slowly twisted in the frictionless vacuum of space, pointed its tail in the direction of travel, and nosed toward the blue giant directly above South Africa.

CHAPTER 10

Mountain of Opportunity

During his drive up the mountain, Mark had much to think about. His mind was distracted as he drove by the second-generation Allen Telescope Array (ATA) situated on a flat part of the mountain. As he pulled up to the center's parking lot, the sun was just breaking over the horizon. This was his favorite part of the day. He stepped out of the car. He noticed a light on in the house.

He paused in thought, looking at the house. He closed the car door and walked toward the house. As he reached the door, it opened, and Jo's voice bounced out.

"Well, Mark, the mystery man. Entrez."

"Thanks, Jo. What's this mystery-man stuff?" Mark asked.

Mark stepped inside, and Jo wrapped her arm in his and escorted Mark as she spoke.

"When you gave us the envelope and asked us to open it after you left. Don't you think that's mysterious?"

Mark slowly nodded. As they entered the study where Cory was standing, he took Mark's hand and said with a laugh, "I would say so."

Mark was somewhat cautious and concerned with the levity. He spoke slowly and deliberately, "You two don't act like you read the letter."

"Au contraire," Cory quipped. "It's right here." He took it off the table and waved it in front of Mark.

Mark sat down. Feeling more at ease, he said, "Well, then I've got one question." He paused. "Where's my glass of wine?"

Jo laughed and reached under the bar and grabbed a glass and a decanter of wine.

"Red or red?" she queried.

"Red will do...with some ice," Mark replied.

"Of course." She put the wine glass on the counter. Cory looked at the glass, then looked at Mark and nodded toward the glass. Mark stretched his eyebrows.

Cory smiled and said to Jo, "Make it a big glass."

Jo smiled and replaced the wine glass with a drinking glass and, setting it down sharply, looked at Mark for approval. Mark nodded sharply.

Jo began talking as she poured his drink, "You know, after we read the letter, we were both excited and disappointed."

Mark fell into his insightful self and began to listen intently and asked no more questions.

Cory paced somewhat as he spoke.

"Yeah, the full gambit of emotions. Anger at the audacity, the thoughtlessness, the thanklessness—"

"The balls!" Jo added.

"Yeah, big ones at that." Cory continued, "To think that our dreams, our purpose, our life's ambition, our—"

"Friendship," Jo added once more.

Cory paused and reflected for a second, then softly said, "Our friendship..." then continued deliberately, "could be bought or sold."

Jo sat next to Mark. Cory circled and sat on his other side.

Jo spoke, "Yes...yes, it could...if. We began to talk about the offer. We'd still get credit for the work, even though it might not be disclosed to the people. But we'd have the money. Yes, the money. Travel, houses, cars, clothes, we could buy or do anything we wanted."

Cory picked up the thoughts with excitement.

"You know we always wanted to travel. Arizona, Idaho, Manitoba, Australia, all the new and quiet places, maybe even Mars."

"Wouldn't that be great?" Jo continued the excitement. "Mars... research, discovery..." She stopped. She and Cory gazed at each other and said simultaneously, "Children!" They paused. Cory continued slowly and emotionally, "That's when we began to realize that 'we' already had what we wanted."

Cory smiled at Jo and continued, "We travel every day, billions of miles, through galaxies. Research and discover new stars, systems, concepts…new life."

He paused.

Jo broke the spell with a harsh tone. "That's when we knew that our first reaction was right. We were angry."

Jo looked at Mark, goading him, "Why? You ask."

Mark raised his brows and shrugged his shoulders.

"Because…" Jo dragged out the response. "We're pregnant!" she shouted in excitement.

Mark was following intently, but now his brows and eyes strained in the twist of information. He shook his head back from confusion.

"What!"

Cory was enthusiastically nodding his head and grinning. "Yes!" he shouted.

Mark joined the excitement. "All right!" He stood and hugged Jo as she giggled.

Cory stood and put his hand on Mark's shoulder. "The bad news is," he said in a matter-of-fact tone. "You're not the father."

They all hugged and laughed and patted one another on the back.

*****

They were sitting at the kitchen table finishing their meal. Mark sat opposite Cory and Jo.

"That was the best chicken I ever had," Mark declared.

Jo replied, "You're part right. They were egg noodles, but the meat was vegan chicken."

She stood and walked to the counter.

"It was still the best," Mark said.

"More water?" Jo asked.

Both Cory and Mark waved a decline.

"*So…*" Mark drawled. "You see why I had to give you a choice?"

Cory nodded and spoke, "It was one way of quickly finding out if the information we were supplying was fabricated."

Jo followed up, "And to test our loyalties."

Mark quickly jumped in, "No, not loyalties…priorities. I've known you too long to question your loyalties. It's part of your character. But priorities can and do change."

Mark continued, "However, you did have cause to be angry, if you felt that I, or Richard, questioned your veracity. We both knew what your choice would be, and it would lend credibility to the cause down the road."

Jo questioned, "It seems to me that if this test got out, it would smell of a cover-up."

"If it got out, yes. But this whole episode has already been documented and released to certain persons." Mark took a sip of his drink. "And the best part, your data has been verified by all SETI links."

"How could THIS already—" Cory was interrupted.

"Trust me," Mark said with a knowing smile. He continued, "Anyway I'm thrilled for both of you—a baby!"

*****

Agent Fuller was talking from his van, "Yes, I left the JC an hour ago when the bug died."

CHAPTER 11

Visage

Davis and Yost were exchanging conversation with a VIC (Voice Interactive Computer) when the door to the debriefing room slid open. A man and woman entered the tank and walked past several tables and their occupants, en route to the two.

Yost saw them approaching and stood, extending his hand.

"Hi, Yost. How are you?" the woman said, taking his hand.

"Good, Kamazov, good," Yost replied.

"Commander, I'm Parker, NSA," the man offered.

"Glad to meet you, Parker. Jim, isn't it?"

Parker was surprised. "Yes."

Yost continued, "Jim, this is Lieutenant Colonel Marta Davis, and, Marta, you know Kamazov."

Marta nodded, extended her hand. "Hello, Jim, Kamazov."

"Jim," Yost said, "Marta is a big fan of yours."

Parker looked puzzled, as did Marta.

"Yeah, she saw you in the lobby on the secure scan and said you were 'HOT.'"

Marta interrupted and suggestively said, "Actually I said you LOOKED hot." He tugged lightly on his somewhat-heavy coat. She elbowed Yost in the ribs.

"Oh, I got tired of carrying it. I forgot to leave it in my room," Parker explained, taking it off and draping it over the chair.

"Well, anyway. Marta can help you with any HEAT problems." Yost smiled, as did Marta.

"Doc, can I talk to you a moment? Excuse us for a moment, will you?" Yost nodded to Parker and Marta and led Kamazov away to another table, and they sat down.

Kamazov settled in her chair and leaned her forearms on the table.

"Okay, Steven, what is it?" she said with interest.

Steven pondered for a long moment.

"Steven?" she prompted.

Steven finally spoke, "Look, Kate. You know I'm not given to hysteria, hype, or fabrication."

Steven was serious, and Kate was silent as he continued.

"I've documented this in my report, but I want you to get it firsthand. Then you can help explain it to the NSA."

She continued to listen.

"Before I start, I want you to know what won't be in my report. In my report, I reported seeing a figure, a man, and he was saying something. I couldn't hear it, as there was no sound. But I read his lips."

Parker and Davis stepped to the table. Parker said, "Okay, Commander. I'm ready."

Steven shelved his thoughts. "Okay, let's do it."

Parker asked, "Here?"

Steven replied, "Here! Why not? Everyone here knows about the incident or has clearance to know."

Parker ticked his head and raised his brows, and he and Marta, who was with him, sat down. Parker pulled out a COM recorder pod and turned it on.

As Parker prepped the recording with date, time, place, and participants, Steven gathered his thoughts.

"Okay, Commander. You may begin," Parker prompted.

"As my report states, two days ago, I was EVA on Shuttle Flight 6, when something caught my attention. It was about forty feet away. I flipped up my sun shield and saw that it was a figure, suspended in space, as I was. It was a three-dimensional human form, appeared to be male, with no space suit. It was slowly turning and twisting. I notified the ship of its location and to sensor scan the figure.

"As the figure became vertical to my axis, I saw the figure plainly at about twelve feet away. It had loose-fitting clothing, like a belted garment or robe, medium brown or gray in color, with a hood. Its hands, bare feet, and face were human, lighter in color than the clothing. Its mouth was moving. The eyes were open and began to widen. At that moment, the figure was absorbed by a dull-gray light and completely disappeared."

Steven took a breath. "The scans were recorded. Preliminary indications were that the figure wasn't human, as it had no organic substance. In effect, there wasn't anything there, just an energy anomaly."

Parker asked in a confused tone, "If it wasn't there, then what did you see?"

Steven explained, "What I saw, according to the scans, was an energy emitting convergence, very similar to our own light convergence and dissemination process we know as a hologram."

Parker spoke again, "A hologram, like our video cube."

Steven nodded and added, "But with a very big difference. We see the figure because our cubes have a receiver. I saw no receiver. Although I could have just gotten a little space happy or went temporarily berserk."

Marta stepped in, "Well, I didn't see 'it,' but the sensor scans say something was there, and even without the SSs, if Steven said he saw it, then you better believe it was there."

"Thanks, Marta," Steven finished and stood. "Well, I'm done and I'm fadin'."

Marta agreed, standing up, "Me too."

Parker became anxious. "Hey, hey. Not yet. I have more questions."

Steven responded, "View my report, it has more details. I just wanted to give you both a personal report first. If you have more questions, see me later."

Steven and Marta began to leave. Parker and Kate stood, looked at each other, and shrugged their shoulders in unison.

"I guess it's over," Parker said.

Kate became pensive and prophetic. "No...I think it has just started."

*****

Steven and Marta had just stepped into the corridor when Sal tapped Steven on the shoulder. A smile came to Steven when he saw Sal.

"Hey, Stevie. Welcome to earth. Take me to your leader."

Sal's kidding around was welcomed.

"How about I take you to a whiskey instead?" Steven suggested.

Steven grabbed Sal by both shoulders and shook him.

Sal prompted, "Ply me with liquor, sing me a song, and I'm yours."

"You're still an easy mark, you old shit-faced dog," Steven stated.

"Getting easier every day," Sal responded.

Sal tipped his head toward Marta, saying, "Want to make it a threesome?"

"That could be interesting," Marta said, smiling.

"I suppose you have come for the 'notes,'" Steven said.

"Yes, but I've got about an hour to kill," Sal said.

"Well, let's do it," Steven said and started walking.

Sal began to walk also, but Marta was looking back into the tank.

She said, "You two go on. I think I see my ride."

She walked back into the debriefing room, picked up Parker's coat off the chair, and dangled it in front of Parker. She looked at Parker and suggested, "Why don't we take your coat back to your room?"

Sal was watching her.

"What was that?" he asked.

"Body heat, buddy...body heat," Steven explained, slapping Sal on the back.

They proceeded down the corridor.

CHAPTER 12

Conspirators

The silver car glistened in the morning sun as it twisted and turned its way through the streets of the city. Finally the turns changed to lazy uphill curves. Near the top of the hill, the car turned into an entrance with a large gate with a guard post just inside. The sensor board inside the guard post showed only a slight change with the presence of the car. Virtually invisible lenses and other electronic devices strategically decorated the gate and entire fence line and guard towers. A man in a suit stepped out of the entrance building to get a full view of the car and its occupant as the gate slid open. The car was still moving as the gate completed its journey. Finally the car slowed and stopped.

"Good morning, Reager," the decidedly female voice greeted the man.

"Good morning, Jennifer," came the reply.

"Good morning, Paula," Jennifer said, waiving to a uniformed woman in the doorway of the entrance building. The woman waved back.

"Keep it under fifty," he said with a smile as the car started to move again and picked up speed. The car reached fifty twice in the short drive to the main house. The car stopped in front, under the covered part of the driveway. Jennifer opened the door and slipped out of the driver's seat, the only way her tight skirt would permit a lady to do. She tossed her sunglasses in the front seat and closed the door. Her body bounced pleasantly up the steps to the front door.

She opened the door and swung it closed behind her. Richard was coming out of the kitchen when he saw Jennifer. He waited for her to get to him. He had a cup in one hand, and smiling, he gave her a big one-armed hug and kissed her on her cheek.

Then with a curious look, he asked, "Who are you?"

Jennifer slapped him on the shoulder and said, "*Dad!*"

He led her down the hall, and upon entering the living room, he announced, "Guess who's here."

Paul was sitting on the sofa. He and Jennifer, at the same time, said, "Who?"

At their words, they noticed each other. Richard shrugged his shoulders and continued walking.

"Oh, Jen!" Paul was elated.

"Uncle Paul!" she exalted.

She went to the sofa as Paul stood, and they hugged.

"Richard didn't say you were coming," Paul said.

Richard jumped in, "That's because my daughter, the 'agent,' didn't tell Richard."

"Well, your daughter, the agent in training, didn't know she would be in the area until an hour ago," she said in a matter-of-fact tone.

"You still could have called. You might have caught me in a compromising position."

She looked at Paul and joked, "You mean I didn't?"

Paul laughed.

"This old gate may have rust spots on it, but it still swings only one way, but for the wiles of woman," he finished dramatically.

Jennifer smiled as Paul still held both of her hands. He held her away to look at her. He tilted his head at the sight of her skirt and said, intentionally leeringly, "Nice skirt."

She turned to model it and asked, "You like?"

Richard chimed in, "It's standard issue for an agent going undercover?"

Jennifer tried to make her case, "After wearing nondescript clothes on the job, I need to feel like a woman off duty."

Paul raised his brows and said, "And woman you are."

Richard walked up behind her, put his hands on her shoulders, and rested his forehead on the back of her head and said with finality, "Yes, she is."

Jennifer smiled the warm smile of a loving daughter. There was a pause in conversation. The pause was short-lived. It was displaced by a door tone.

"I'll get it," Jennifer declared as she bounced out of the room. She was yet full of bounce when she opened the door. She settled into a somewhat-composed state on seeing Evelyn Walker at the door.

Jennifer spoke through a tone of curiosity, "Hello...Ms. Walker, isn't it?" She extended her hand.

"Yes," Walker said, smiling and taking her hand, and continued, "and you're Ms. Natás."

Jennifer laughed and said, "Now that we've been introduced, come in."

Jennifer gave her a royalty sweep of her hand.

"Thank you. The vice president is expecting me," Walker said as she stepped through the door.

Jennifer, silently nodding approval of Walker's knockout business attire and her womanly charms as Walker eased by her, said softly to herself, "I'm sure he is."

They walked down the hallway, and as they entered the room, Richard and Paul were scanning a monitor. Richard caught their entrance out of the corner of his eye. He approached Walker and took her offered hand, saying, "Good morning, Ms. Walker."

"Good morning, Mr. Vice President," she returned.

"You've apparently met Jennifer," Richard said.

Walker smiled and said, "A quasi introduction." She nodded to Jennifer.

"Good enough," Richard said and waved his hand toward Paul. "And of course, you know Paul."

Paul started toward her, and she met him halfway, and she said, "Of course. Mr. Le Cross. Good morning." They shook hands.

"Okay. Now that we've met, let's drop the decorum."

He gestured at each person as he called their names, "Paul... Jennifer...Eve, Evelyn?" he queried.

Walker smiled and offered, "Eve is fine."

Richard put his hand to his chest and looked at Eve and said, "Richard."

He looked at Eve for approval, who gave an uneasy but gracious nod.

Richard continued, "Now that we won't be tripping over protocol, let's get to work."

"Yeah," Paul said, looking at Jennifer, who knew what he was about to say, and said it together, "Let's eat."

They glanced at Richard and Eve; Paul and Jennifer went arm in arm out of the room. Richard put out his arm for Eve to take, which she did. Richard said, "Bring your briefcase. We eat while we work, or work while we eat."

They followed the other two.

The dining table was large and held various breakfast items and beverages. Smaller tables were placed strategically to hold briefcases and electronic devices. Each included a monitor. A servant was busy with table preparations. Each person selected their food choices from the table and sat down. Eve was offered a seat close to Richard, which she dutifully accepted.

Richard spoke to the server, "Oh, Chuck."

"Yes, sir," Chuck replied.

"After you finish this, can you refill the beverage cart? And then you and Inca may leave," Richard requested.

"Of course, sir. Thank you, sir."

Chuck finished gathering some plates and left.

Eve leaned slightly toward Richard and asked, "Inca?"

Richard smiled and stated, "Direct bloodline."

"Really," she said in an approving tone.

Everyone began settling at the table with their choices. Eve felt as ease with her unpretentious breakfast mates. It was more of a family breakfast. She took a bite of pastry and a sip of her coffee and put it down. She turned to her already-opened briefcase and retrieved a pen, writing tablet, and a COM that turned on as she opened it.

She turned to Richard and said, "Mr. Vice President..." She stopped talking when she noticed Richard's brow wrinkling. "Richard." She paused. "It's a little difficult to call you—"

Richard interrupted, "Eve, I trust you'll work through it."

"Okay," she resigned. "I'm ready."

Richard nodded. He caught Jennifer's and Paul's attention, who were deep in conversation.

"Okay, you two. Ms.—" Richard smiled at Eve. "Eve has 413 questions that need answers."

Paul added, "And I still have some questions left over."

Richard settled back into his chair with a glass of iced tea and asked Eve, "What can I tell you that would give us a base to build on?"

She looked at her notes for a moment and said, "I have a lot of questions, but perhaps a general overview of the situation would be the best place to start."

Richard acknowledged her statement and pondered deep within his mind, touching all the aspects of response.

"It may better serve you to know who the players are and their roles."

She searched her reason and stumbled into a response, "I... guess that...would help cover it."

He began, "First of all, even though Jennifer is with the Secret Service, she is yet covered by executive privilege and...my trust."

Jennifer nodded kind acceptance as he continued, "She is not involved in the scenario, but I don't talk AROUND her. She knows when to shut up, a trait not consistent with much of the younger generation, and fortunately she has demonstrated her accountability."

He continued, nodding toward Paul, "Paul...what can I say?"

Richard smiled. "Paul handles my thoughts and actions and assimilates them and tosses necessary information to the public via, leaks, misinformation, disinformation, and sometimes press releases."

"That aspect of Paul I've seen for several years," Eve announced.

Richard continued, "Also he is my sounding board, albeit unwilling at times. He gives me a good feel as to the reaction or mood of the people. And at that, he is very good."

Paul stifled a chuckle.

Richard turned toward Eve. "You, Eve…are my mind's eye, if you will, to see what I see, but more important, to perceive as I perceive. That is what I want of you." He cupped his hand around his glass, looking at it as he formed his words.

He continued, "Yours is an important position, an awesome task. Your interpretations, your intuitions, your dissemination of information may very well be a safety net for humanity."

Eve's eyebrows sagged as she felt somewhat uncomfortable at his words. He continued, less intense, "Your responsibility is not as grave as I paint it, nor are you the only safeguard. But assuredly, your credentials and credibility play a major role. I may seem to border on insanity with some of my oratory, but my intent is to bridge the gap between reality and hope, which may very well be madness."

He took a drink, then continued, "All philosophy aside, Eve, I want you to do your best to chronicle events as a backup to show credibility, i.e., to lend some measure of proof of no malfeasance."

Eve was absorbing all that he had said. She began with a purpose, "That 'story' we spoke about before?" Begging acknowledgment, and Richard nodded. "I'm ready to take the first step."

She had a pleased look on her face.

Richard's face smiled approval.

He lifted his glass, as if to toast, and said, "To the first step."

He drank.

CHAPTER 13

We Are Not Alone

Hat Creek Radio Observatory has evolved immensely since its inception in the late 1950s. The arrays have been tripled and an onsite residence and research center are some of its attractions.

Doctors Edmonds and Mitchell were listening to radio signals and watching the frequency modulation charts on the six-foot SETI screen.

Amir Hadad, the translation expert, was busy poring over the translation printouts and verifying them with audio and the modulations on his monitor. He tapped a keypad on his desk that was wirelessly connected to his headset. He was extremely focused as he typed to replay the video and audio files.

He spoke into his headset, "Has anybody received signals from Array 14, 1,500 MHz?"

There was a momentary pause, and an answer was given, "This is Dominique, I have 25.2 minutes received at 0324 hours today."

Hadad typed on the keyboard and watched and listened for a moment, then said, "Wow thanks, Dominique! I think you just verified the contact." He tapped the keypad to disconnect the call. He typed for a few seconds, then got up and stepped over to the printer and picked up several pages. He looked them over as he walked briskly to Edmonds and Mitchell standing at the SETI screen.

Hadad spoke excitedly, "Okay, okay, you got to look at these printouts and—" He paused and reached down to the keyboard on the desk and typed. The SETI screen display changed.

Edmonds read the first page and handed it to Mitchell and did the same with the other two pages. Edmonds read each page, then looked at the screen. Mitchell, in turn, did the same. As he finished reading and looking at the screen, Mitchell was in a state of shocked comfort. He sat firmly down on a chair.

Edmonds looked at Hadad, then at Mitchell.

Hadad was the first to speak. "This is verification of the Johannesburg interactions!"

Edmonds stood, absorbing the moment. "I, uh…this is…"

Mitchell finished Edmonds' thought, "Amazing…after thousands of years of wonder…"

Hadad and Edmonds sat down slowly. They all sat in silence for a long moment.

Edmonds asked Mitchell, "We need to share this. You want to do the honors?"

Mitchell thought for moment and finally said, "No, Amir got the last piece of the puzzle."

He turned to Hadad and said, "Amir, you do it."

Hadad said, "Me? I'm just a peon, not the director. That should be your honor."

Mitchell laughed emphatically. "I think this discovery shows that relatively, we are all de facto peons."

"But what do I say? How do I say it?" Amir asked.

Mitchell said, "This is your Armstrong moment 'One small step…'"

Mitchell stood and stepped over to the panel on the desk, picked up a microphone, and, using the console, connected it to the SETI units worldwide.

He paused and spoke, "This is SETI Hat Creek, may I have your attention, please?" The announcement caused a lull in the center.

"Mr. Amir Hadad has an announcement."

He handed the mic to Hadad. He stood and looked around the room. He sighed deeply.

"All of the SETI communities have long waited, with ambivalence, for proof. Today we have confirmation…"

He said the next words with pride, "WE ARE NOT ALONE!"

The applause was overwhelming and gratifying.

CHAPTER 14

Of Clouds and Apparitions

The presidential coach came to an easy stop at the side entrance of the residence. Tsirch stepped out as the door was opened. He greeted his domestic staff with his usual charisma, smiling as he spoke to each one he approached.

He stopped at one young girl who had a bandaged finger.

"Carla, how's the finger?"

"Four more days, and I'll be good as new," she said, smiling.

"That's fine," Tsirch said and, using his unbandaged finger, continued, "It'll be good to see you poke fun at the other staff." He chuckled.

A woman's voice interceded, "Tsirch. Quit pestering people."

Tsirch turned his head, then his body, toward the voice.

"Well, the First Lady herself." He looked at his watch. "Do we have an appointment? Did I forget?"

He walked up to her and looked warmly into her eyes and said softly, "I guess I can squeeze you in somewhere."

The staff was smiling and began to go about their duties.

With an equally soft tone, she said, "I think you had better."

They smiled, and he gave her a modest kiss, which she returned. They turned and walked down the hall, hand in hand.

Tsirch stopped at the Oval Office and said, "I should make a call. I'll be right in."

"Okay, but not long." They parted.

He went into the room but quickly popped back out and said to her, "Vicki?"

"Yes."

"Can you send me a tall one? I'm thirsty."

"Sure."

The door closed behind Tsirch. He sat on a plush swivel rocker.

"Vic, open com," he said aloud.

"COM open," the male computer voice stated.

"Silver, scramble, two."

Silver, scramble, two," the voice repeated.

A woman appeared in the cube and saw Tsirch. "Good morning, Mr. President."

"Good morning, Jan. Is Silver in?" he asked.

"No, I'm sorry, but I can forward," she said.

He said, "It's not necessary. Just tell him I'm back at the House."

"Yes, Mr. President. You're back at the House. Is that all, Mr. President?"

"Yes. Thanks, Jan."

"You're very welcome, Mr. President."

The cube went dark. Tsirch sat looking at a monitor. There was a knock on the door.

"Enter," he said.

A casually but well-dressed man came in. "Your tall OJ with ice. Sir."

Tsirch stood and lifted the glass off the tray. "Thanks, Kevin. Who's winning?" he asked.

Kevin sneered. "Yankees, 3–2 in the fourth."

"Is Baker pitching?" Tsirch asked.

"She's still in," Kevin replied.

"She'll hold 'em," Tsirch said as he patted Kevin on the shoulder.

"I hope so," Kevin pled. He turned and left the room.

Tsirch spun partway in the chair and intently stared out the window, focusing on a lone single cumulus cloud.

There was a knock on the door, and Tsirch, without leaving his focus on the cloud, called out, "Come in."

Philip came in with some papers in his hand and said, "Mr. President, I have—"

Tsirch interrupted him, and still eyeing the cloud, he said, "Philip, you see that single cloud out the window?"

Philip slowed his walk and stepped over toward Tsirch and looked out at the cloud and said, "Sir, yes, I see it."

"Do you see any other clouds out the window?"

Philip scanned the windows and saw no other clouds. "Actually, Mr. President, I don't see any other clouds."

Still looking at the cloud, Tsirch asked, "Without getting technical, you know what clouds are made of and how they are formed, right?"

Tsirch spun toward Philip, half-smiling.

Philip said, "Meteorology was not my major, but yes, I do know."

"Just follow along philosophically for a little bit." Tsirch paused. "If that was the only cloud you had ever seen, would it be reasonable to think that no other clouds exist?"

Philip paused and extrapolated his best philosophical answer. "Knowing how clouds are formed, it would be absurd to say that no other clouds exist."

Tsirch listened closely to his answer and chewed on it. Finally he initiated his next question.

"Could you also say that no other cloud could ever be the same shape and size as that one?"

Philip realized that this existential exercise was not over. He saw that the president was totally serious.

He thought for a long moment and replied, "Although it seems unlikely that any other cloud would exist identically to that one, I, yet, could not rule out that possibility."

Philip seemed satisfied with his logic, and a partial smile showed on his face.

The president thought and slowly nodded. He pursed his lips and said, "Very good, Philip."

He paused and said, "And they are yet, all clouds."

Philip nodded and handed Tsirch some papers. "Here are the energy reports. There are priority docs from Director Silver in your printout cabinet."

Tsirch took the reports from Philip and said, "Thanks, Philip."

As he left the office, Philip had a pensive look on his face.

The call light flashed on the desk along with a soft buzzer tone. Tsirch saw the CIA director's face on the COM prescreen.

"Vic open com, COM 2."

Silver appeared on the video cube.

"Mr. President, good morning," Silver said.

"Morning, Silver, I trust you're doing well."

"Yes, sir, thank you, sir."

"I hope I haven't put too much on you and the agency as of late."

Silver eased back into his chair. "Mr. President, we endeavor to please."

Tsirch smiled and got up from his swivel chair, taking the energy reports with him. He walked over to his desk, put the reports down, and sat on the chair at the desk. He swiveled to reach over and put his hand on the hand lock on the printout cabinet. He retrieved a packet of papers out of the cabinet.

"Good answer, Silver, guess I'll keep you in that job for a little longer," Tsirch quipped.

Silver smiled and noticeably stifled a chuckle. "Thank you, Mr. President."

"Okay, Silver, I know you have a mountain of information to throw at me," Tsirch suggested.

"Speaking of mountains, Jo and Cory James at the Johannesburg COM Center sent more information to us. You should check your printouts…and their data is more intriguing than ever," Silver stated, then added, "Lucas Makiev, Mark Narkiewicz, and Peter Simmons also sent reports."

Tsirch swiveled back and set the printouts on his desk.

"I have the printouts in front of me. Can you give me the proverbial *Readers Digest* version?"

"Well, Mr. President, I think you'll want more to dig into this report with more than a cursory read."

One of Tsirch's eyebrows sagged with interest. "Okay, Silver, you start and I'll play catch-up."

Silver shrugged his shoulders and began, "As an overview, I'll start with…WE—that's a capitalized WE—have practically verified contact with ET, not only in English but also several other languages. We have been apprised that there is, as yet, an undefined threat to Earth and our moon of a biological, chemical, microbiological, and or genetic nature. It is proffered via this contact that the threat was sent from the non-Earth entity but was not intended to present a threat to humanity."

Tsirch's other eyebrow sagged also. He sat in silence.

Silver watched the president on his video cube and waited for a long, long minute. The president's head rolled slightly in various positions, reflecting deep thought.

"Mr. President…" he said.

Tsirch held up a couple of fingers to further pause Silver's entreaty. Tsirch finally responded with a slowed down, "Oh…kay…"

He put his hands on the stack of printouts and slowly started to thumb through the first few pages.

Silver waited and watched patiently.

Tsirch, at last, spoke, "Okay, I'm trying to organize the sequence of my questions?"

"Understandable, Mr. President," Silver stated.

"Am I to assume that the confirmation of contact came from most of our sources?"

"Sir, Hat Creek and ALL of the SETI sources are in agreement and are, and have been, sharing all the data."

"Do we know where the signals originated?"

"There appears to be at least two points of origin, and the amazing aspect is that the contact is virtually in real time."

"Real time? Like us talking now?"

"Yes, sir, but not really." Silver became perplexed. "Sir, I'm not the one you should be talking to. It's beyond my technical capabilities. You should be talking to Dr. Uschin or Lucas Makiev."

Tsirch was somewhat surprised. "I thought Uschin was busy going over 'Gemo's notes."

"He is, but he said he would be willing to answer any questions via COM or personally, whichever you so choose."

Tsirch was multitasking—reading the printouts and listening.

His listening was aborted as he read a printout.

"Whoa, what is this? Commander Yost saw a mysterious male figure without a suit floating in space during a shuttle EVA?" Tsirch exclaimed.

"Yes, Mr. President. I had to read that at least twice and tried to contact the commander, but he wasn't available. But again, Dr. Uschin has more information."

Tsirch's tone became more urgent. "I want to meet with both Uschin and Makiev. We need to control the situation before the public falls prey to misinformation."

"Mr. President, I feel that proverbial ship is about to sail," Silver stated.

"And who is launching that ship?" Tsirch queried.

"It seems that Paul Le Cross wants to schedule a vice presidential press briefing regarding the Hat Creek revelation, and I'm sure Peter Simmons will be there to give a synopsis of the vice president's actions. However, they will delay it to give you a chance to break the news as you see fit," Silver related.

Tsirch's face flushed pensively. "Okay, Jack, I have to set up some meetings. Thanks for the info."

"Certainly, Mr. President," Silver replied.

Tsirch disconnected the video call and buzzed Philip and sat, continuing to scan through the printouts.

Momentarily Philip knocked on the door.

"Come in," Tsirch directed.

Philip entered and asked, "Yes, Mr. President."

"I need you to find Lucas Makiev and Dr. Uschin and set up a meeting ASAP."

"Where do you want the meeting?"

"Time is of the essence. I prefer face-to-face, so wherever that can happen the quickest. If not, then make it a video conference. It's extremely important that we meet today."

Philip understood the urgency of the request. "Yes sir, at once."

Philip left, and Tsirch continued to pore over the printouts.

CHAPTER 15

Meeting of the Minds

Richard sat at his desk in his residence, reading off a monitor and talking to Sal Uschin on a video cube. Pictures of Lucas Makiev, Jo and Cory James, Perry Edmonds, Amir Hadad, Paul Le Cross, Mark Narkiewicz, Jack Silver, Julia Van Hook, Eve Walker, and Peter Simmons began to appear on the eight-foot monitor as they accepted the invitation to the joint video conference.

"Is there any new progress on the samples?" Richard asked Sal.

"So far, we cannot get an exact match to the criteria suggested by the source. I'm waiting for more information from the JC, Hat Creek, and other SETI sites." Sal paused. "I'm so damned intrigued as to how the stream or *diffusion* was delivered through space and time, that I get distracted in my analyzing the data."

Richard nodded. "I can only imagine the quandaries your team and the SETI group are facing." Richard paused and continued, "I've invited Perry, Lucas, Mark, Jo, and Cory to join us on a conference call. Maybe they have more updates."

Richard paused and added, "I also invited Secretary of State Richter, DHS Van Hook, and January Yee, the president's press secretary, but I'm not sure they will make it. And," Richard sighed and added, "of course I reached out to Ren Lang as a courtesy."

Sal shook his head in surprise. "You really think he will show?"

"You know me, Sal, all inclusive," Richard offered.

"Keep your enemies closer?" Sal chuckled.

94

Richard shook his head in despair. "Sal, you know, above everyone, that Tsirch and I have always been friends.

"I know, Richard…just had to say it." Sal chuckled once again. "But asking for your resignation?"

Richard became introspective. "That's just Tsirch being presidential. He had no choice." Richard added, "Regardless this whole conference will be sent to him as it happens."

Richard looked up at the monitor, noting the participants' images being displayed.

"Looks like we have a quorum," Richard said. "You ready, Sal?"

"Yeah, this is me being all inclusive," Sal quipped.

Richard spoke to the monitor, "Baker 2, acknowledge."

A voice replied softly in a decidedly female tone, "Baker 2, ready."

"Baker 2, engage screen 1 and VC."

Each participant was notified on their individual units that the conference was open. As each one accepted the invitation, their live image displayed the word *Active* below it.

Richard saw all the images active except for Paul Le Cross.

He waited for a moment. Although Paul's image wasn't active yet, Richard began, "Good morning, everyone."

A smattering of "Good morning, Mr. Vice President" responses, were audibly registered. Many of the participants looking at their respective video screens were surprised at some of the people on their displays, most noticeably that of Evelyn Walker.

"Thank you for your participation in this extremely important conference."

Richard leaned somewhat left and forward in his chair, resting his left elbow on the chair arm.

"First, I want to set some ground rules…"

Paul's live image finally showed *active*.

"Good for you to join us, Paul," Richard said, smiling.

Paul said, "And good morning to you and everyone else."

Richard continued, "I'll introduce everyone for the record, as this is being recorded and delivered to all participants, including those who may or may not join us—Commander Steven Yost, the president's press secretary, January Yee, Julia Van Hook, Director of Homeland Security, Secretary of State Marilyn Richter, and President Ren Lang." Many in the group reacted in surprise to the president's inclusion.

"If anyone wishes to disengage, you may do so now."

Richard noted that everyone decided to continue. "Okay, this may take a while, so settle back and relax and if you need to. Take notes."

Richard looked at the monitor and began at the top left.

"Lucas Makiev has been my coordinator of Operation Haystack, analyzing the mountains of information from hundreds of sources, including some of you."

Richard moved on, "Jo and Cory James are part of the SETI operation. They are stationed in Johannesburg. They are shown together, but make no mistake, each has their own expertise in the field."

Richard nodded to them. "Next are Perry Edmonds, director, and Amir Hadad, translation expert at the Hat Creek SETI facility." Richard nodded to them also.

Jack Silver was next.

"Jack Silver, the director of the CIA, needs no introduction to most of you. He has an extensive network that has tracked almost all of us at one time or the other."

The CIA director smiled in silent acknowledgment.

"Mark Narkiewicz is the foremost Multi-Modal/Directional Signal research expert working closely with SETI."

Richard continued, "Peter Simmons, of course, most of you know is my right and left-hand man and confidant." Richard gave him a knowing smile and rolled on.

"Of course all of you should know Paul Le Cross, my highly valued and competent press secretary that I forever confuse."

Richard next focused in on Eve.

"Now I'd like to introduce an extraordinary journalist and attorney, Evelyn Walker. She has accepted my offer to chronicle my/our endeavors with an eye as to any legal ramifications."

Richard paused. "I want to be clear. I've placed no restrictions on her legal obligations. She is to keep us from coloring outside the lines…or at least too far outside the lines." Richard paused.

Richard turned to Sal. "Dr. Sal Uschin, or just Sal. Sal wears too many hats to itemize. His team has been encompassed with the critical daunting task of determining if there is a real biochemical threat to human existence and, if so, how to eliminate the threat."

Richard sat back in his chair. "Now let's see if we can suspend some of this awkward decorum. Each of you can tell us how you want to be addressed during this call. I'll start, Richard!"

The group was summarily surprised at calling the vice president by his first name.

Amir Hadad spoke first. "Are you sure, Mr. Vice President?"

"Yes, I'm sure," Richard replied.

Hadad took a breath. "Okay, call me Amir."

Richard sort of chuckled and added, "For a moment there, I thought you were going to say, 'Call me Ishmael.'"

The group collectively smiled, then followed suit.

"Perry."

"Paul."

"Mark."

"Lucas."

"Eve."

"Peter."

"Silver."

"Jo."

"Cory."

"Sal."

"Amir."

Richard leaned up and started to speak, "All right, let's—" But he was interrupted by the appearance of a new face on the screen.

"I'm sorry. Am I too late to get in on this?" Marilyn Richter asked.

Richard smiled and said, "Of course not, Madam Secretary."

"Thank you, Mr. Vice—" She stopped and then continued, "Richard. I am Marilyn."

Richard sat back into his chair. "I think we should start with the SETI group. Perry, you want to start, or how about we hear from 'We Are Not Alone' Amir?"

Amir seemed a little embarrassed but shook it off and began.

"I don't have much to report except that the signals from the source have been translated digitally to at least seven of our languages—English, Spanish, Arabic, Mandarin, Japanese, Russian, and Hindi. Each of the translations is directly correlated to a related religious belief of each language, such as Christianity, Judaism, Islam, Hinduism, and so forth. I don't know what it means, but it delineates loosely each religion's goals or purpose."

Marilyn jumped in, "Amir, how do we know that the signals are coming from…out there, as opposed to intrasolar?"

Amir started to reply, "Madam Secretary—" Amir was interrupted by the Secretary.

"Amir, ground rules…Marilyn!"

"Of course, uh…Marilyn. Perhaps Director Perry should answer that."

Perry Evans nodded and spoke, "Marilyn, the source of the signals has been verified by every SETI facility as well as several independent observatories."

"And what I understand, that source is the Alpha Centauri system. Is that correct?" Marilyn asked.

"That's correct, Alpha Centauri A to be precise. The signals have been generated for at least a year and were deemed, at best, a level 4 on the RIO Scale, denoting of moderate importance. However"— Evans became more deliberate—"in last September, coinciding with the Lunar Fall, the intensity, strength, and clarity elevated to a level 10 on the RIO Scale, extraordinary.'"

Jo James interjected, "That's when Cory and I contacted Hat Creek to verify the content of the signals as being digital signatures representing that of several languages. Since Amir is the foremost in the linguistic and language field, we asked for his input."

Jack Silver broke in, "Let's get back to the Lunar Fall reference. What specifically happened during that event?"

Richard interjected, "Silver, I realize you have security concerns, but could you hold that question as it will be clearer after we lay a foundation? Most of our participants are familiar with the scope of this get-together and will add more blocks to the foundation."

Silver nodded.

"Thank you," Richard said and asked, "Cory, can you add anything?"

Cory James said, "I can partially answer Silver's question. Our part of the Lunar Fall event entails the discovery of not only an accelerated signal burst from the source but also some type of particle infusion, or what we called a *diffusion*. We have yet to completely analyze the digital and physical characteristics of that physical *diffusion*."

Lucas Makiev tacked on to the conversation,

"When the president and Richard called for an investigation of the Lunar Fall event, Richard added me to his list of investigators."

Marilyn chimed in, "Did the president authorize you to investigate the event?"

Richard broke into the conversation, "Marilyn, you were in the room when the president asked for my assistance in the investigation, primarily due to my connections with my science resources. I accepted his offer and recruited perhaps twenty or more contacts to assist me. I didn't believe that I required individual permission to recruit assistants. Additionally the president was aware of most of my selections. So if you please, let's not make this a political exercise."

"I understand, Mr. Vice President," the Secretary stated.

"It's still Richard."

The Secretary took a breath and said, "Sure…Richard."

"Thank you, Marilyn." Richard sighed and asked, "Lucas, you have more to say?"

Lucas said, "Sure." Then he continued, "As I delved into the event, I found that I was spreading myself too thin, and the leads went into several directions. So I reached out to several friends—Sal, Mark, Jo and Cory, Perry, and others. As the information was gathered, we found out so much more than we expected. The search for a specific answer became more complex. Richard suggested we call the investigation Operation Haystack, as we were basically looking for needles."

"Okay," Marilyn said, "the president read me in on much of this. From what I gather, there are three aspects in play—the effects of the *diffusion* on the earth, the meaning of the religious connotations, and the threat of yet another *diffusion*. Have I got that right so far?"

Richard nodded. "Yes, a simplified summary. However, to your first point, the physical contents of the *diffusion* itself represent a possible threat to the earth. Also the interpretation of the signal data from the source seems to point to the *diffusion* having been unintentional. This leads us to the possible effects of an imminent threat of a second *diffusion*. Sal and his team at the Bio-Safety Level 4 lab, along with six other BSL-4 labs, are working to isolate possible toxins, be they viral, bacterial, or alien, which may present a threat to humanity. Additionally they are trying to ascertain what additional toxins another *diffusion* might contain. Lucas has literally been all over the earth gathering samples of air, water, and land and dropping them off at the closet BSL-4 Lab."

He paused.

"Sal, would you like to add to the confusion?" Richard asked.

Sal took a measured breath. "I have more questions than answers." He paused in thought. "What am I looking for and will I even know it if I find it. What could be delivered in a second *diffusion*? How did these ETs send this *diffusion* by both electronic and physical means simultaneously? Who or what the hell are they, and what do they want? Where does God and religion fit into all this?"

Sal thought for a moment and leaned forward in his chair. "I must impress upon all of you that there is no evidence of an alien virus or bacteria present on Earth or the moon." He paused and said emphatically, "WE ARE NOT UNDER ATTACK!"

He sat back in his chair. "And then there are 'Gemos' notes."

Eve's senses took hold. "Sorry, but are we talking about Dr. 'Gemo and the lunar lab?"

Every face became focused on the answer. "Yes, Eve, I've been entrusted with his notes that were found on the moon three days ago."

"I didn't know anything survived the lab explosion," she added.

"Apparently he kept them in a sealed container just in case something happened," he explained.

"And what about the notes?" she prodded.

"Well," Sal continued, "basically he discerned most of everything we now know, but with a twist. The data he got from his array foretold that a second *diffusion* was coming and that the first was a mistake, whatever that means. He gave thanks to Edward Narkiewicz for finding a particle mass. He used an electromagnetic sensor to find the particle mass from the *diffusion* that was captured in the Aitken basin in a subzero state before sunrise on the moon. 'Gemo analyzed the particles from the *diffusion*, and his research showed that the alien particles have an incubation period of about six months in an earth-like environment. We are still analyzing the data to find what the particles/agents are. It appears that even after the incubation period, the particles/agents would NOT develop into a hazardous substance. At least we have a starting point."

Sal took a slow breath. "There is another small tidbit that you may find interesting, especially you, Mark. It seems that Dr. 'Gemo had a visitor not long before the lab exploded."

Jack Silver leaned forward in his chair and asked, "Okay, Sal, who was it?"

Sal stated, "While he was outside the lab working on a circuit panel, he saw a figure, probably a hologram, sans a space suit, he described as male, dressed in loose clothing. He was standing, or floating somewhat, and was saying something, yet there was no sound. It stayed for about a minute, then disappeared."

Marilyn's interest was piqued. "Sal, this figure/hologram, was it captured on video, or were there any witnesses?"

"I've yet to find any chips that can verify the sighting, but we haven't completed the inspection of the container. As to any witnesses, as far as I know, it only was seen by Dr. 'Gemo."

Perry Edmonds excitedly added a comment, "Wow, that would be amazing to have verification of such an event. I'm sure that our own expert, Mark, would be completely absorbed by such a sighting."

Mark listened and smiled. "Yes, Perry, I am intrigued by this, but even more so since it has not been the only sighting."

Perry was perplexed. "Not the only sighting? You're holding out on us."

Richard broke into the discourse. "Mark met with Commander Yost and Jim Parker of the NSA and was debriefed that an additional similar sighting was made by Commander Steven Yost several days ago during an EVA of a space shuttle. Some of you have already been made aware of the incident."

He looked at the Secretary and asked, "I believe that you and the president have knowledge of the event?"

Marilyn nodded. "Yes, the president has met with Dr. Uschin and Commander Yost, and yes, we are aware of the incident."

Richard added, "I was hoping that Homeland Security director Van Hook would have joined us to get her input."

Marilyn added, "The president and the director are meeting about the same topics we are discussing here."

Richard looked down at his notes on his desk. He addressed the group, "So are there are any subjects we haven't broached?"

There were no immediate takers.

"We've covered a lot of ground. If there are questions about specifics, that is why I brought you all together so you'll know who to ask. And if anyone is asked for more information from you, please, please be transparent. I would like to add a caveat before we finish."

Richard had his most earnest look on his face.

"You all must realize that the information we have shared here will get out to the people. I have to defer to the president's agenda. Hopefully soon he will address the nation. Follow his lead. He, as I do, does not want to cause disruption or panic. However, aside from the *diffusion* and its contents, you have to realize the religious ramifications of the revelation of the hologram/figure and the SETI contact. There will be those who will use this to cause dissention. You must impress upon the public that we have only made contact. Aliens are not here and have indicated that they do not pose a threat."

Richard took a breath.

"If anyone needs to address the group, do so."

Again there were no takers.

Richard said, "Thank you for your indulgence and...have a good day."

One by one, the images disappeared from the monitor.

CHAPTER 16

They Saw WHAT?

In her alternate office in the White House, the Secretary of State sat at her desk, cupped her hands around the mug on the desk as she regurgitated the information from the video conference. Deep in thought, she took a sip from the cup and held the cup with both hands in front of her, while resting her elbows on the arms of her chair. After a long moment, she set the cup down and gathered a few papers off her desk and put them into a valise. She pushed her chair back from the desk and stood up. She took a breath and picked up the valise and her cup. She turned and walked toward a door and opened it. She closed the door and turned to the left and walked down the hallway. She made a few turns and came to the door of the Situation Room. She punched in a code on the key-pad and opened the door. She stepped into the room, and the door closed behind her. Seated at the long and wide table was Secretary Julia Van Hook, Homeland Security; Defense Secretary General Walter Porter; Attorney General Jerry Jameson; and the president. The president stood as she entered.

Several smaller tables were scattered along the walls around the room. Large monitors were mounted on each of the four walls.

Marilyn walked around the table toward the president who offered her a seat to his right. She accepted and sat down. Julia Van Hook sat next to the president; General Porter and Jameson were seated directly across the table.

She nodded to each as she said, "Good morning, Director Van Hook, General Porter, Mr. Attorney General, and"—also nodding and smiling to Tsirch—"once again to you, Mr. President."

They all returned good morning wishes to Marilyn.

Tsirch returned the smile. "As you probably assumed, we were also watching the COM conference."

"Yes, Mr. President. Am I also to assume that you were not too surprised about the revelations?" she asked.

"Actually there were some interactions that were surprising to all of us," he stated.

Marilyn dropped her head slightly with a look of curiosity at the president.

"While I did share my video briefing with Dr. Uschin and Commander Yost about the apparition during his EVA, it was intriguing and somewhat unnerving that Dr. Uschin discovered there was a previous sighting on the moon."

Marilyn interjected, "But, Mr. President, I don't believe that Dr. Uschin hid that from you."

Tsirch shook his head. "No, I'm sure that the doctor found that out after going over 'Gemo's notes, subsequent to our meeting."

Tsirch panned his hands toward the other tablemates. "We had a short discussion about the validity of the sightings, what they could be, and the ramifications relative to the public."

Tsirch paused, then asked, "What's your take on the sightings?"

Marilyn took a modest breath. "A pragmatic take could address the sightings as fact, since neither source is given to embellishment or mental defect. That coupled with the actual contact with non-Earth entities and that most everyone wants to believe there are other intelligent life-forms out there—" She stopped momentarily. "I'm not sure what to think, but I cannot discount either the sightings or the signals."

Director Van Hook took a turn. "The general and I were concerned about the particle *diffusions* and how to address the possible threat to the nation and the world. We haven't had much opportunity to interact with Bio-Safety labs in the past, and not to question

Dr. Uschin's credibility, we are unsure with the security of the BSL-4 labs."

Marilyn replied, "Julia, you said it yourself. If Dr. Uschin is involved with anything, you can rest assured that he is on top of any security or safety concerns. He has always been available to meet with anyone. You just have to ask."

General Porter entered the conversation, "I've worked with Colonel Edward Narkiewicz, but what is his brother, Mark, like? Can he be trusted?"

The President broke in, "Director Silver has vetted all of the actors on behalf of the vice president, and to my surprise, I have found them all to be above board and approachable. As a matter of fact, Mark Narkiewicz and Lucas Makiev have delivered all of their findings to me, much of which I've shared with all of you."

Tsirch looked around the table and asked, "Are the any concerns that I need to address?"

Marilyn spoke up, "How do you want us to handle questions from the public or the media?"

Tsirch thought for a moment. "Well...while I don't want to hide information, I prefer you to use no comment for the moment. I will be delivering a press conference, and after that, you can follow my lead from there."

The president stood, and the others stood also.

"Thank you." Tsirch added, "I'd like Marilyn and Mr. Attorney General to hold on for a moment."

The president nodded to Van Hook and Porter. As they left the room, Tsirch sat back down, and the other two sat back down also.

Tsirch turned to Jameson. "Jerry, I guess you are wondering why I included you in the get-together this morning."

Jameson said, "Yes, Mr. President, I was wondering just that."

"I wanted you to witness the exchange of ideas as a matter of inclusion in workings of national security. Also I want your opinion concerning the vice president's counsel selection, Evelyn Walker."

Jameson nodded. "Thank you for including me, Mr. President. As for Ms. Walker, I know her as an excellent case law and trial attorney. Her journalistic ability is tenacious, honest, and direct. I know not his reason for choosing her, but she is up to whatever task he would give her," Jameson concluded.

They all stood up, and Tsirch and Jameson shook hands.

"Thank you, Mr. Attorney General, for your input and for joining us."

Jameson said, "It was enlightening and a pleasure."

Jameson left.

Tsirch and Marilyn sat back down.

Tsirch sat back in his chair deep in thought. Marilyn was used to Tsirch's tells. She knew he had to get something out in the open. She waited patiently. He swiveled slightly back and forth in his chair.

Finally he spoke, "Have I been wrong?"

She knew what he was thinking but decided to let him think some more. He stopped swiveling and sat back in his chair.

"Silver checked out Browning's sources, and they were all found credible. The information was verified, and it was clear that his actions presented a threat to national security." He swiveled a little more, then stopped. "I should have asked myself, what is his motive?"

He leaned forward and put his right elbow on the table and rested his chin between his fingers and thumb in a modified thinker pose.

"I should have listened to you."

Marilyn yet said nothing, still biding her time.

He put his elbows on the arms of his chair.

Marilyn finally broke her silence. "Why don't you talk to him?"

His brow sagged, and he pursed his lips.

"Yeah, I should. Set it up," he directed.

Marilyn spoke the word that should not be said to the president, "*No.*"

Tsirch looked at Marilyn, smiled, and laughed.

"You're not going to make this easy on me, are you?"

"He reached out to you before. You call him and go talk to him face-to-face," she stated.

He smiled and said, "Damn you."

CHAPTER 17

Of Microbes and Men

Working in a positive-pressure suit is a challenge in itself, without the need for meticulous use of tools, valves, and cool-vac chambers. Fortunately the new version of the suit allows for maximum flexibility and durability using nanofibers.

Susan Byers carefully separated the inorganic layers from the organic samples. She placed the organic samples into a container and sealed it. She carried it over to an access door of a chamber in the nanoglass wall. She pushed a button on the wall. The chamber pressure neutralized, and she opened the access door, placed the samples inside, and closed the door. On the other side of the nanoglass wall, Eric Mimilis pressed a lever and pressurized the transfer chamber. He put his hands into the gloves inside the holes in the cabinet and opened the door of the transfer chamber. He took the samples out and placed them on a tray and closed the door of the transfer chamber. The nanoglass wall of the cabinet lab had ten pairs of glove holes along its thirty-foot length. Eric pulled his hands out of the glove hole and pressed another lever. The sample tray moved slowly on a conveyer belt. Eric followed it for several feet and pressed a lever to stop the belt.

Sal waited in the entry room for it to pressurize. When it finished, he opened the door and went into the cabinet lab.

"Are these the new samples, Eric?" Sal asked.

"Yes they are. Just came out of the cool vac," he announced.

"Guess all we can do now is wait," Sal said.

"Have you found anything that will help in 'Gemo's notes?" Eric asked.

"Maybe, but I want to bounce things around with Alan and Susan also."

Sal looked into the room where Susan was working.

"Where is Alan?" Sal questioned.

"He was helping Susan. He should be going through decontamination right now," Eric explained.

Sal walked over to the wall between the cabinet lab and the suit lab and activated a COM between the labs.

"Susan, can you meet us in the office?" Sal asked.

Susan looked over at Sal and gave a thumbs-up.

Sal walked over to the lab door and waited for it to pressurize. When it finished pressurizing, Sal stepped in and sat on a bench and began taking off the protective suit.

His mind flashed back to the encounter with Johnny in the hotel room.

She was playfully laughing and teasing him with her dress straps sliding sexily off the shoulders. He followed each strap with gentle kisses from her neck to her shoulders. He helped her to complete the journey of the dress, and it fell to the floor. He spun her around and embraced the flesh of the breasts with his hands and arms while meeting her neck with his lips.

She slinked away from him and led him enticingly toward the bed.

As he leaned with her to the bed, a voice stirred him from his memory.

"Sal, Sal?" Eric's voice was an unwelcomed interruption.

Sal took a well-deserved breath and looked over at Eric waiting for Sal to exit the pressure chamber.

"Where were you?"

Sal shook his head awake and answered, "I was going over microbes and bacteria in my mind."

Eric smirked and said, "Must have been some pretty happy microbes from the look on your face."

Sal finished removing the protective suit, placed it in a bin, and activated the exit door.

*****

Alan Olguin has a multifaceted history: military and private sector leadership coupled with his biochemical expertise. He and Susan worked together during the Congo SARS virus epidemic. They were credited with preventing a serious pandemic.

*****

Susan and Sal seemed to have been cut from the same genetic cloth. Susan also took the road not traveled and became renowned for her out-of-the-box approach in solving problems.

Sal met Eric literally by accident. He was flying an old Huey for a medical transport of a guy that became exposed to the Marburg virus when a lab worker broke protocol and opened the wrong door. He was the only pilot that would pick up the infected lab guy. Yes, that lab guy he picked up was Sal. Eric, also a biochemist, had contracted and survived the virus and was willing to take the risk.

Sal and Eric sat at a table in a rather large office. The door opened, and Alan and Susan came in. Susan took a chair across from Sal, and Alan sat next to her across from Eric. There were pitchers of water and iced tea on the table, along with several glasses.

Also on the table were four stacks of papers in front of each chair.

Sal stood and went over to a desk and picked up a control module off the desk and sat back down. He pushed some buttons on the control module, and a monitor on the wall lit up.

Sal took a drink of iced tea from his glass. Susan poured herself a glass of tea also and doctored it to suit her taste.

Sal looked at the monitor and said, "I'm waiting for Mara Goya in Milan, Harry Holland at Parks in New South Wales, and Mike Mitchell at Hat Creek. Maybe we can narrow our focus a bit."

Eric selected a glass and started to pour a glass of tea but stopped and put the glass back. He got up and walked over to a cabinet and took out a cup. He picked up a carafe and poured a cup of coffee and went and sat back down.

Mike Mitchell was the first image to appear on the monitor. Sal pressed a button.

"Good morning, Mike," Sal said.

Mitchell was reading but looked at his monitor and saw the image of the group at the table.

"Yes, good morning to all also."

"Mike, you know these faces, don't you?" He panned his hands at his tablemates.

"Most assuredly, Sal. I—"

Mitchell was interrupted by the appearance of two other images on the monitor.

"Oops," Sal said. "I guess I should have waited. Sorry about that. I'll start again."

Sal began again, "Good morning, *buona sera*, and g'day to all of you."

Harry replied, smiling, "G'day to you, mates."

Mara said, "Good morning and buona sera also."

"I was asking Mike if he knew everyone, but I'll extend that to all of you," Sal asked.

Mike, Harry, and Mara looked at the images on their monitors.

Harry nodded and said, "I know everyone but haven't actually met the gentleman from Hat Creek. Mike, is it?"

Mike smiled and replied, "Yes, Mr. Holland. G'day. But some may take issue with you calling me a 'gentleman,' though."

Harry smiled. "I here ya, mate."

Mara smiled also and added, "Harry, I've met Mike, and he truly is a gentleman."

Susan laughed and said, "I can see how this session is going to go."

Sal smiled and stifled a chuckle. "Okay, okay." Sal picked up some papers off the table and asked, "I hope we all have read the daily activity logs."

Harry, Mara, and Mike all nodded.

Alan was reading one of the papers and put it down. He looked at Sal and asked, "Sal, can I ask Mike some questions?"

Sal answered, "That's what we're her for, Alan."

"Michael, your Hat Creek report is somewhat ambiguous regarding the English translation and the French translation of the meaning of *microbes* and *microorganisms*. What is the differentiation?"

Mitchell was nodding.

"Alan, we've had conversations with several SETI sites about the same thing. The actual translation of English, French, and also the German phrasing presented that specific question."

Mike paused. "You know, perhaps I should get Amir to join us, since he was the first to address the issue."

Sal interceded, "That would be great, Mike. Could you get him to join us?"

Mike stood and looked around his room and called out.

"Amir, Amir. Can you join me?"

Mike sat back down and moved over to make room for another chair.

"Amir is coming."

Amir appeared on the monitor and sat down.

Mike spoke and pointed to his monitor.

"Amir, these are some BSL-4 workers, and they have some questions."

Amir said, "Of course, however I can help."

He looked at the monitor and appeared to be intimidated by the participants.

"Wow," he said, "didn't know this would be a who's who gathering. I'm in awe."

Sal smiled and offered, "Amir, you'll have to get used to your being included in the who's who category, as your notoriety precedes you."

"Really?" Amir took a breath. "Okay, what can I do to help?"

Alan nodded to Amir. "Amir, I'm Alan Olguin. I work at the BSL-4 in Fort Detrick and—"

Amir broke in, "Yes, yes, Mr. Olguin. I know your work. It's a pleasure to—"

Sal interrupted, "Amir. Take a breath, relax. You need to realize that WE, including you, are all just people. We are of equal status. While we appreciate the adorations, we'll better be served if you focus on the expertise you bring to the table. Treat us like the friends that we are."

Amir took a couple of short breaths and said, "Okay, sorry, Alan."

Alan smiled and bantered, "Okay, Mr. We Are Not Alone."

Amir smiled.

Alan continued, "Anyway, Amir, can you elaborate on the different translations of English, French, and German relative to the words or phrases of *microbes* and or *microorganisms*?"

Amir thought for a moment. "The discussions I've had with my counterparts in SETI have a general consensus that the translation leans to what we understand as archaea or algae microbes, or a combination of both. The difference lies in that, in our opinion, the aliens themselves aren't sure of their own technology's efficacy."

Eric added to the discussion, "Okay, is that why the subsequent signals imply that 'they' made a mistake?"

Amir shook his head and continued, "It appears that for all their presumed intelligence, they're not as smart as we think they are."

Alan settled back in his chair. He summed up many of the collective thoughts with a decisive word, "*Huh!*"

Eric smiled and said, "Sal, you thinking what I'm thinking?"

"Yeah," Sal said, "it may be a case of one of their 'lab workers' opened the wrong door and exposed us."

Mara tacked on her observation, "You know, my group was also under the impression that these guys—aliens—are so supersmart that we are at a lower rung of intelligence. Are we wrong? Maybe we aren't that far behind them."

Harry made his own observation, "Well, that may be so in one aspect, but they yet have the ability to make contact, seemingly in real time. That in itself does separate us on that level."

Sal asked the next question, "Okay, now that we have this information. What do we do now?

Susan posed a question for the group, "Could it be that the survivability of an archaea microbe was infused/combined with the growth and life-giving/altering characteristics of an algae microorganism? Is that possible?"

Mitchell shook his head and offered, "You know, you geniuses are getting way beyond my expertise in biological science. I'm gonna stick with what I know. But please continue to ford the stream of information. I'm going see if there is more information out there."

Mitchell added, "Amir, you want to stick around?"

Amir nodded. "Yes, I would like to hear where this goes."

Mitchell said, "Okay, buddy, have at it." He looked at the other images on the monitor and said a collective, "Later, guys."

Sal and the others chimed in with various thank yous and goodbyes. He stood and left the monitor, and Amir took his place in center screen.

Susan continued, "Amir, I'm glad you stuck around, 'cause I'd like to see if you and your cohorts can refocus on the technical interpretation of the microbe data."

Amir asked, "I'll try to relay the request to the others, but I'm not sure how to convey the request. I'm not that biologically savvy."

Susan questioned, "Okay, if you can break down the information with only one of the clearest language you have, English, French, or German, in a linguistic sense, did they intentionally combine the two microbes or was that a mistake. Also if you can glean the purpose of sending the microbes, that would be great. Any additional words or interpretations, however insignificant, may be of help."

Amir thought for a moment. "Actually we were just going over some new signal data translations that may help."

Amir became excited. "Yes, yes. I'll go check that now. Thank you for including me in this."

Susan said, "Amir it was our pleasure to—"

Amir abruptly stood up and left, not turning off the screen on his end.

Sal smiled and commented on Amir's hasty exit, "Guess his excitement couldn't be contained."

Harry posed a question, "Susan, what's your thinking about the combination of microbes? What do you think would be the objective?"

Susan responded, "I'm trying to ferret through the data to see what their intent might be." She paused. "I know you and Mara have held symposiums about the benefits of algae for furthering our bio-fuel production. Are they trying to help us increase that efficiency? It's already at 95 percent. Of course I'm assuming that they don't know how far we've come in biofuel."

Alan tried to help, "It's strange that they wouldn't know about our biofuel status when they took the time to learn our various languages and religious proclivities."

Sal asked, "That begs another question...where did they get the information about our languages and religion? It's not like we sent out a primer on those subjects."

Alan took issue, "Au contraire. We've been beaming out media waves since the radio days."

Sal accepted the issue. "True, Alan, but much of the information that was sent back to us was not out there until the last three years or so. And unless the waves are moving faster than the speed of light, that would indicate that they' are closer than Alpha Centauri—4.3 light-years away. That begs yet another question...Where are they?"

Eric continued on course, "Let's follow Susan down the rabbit hole."

Susan laughed in her taking issue with the characterization. "Beg your pardon."

Eric laughed and said, "Susan, don't beg, it's beneath your station."

Susan smiled. "Okay, Alice, let's fall together."

Eric continued, "Combining the survivability of archaea microbes with the algae microbes would theoretically make the algae more survivable. That's one aspect of what we've been assessing, but how would it change the characteristics of the algae or the archaea microbes?"

Mara furthered the quandary, "We've also used your research to extrapolate the uses of a combo microbe in a variety of environments. It's extremely interesting that we found that regardless of the environment, a computer simulation of a combo microbe theoretically would survive all of the scenarios."

Harry added a caveat, "The question remains—is it possible to combine microbes and maintain the integrity of each microbe? I've come to suspect that such a combination would create an inextricable ionic bond."

Sal tried to create an escape from the rabbit hole, "Unless there was an antigen of some type, that would prevent the ionic bond."

Sal sat forward in his chair. "Enough for today. We have more samples and data to go over. We can grill our minds another time."

Harry asserted the same sentiment, "Hear, hear, mate. Gonna hit the proverbial hay and dream of Operation Haystack."

"Sounds good to me," Mara added.

"Okay," Sal offered. "Thanks, Mara and Harry, be safe."

The monitor's images disappeared.

Alan said, "That was a deep conversation."

Susan added, "And tiring."

Sal agreed. "You guys take a few hours and unwind. I'll cover the progression of the samples."

Susan asked, "Alan, Eric, want to take a long lunch at Sal's favorite place, Makos?"

Alan asked, "Does a bear shit in the woods?"

Susan replied, "Not a polar bear."

Eric laughed. "You two go ahead. I'll babysit Sal."

As the two got up and left, Sal sat deep in thought for a long moment.

Eric looked at Sal and said, "I think I can read your mind, Sal."

Sal stirred a bit in his chair, then asked, "Who are they?"

CHAPTER 18

Gathering Forces

The Pentagon hadn't changed much since the repair and remodel after the 9/11 attack. Most of the office locations were basically retained. Defense Secretary General Porter's office was located in the same army offices that suffered only minor damage.

Porter sat at his desk talking to Homeland Secretary Van Hook. There was a knock on the door.

Porter answered, "Yes."

Porter's secretary, Lieutenant Rosa, stepped in. "Colonel Narkiewicz is here."

"Show him in," was the response.

Edward Narkiewicz walked in several steps and snapped to attention. Lieutenant Rosa closed the door.

Porter said, "At ease."

Edward took off his hat and assumed the position.

The general smiled and said, "Okay, Colonel, you've shown you have decorum, so sit down."

Narkiewicz relaxed somewhat, took off his hat, and walked over and nodded to Julia.

"Madam Secretary," he said in a formal address.

"Colonel," she responded.

He sat down next to her and put his hat on his lap.

The general asked Edward, "You know Julia Van Hook?"

"Yes, sir, I met her on 7 January at the White House."

The secretary smiled and nodded. "Wow, a memory and rank, impressive."

Porter laughed softly. "He can be insufferably regimented also."

He looked at the colonel and directed, "Edward, you can break ranks and be yourself."

Van Hook looked at the colonel and suggested, "You may call me Julia."

"Thank you, ma'am, I'll try," he replied. He yet sat in a rigid attention posture.

Porter looked at the Colonel and ordered, "Edward, relax. We need your free thinking now."

Edward finally broke his facade and smiled. "All right, General, I'm here now."

Van Hook spoke, "The general and I were discussing your Lunar Fall reports and your tactical containment expertise."

"Yes, ma'am?" he replied.

"We want to get your take on the potential threats from alien technology."

"Ma'am?" he asked.

The general interrupted, "Julia, the colonel is holding on to his classified-information defense training."

He turned to the colonel and said, "Edward, you can speak freely. She has been read in on your debriefings and your brother's work with the vice president. There are no limits in our discussions."

Edward thought for a moment and asked, "Okay, ma'am… Julia, how can I help?"

Van Hook smiled and said, "Finally we can get down to business."

Edward leaned up and offered to place his hat on the general's desk. The general nodded, and Edward put it on the desk.

Van Hook began, "Colonel, what do you know about Operation Haystack?"

Edward responded, "The operation was initially created by the president and given to the vice president. It was created, partially, in response to the Lunar Fall particle *diffusion* and the discovery of possible alien signals and subsequent proof of contact with said aliens.

The data from the signal has been partially translated and indicates that the *diffusion* may contain biological or biochemical agents that could be a threat to our environment. Ongoing data translation has pointed to the *diffusion* as being an unintentional act, or accident, if you will.

"The search for possible remnants of the *diffusion* on the moon and sections of Earth are ongoing. The samples that have been collected are being analyzed by various BSL-4 labs, including Fort Detrick. Worthy of note is that the translations of the data streams are found to be in the form of various Earth languages, and as an aside, references have been made to our various world religious dogmas."

The colonel finished with, "Ma'am!"

The Secretary was totally impressed and rhetorically asked, "Who are you? And where is Jimmy Hoffa?"

Edward smiled and stated, "Hoffa's whereabouts is classified level 7." He chuckled and shook his head.

Porter smiled and said, "Well…that was asked and answered."

Van Hook gathered her thoughts and asked, "As a protective measure, what would you suggest should be done to contain any alien threats?"

Edward cocked his head a little to the left and said, "Seriously, ma'am, I would get onboard with Operation Haystack. They are on the right track."

Porter stated, "I've suggested to the president that he maintain the military threat level at DEFCON 5, normal. Julia here thinks that the domestic level might be better addressed at Alpha."

Edward saw them anticipating his response. "Whoa, you're asking a peon to weigh in on national-security issues? I respectfully decline."

Porter took a shallow breath. "I'm sorry, Colonel. That's not what we are asking. What we would like to know, given your military/tactical expertise, what would be the likely public response to raising the domestic threat level to alpha and not raising the military level. Wouldn't that be sending a mixed message about the potential alien threat?"

Van Hook added, "The president is going to deliver a press conference to apprise the public of the recent revelations. We are asking how you might mitigate the likely negative reaction to the revelations."

Edward sat in silent contemplation.

He began cautiously, "As far as the levels of threat goes, the public would expect the threat level to increase, at least to a 'possible' threat. The issue of how to contain public reaction is another matter. Depending on how the information is delivered, there will be at least mild chaos. An uncertain future will elevate desperation, leading to economic instability. There can be no military containment."

Van Hook asked, "How can we mitigate the reaction?"

He continued, "One thing should not be done, and that is to downplay the situation. Again the delivery of the information is critical. However, given the political schism, there may be little chance of showing unity. The people—WE—need to have a united front and a cause to rally around, and this could be that cause. If the TRUTH is told, the people will know it and accept it."

Van Hook had listened to the words and prepared her thoughts.

"I think I should be waving a flag and have the general salute it."

Porter exalted, "Well said. That's the colonel I know. You and your brother are so much alike."

Edward commented, "I didn't know that you knew Mark."

"My daughter, Carrie, and Mark worked on military communications together," Porter explained.

Edward made the connection, "Oh, Carrie Wilson. Of course, that's her married name."

Porter added, "She doesn't use the my-dad-is-a-general line to get ahead. She's her own person, as is Mark. As a matter of fact, I recommended Mark to the vice president to work on Operation Haystack."

Porter had a realization, "By the way, how is your dad doing?

Van Hook looked at Edward and asked, "Oh my. What happened?"

Edward replied, "He's fine. He was in a minor automobile accident. He suffered a broken wrist, but he has to have everyone sign his cast."

"Hope he gets well soon," she said.

"Thank you. Ma'am." Van Hook gave him a look. Edward retracted, "Julie."

Porter changed direction.

"When you came in, the Secretary, uh, Julie and I were discussing the coordination of the Coast Guard with the National Guard to secure likely hot spots and critical areas in the event of any unrest."

Van Hook reached on to the desk and picked up several oversized maps and put them in front of the colonel. "We'd like your input."

He looked over the maps and sorted back through a few of them a couple of times again. He nodded a few times as he scanned them again.

Eventually he spoke, "I like the contingency plans for the BSL labs."

He looked at a couple more maps. "You might consider different drone positioning and increase the ground-troop placement for the SETI sites. The topography may present a response time lag."

He gave two of the maps to Van Hook and pointed out his concerns, "It may seem premature, but you might consider that an organized incursion may develop sooner than projected, especially if the situation drags on for more than a week."

Porter asked, "You think that could happen sooner?"

Van Hook agreed, "Walter, if only 2 percent of subversives find a particular cause, it would not take long to organize an assault on a single target."

Porter thought for a moment. "Yes, you're right, but what cause and which target?"

She continued, "We've spent years fine-tuning our defense of the usual targets, but the colonel is right. BSL labs and the SETI sites are new to our overall protection structure."

The general sat back in his chair in thought. Van Hook continued to look at the maps.

The general leaned up in his seat and looked at Van Hook.

"Julie. Who do we have that could command that aspect of the project?"

He caught her eye and directed it toward Edward.

The colonel was looking at the maps, half-listening to their conversation. He noticed the silence between the two. He looked up and saw that they were smiling and looking at him.

He shook his head and sat back in his chair. "Hold on!"

His head leaned downward slightly, and his brows dropped as he continued, "That's job for a general, not a lowly colonel."

Porter said, "So…are you saying that you aren't capable of commanding more than five thousand troops?"

Edward sat up in his chair. "Sir, I'm saying that the command structure says—"

The general interrupted the colonel, "Blaa, blaa, blaa!"

Edward stopped talking.

Porter continued, "Colonel, you have time in grade. But a promotion isn't the only workaround. The president can designate a 'special commander' in this case. See it as a field promotion."

Edward shook his head. "This, sir, is a set up!"

Van Hook added, "Not really. We've been interviewing candidates for this particular job and YOU, sir, are our choice for it."

Edward sat in thought. "Sir, you realize that—"

Porter, somewhat exasperated, again, strongly interrupted.

"Soldier, stop!"

Van Hook stood up and extended her hand and exclaimed, "Welcome, Commander."

CHAPTER 19

Celebrate: They Be Aliens

Jo James sat, looking at the signal monitor and entering data into the keyboard. She glanced down at a paper on the table and input more data. At the next station, Cory was talking, on a monitor, to Perry Edmonds at Hat Creek. Several lab workers were busy at their own stations, inputting data and comparing that with documents and charts.

"Perry, are you certain?" Cory asked.

I'm waiting for verification from Berlin and Berkeley, but yes the coordinates are the same. Are you getting the same readings?"

Cory called out to Jo, "Jo, can you join me?"

Jo got up and walked over to Cory. She saw Perry on the monitor.

"What are you two up to now?" she quipped.

Cory had a devious look on his face. "We were trying to ascertain if you are really the mother of our child."

Jo answered in a doubtful tone, "Really?"

Perry shook his head and smiled. "Actually we were going over the source coordinates, and so far all the verifications match."

Perry looked at another monitor at his station and exclaimed, "Just got verification from Berlin and Berkeley, they all match."

Jo sat down easily on a chair. She looked at Perry and then at Cory.

"So…we have always fantasized and bantered about life in the Alpha Centauri A system, but to have proof…"

Cory said to himself, "Proof."

Perry partially nodded his head. "Yes, but now what do we do with that *proof?*"

Jo, still seated, leaned to one side. "Yes, after we shout it to the rooftops, how will that help explain the data?"

Cory added, "And that doesn't explain the technically *real-time* communications."

Perry commiserated with Jo and Cory, "We have all been working on verifying the source of the signals but actively ignoring what that means."

Jo added a next step, "First we have to notify the other SETI stations so we can all celebrate the news, then we have to regroup and combine our quantum minds to hypothesize and theorize a new understanding of *time* itself."

She asked, "Okay, who wants the honor of breaking the news?"

Perry offered, "Let's put it on an all-call audio/video stream."

Cory said, "Great idea. Can you set it up, Perry?"

Perry said, "Of course, but just a minute, I've gotta go get Amir."

Cory laughed. "Yeah, do it."

Perry left the screen and returned shortly with Amir in tow.

Amir asked, "What's up?"

Jo said, "We want you to be a part of this."

Amir asked, "Part of what?"

Perry said, "The signal data is coming from the Alpha Centauri A system."

"Really? It's verified?" Amir asked.

Perry nodded. "Okay, here it goes."

Perry engaged a red button on his console. Images began appearing on the monitor, each one making the next image smaller to accommodate a new connection. After a few minutes, the monitor was filled with small icons, perhaps a hundred. Each contact added an audio acknowledgment of contact. Perry made an announcement.

"Everyone, please, may I have your attention?"

He waited for relative silence. "I realize you probably can't see us among the many icons on your screen. This is Perry Edmonds at Hat Creek, and Jo and Cory James at Johannesburg."

The noise level again increased.

"Okay, quiet please."

The noise mostly abated.

"We wanted to make this announcement on all-call. You probably have all suspected the source of the signal data streams. But it has been verified that the source is, in fact, coming from the Alpha Centauri A system from a lower-mass exoplanet. So…everyone, celebrate our work and on to the next task. How are they communicating in practically *real time*?

"Congratulations and thanks, everyone," Perry ended the connection.

CHAPTER 20

Living on Alpha Time

Sal and Lucas were just walking into Peter Simmons' office when Sal's COM activated. Lucas and Peters COMs went off also.

Peter looked at the message and said, "This is from SETI, how about yours?" Sal and Lucas looked at their COMs and nodded.

"Why don't we take it together on my monitor?"

They both walked over to Peter's desk and watched the monitor as Peter accepted the COM. They listened intently at the replay of the SETI announcement concerning the verification of the signal source as coming from Alpha Centauri A.

Lucas said, "That's not really a surprise. Mark was in the know with the data source in Johannesburg. Jo and Cory were almost certain of the source."

Sal and Peter started walking back around the desk.

Peter commented, "Keeping us in the dark, eh?"

Sal took exception, "Well, not all of us were in the dark."

As he sat down, Peter asked, "Sal, you knew?"

"Just waited for confirmation, but there wasn't any other likely source that aligned with the time line and direction of the diffusion that struck the moon and Earth in those precise locations." Sal also sat down.

Peter was surprised. "That's something I was kept in the dark about."

"Wasn't a secret, just had to ask the right people the right questions, and…going over 'Gemo's notes didn't hurt," Sal said with a chuckle.

Peter ceded defeat. "Lucas, that's called burying the lead."

Sal quipped, "A guy's gotta have some secrets."

Sal looked at his watch.

"I wonder if Cory and Jo are awake?"

Lucas said, "You kidding? There are probably still jazzed about the news."

Sal asked, "Peter, see if you can get them on a COM call."

Peter looked at the digital time displayed on the wall. Peter replied, "I'll try."

He pushed a few keys on a keypad. They waited for a connection.

"Let me guess. You want to discuss the time conundrum?" Lucas said.

"Well, we're awake. Why not have a party?" Sal suggested.

"Oh, oh. How about Hat Creek? Let's rattle their cage," Lucas laughingly said.

"Good idea, Lucas. Try them too," Sal said.

Lucas wanted a retraction. "Really, Sal? I was trying to be funny."

"Come on, Lucas, they are three hours behind us. They're just starting their day."

Lucas threw up his hands and said, "Why not?"

Peter asked, "You really want to include Hat Creek?"

Sal responded, "The more, the merrier."

Peter pushed a few more keys on the keypad.

Momentarily the monitor displayed Mike Mitchell's image.

Peter said, "Michael, good to see you."

Michael looked at his screen for a moment and exclaimed, "Oh it's you, Peter. I was expecting a call from the Community Observatory in Placerville. I wanted to tell them the news."

Peter smiled. "We saw the broadcast, congratulations to all of you."

Sal added, "Yes, congratulations."

Michael heard the voice but didn't see anyone else on his monitor. "Who's that?"

Peter said, "Just a minute, I'll move the monitor."

Peter slid the monitor to the end of his desk. Sal and Lucas moved their chairs to the other end to be in view of the monitor.

As they adjusted their positions, Michael began to recognize participants. "Hey, Lucas." He looked closer at the monitor. "Oh wow!" he exclaimed. "Is that you, Sal?"

Peter said, "Yes, I found these two lurking about the street, panhandling. I gave them each a dollar, and they followed me here."

Michael responded, "They are sad-looking puppies."

He added, "Great to see you all."

Lucas chimed in, "I'll bet you guys are ecstatic with the confirmation of the source."

Michael replied, "Certainly are, even though we pretty much expected it, we are all excited to get the affirmation."

Sal asked, "Have you heard from Ren Lang or Richard?"

Michael nodded. "Yes, both have sent their congratulatory messages, and each promised a COM conference call also."

Peter began to ask, "Michael. Lucas and Sal were—" Cory James appeared on the monitor.

"Oops, guess who decided to join us. Hello, Cory," Peter said.

Cory looked at his monitor and shook his head. "Peter, you interrupted us for these hooligans?"

Cory looked off screen and yelled, "Jo, no need to hurry. It's no one important on the COM."

Jo was heard off monitor, "I'll bet it's Sal. He has the worst timing."

Sal smiled and asked, "Cory were you guys 'practicing'? You already have one on the way."

Jo started talking off screen, "Sal, I heard that…" And she eventually sat next to Cory and finished her sentence, "You living vicariously through other people."

She saw the other images on her screen and said slowly, "Oh… we have company." She backhanded Cory on the shoulder as she finished buttoning up her blouse. "Cory, you should have told me."

Sal chuckled. "Busted again."

Jo said softly and quickly, "You pervert." She spoke more lively, "Lucas, Peter…and…Michael! How nice to see you."

Lucas grinned and said, "Sorry to interrupt, but were you guys—"

Cory quickly said, smiling, "Lucas. Drop it!"

Peter maneuvered the dialogue, "So…as you suspect, Sal thought it would be 'fun' to call all of you…as I throw him under the proverbial bus."

Michael laughed. "Don't know about you guys, but I'm awake."

Jo asked, "Sal, are you still playing with your microbes?"

Sal laughed. "Touché, Jo."

Peter said, "Congratulations on the news."

Cory took a breath. "Thanks, we all worked hard on that process."

Sal took a little more serious tone. "I'm sure we all realize that, in addition to the translation of, and the meaning of the data, there is the issue of how the data and diffusion was sent."

Sal settled into his seat. "The latter question intrigues me to no end."

Michael added his thoughts, "I'm with you, Sal. It doesn't promote any logic to find that they can send signals that answer our signals in practically real time."

Jo made a proposal, "You know I would like to give them a name. Calling the aliens them or they is impersonal. Let's give them a name."

Lacus agreed, "I agree. We should give 'em a personality."

Cory smiled at Jo. "Yeah, something we can name our baby after."

Jo sneered at Cory and replied, "Not gonna happen, Cory."

Sal raised his brows. "Think about it Jo, name it Alpha Centauri A, and you could celebrate your baby's birthday every 4.3 light-years."

Jo sneered at Sal. "Sal, Cory doesn't need your help."

Lucas laughed as he added his observation, "How's the couch gonna feel tonight, Cory?"

Lucas then suggested, "Okay, seriously why not just call them Alpha, as in a beginning?"

Sal digressed, "Speaking of real-time responses, how does Alpha do it?"

The group fell into a long collective silence.

Michael finally spoke, "You know I sound like a broken recording, but maybe Amir can shake our minds up a bit?"

Sal nodded. "Is he available?"

Michael related, "Amir is here when I'm here. He hasn't had a life either since we got the first repetitive signals. I'll get him to join us."

Michael picked up a COM and called Amir's station.

While Michael waited for an answer, Sal asked, "Jo, Cory, has the intensity of the signal varied?"

Cory answered, "Now that you mention it, the intensity varies somewhat like a pulse. And the speed of the pulse changes very slightly, continuously. It wouldn't have been noticeable if Dominique at Hat Creek found it by accident. Since then, all of the sites have tracked the change."

Lucas asked, "Is the pulse synchronized with all the sites?"

Jo added, "The sites reported the signal pulses differed by time zones."

Sal questioned out loud, "Varied by time zones...distance between sites...or distance from Alpha?"

Michael hung up the COM, and Amir appeared on the monitor.

Michael announced, "Okay, we have Amir."

Amir said, "Thank you for inviting me."

Sal nodded. "Amir, we are in a quandary and thought you might help us, or possibly confuse us more than we are. But in any case, your input is welcomed."

Amir said, "I'll do what I can."

Sal presented, "Cory and Jo were describing Dominique's discovery of pulse-like change in the intensity of Alpha signals."

Amir looked confused. "I'm sorry what's 'Alpha' signals?"

Sal said, "I'm sorry, Amir, we have thought we'd name the aliens *Alpha*."

Amir thought for a bit, then continued, "That's okay. Yes, Dominique found the slight variance in intensity was consistent, but an anomaly when compared to other radio-type signals."

Sal asked, "What makes this signal an anomaly?"

Amir explained, "If you liken the signals to that of water waves that spread out from a source, that correlates with the pulse-like behavior. However, unlike water waves that subside with distance, these waves remain the same height and distance regardless of distance."

Jo commented, "I was under the impression that the pulses changed when compared to other SETI sites."

Amir continued to explain, "That was the assumption, but further calculation didn't take into account the miniscule distance between the sites relative to the constant."

Sal added, "The constant being the speed of light?"

Amir augmented, "Sorry, yes, the speed of light."

Michael elaborated, "An anomaly was not only noted in the lack of dissipation of the waves, but also that there was no discernable deflection of the signal."

Lucas became confused. "How is it possible not to have a deflection of the signal when it encounters an object?"

Lucas attempted to summarize, "Am I, are we, following this right? Regardless of an obstacle, the wavelengths did not change or deflect."

Sal added another bend in the directions of thought, "However, Dr. 'Gemo's notes identified one additional observation in his calculations."

Lucas said, "Of course, 'Gemo adding more intrigue from the great beyond."

Sal chuckled. "You may not be too far off, Lucas."

Lucas said, "Okay, let's have it."

Sal continued, "'Gemo found that the particles in the diffusion were carried/delivered by the same signal, but they did deflect off objects, those objects being the moon and Earth."

Cory wondered, "But how could the particles travel such a distance, at the speed of light, and not suffer heat deionization or diffusion coming from such a distance."

Sal added yet another piece to the puzzle, "It seems that 'Gemo was working on a theory that there was simultaneous nonparticle diffusion at a different frequency."

Lucas begged out, "Wow, this is getting beyond my comprehension. My head hurts."

Amir said, "I followed along until the particles riding the diffusion, but then the second signal diffusion rattled my brain too."

Sal sat in silence.

Jo said, "Well, it's been a long day. I'm calling it."

Peter had begged out of the discussion. He had tried to follow the discourse but was totally mesmerized by it. "I, like most of you, am calling it a day."

Michael nodded his head in agreement and said, "Catch you later."

Cory and Jo said, "Good night, all." Their faces disappeared from the monitor.

Peter disengaged the monitor. He stood up and asked, "Anyone for dinner?"

Lucas nodded his head. "I'm in."

Lucas looked at Sal. "Okay, Sal. You've gotta eat."

Sal still sat in thought. He eventually shook his head awake and said, "Yep, I need to feed my brain."

CHAPTER 21

Diffusion: Bullet Points

Susan and Eric were in the BSL-4 lab office, going over data printouts and comparing them to the data on the monitor. Alan came through the door of the office carrying several charts under one arm while talking on the phone. Alan straightened out the charts and laid them on the table in front of Susan and Eric. On the monitor was Mara, looking at a monitor in her office in Milan.

Alan pointed to one of the charts. "This is what Mara was talking about."

Mara heard her name, looked at her monitor, and said, "What?"

"Sorry, Mara, didn't realize you were busy."

"That's okay. I was rechecking the algae data from Jakarta."

Eric said, "Alan was pointing out that your assessment of a possible convergence of molecules in those two microbes using an antigen."

Alan looked at the monitor, then back at the chart and asked, "Susan, you could be on to something. The survival of archaea microbe is not contraindicated."

Susan excepted, "That was Mara's hypothesis, not mine."

Mara laughed. "We've been at this so long we're getting punchy. That was Sal's interjection."

Alan added, "Well, regardless of whose track we're following, the train is moving."

Susan made an observation, "Even if that proves likely, we yet don't know where that train is going."

"Why don't we stop for a while and just brainstorm?" Mara suggested.

"Good idea. I need some coffee," Susan said.

Alan said, "I'm already up. I'll get it for you." Alan went over to the service bar and asked, "Anyone else want something?"

Eric answered, "Sure how about a Pinecado?"

Alan thought and nodded several short nods. "That sounds good to me too. Haven't had one of those for a while. Are they in the cooler?"

Eric replied, "Yep, in the back, behind the juice. My private stock."

Alan took a cup out of the cabinet and asked, "Susan? Cream, sugar, coco?"

Susan replied, "Just a touch of cream."

Alan poured the coffee and dropped a bit of cream into it and stirred it with a stir stick. He went to the cooler and opened it. He moved several juice containers aside and discovered Eric's stash. He collected two Pinecados and closed the door.

Alan secured the beverages and deftly delivered them to the requestors. Alan started to sit down but looked at Mara on the monitor and asked, "Mara, I should have asked you if you wanted something. Do you?"

Mara laughed and suggested, "Naw, I'll take sips out of your Pinecado."

Alan chuckled and sat down.

Eric added, "Don't tell Sal I have these."

Alan said, "Oh, that's right. He got addicted to them last year and banned them outright."

Susan added, "Didn't he doctor it with single malt and claim he saw aliens?"

Eric laughed and exalted, "The aliens are coming, the aliens are coming!"

Susan stated, "Thanks for the coffee, Alan."

"My pleasure, Susan."

Mara remarked sarcastically, "Yeah, thanks, Alan."

Eric requested, "All right, let's see if we can make sense of the microbial composition dilemma."

Susan began, "Okay. So far we have modified algae microbes interlaced with archaea and suspended in an antigen with some sort of metallic structure."

She continued, "Mara is that consistent with the Jakarta data?"

Mara looked at her monitor and compared them with some papers on her desk. She checked them again. Finally she asked, "Eric, are you sure 'Gemo's notes support the possible metallic structure?"

Eric looked at a report and looked back at the monitor. "That was the supposed structure in the hypotheses."

Alan suggested, "Let's look at this from the other end of the spectrum. If what we are presuming the possible structure is a given, what is Alpha's purpose for sending it to us?"

Susan stood and went over to a large whiteboard and wrote the number 1. "We could use the microbes to maximize our biofuel production efficiency and"—she wrote on the board "Biofuel Production," and then she wrote the number 2—"create potentially and unlimited food supply and—" She wrote "Food Supply" on the board after the 2; then she wrote the number 3.

"What next?"

Mara offered, "If we include the archaea's ability to live in hostile environments, can we add a sub 2a and b to point 2 to include on Earth, our moon, and other planets?"

Susan wrote under point 2, a "2a: Earth" and "2b: Moon" and planets.

Alan raised a question, "How about the mysterious antigen that seems to shield the microbes in the delivery process, where does that fit?"

They all pondered Alan's query for several moments, looking blankly at one another, at charts, papers, and monitors.

Alan's mind stirred. "Maybe 3 is the delivery process itself."

Susan said, "But the delivery process is complex in itself."

Mara said, "So...Let's add that as 3 and break that down also."

Susan wrote "Delivery process" and added "Diffusion" in parenthesis. Then she added an "a" and "b" under the third point.

"Okay 3a is what?"

"Protection antigen," Alan suggested.

Susan nodded and wrote that down after 3a, and asked, "Next?"

Eric said, "You have to add a sub a-1 and a-2 as the antigen protects the metallic particles and the microbes."

Susan added an a-1 "metallic particles" and an a-2 "microbes" to the board.

Mara asked, "When or where do you insert the delivery mechanism itself?"

Alan took exception, "Ya know…I don't think the delivery mechanism is germane. We should be concerned only with its effects."

Susan said, "That's very astute of you, Alan. Sal must be rubbing off on you."

Alan smiled. "That's a comparison I am pleased to embrace. Thank you."

Eric wondered, "Yes, kudos, Alan. Yet I wonder where a discussion of the delivery mechanism does fit in this whole Alpha enigma."

Susan added, "Yeah, it's not the main focus of the SETI biological, linguistic, or religious impactions. But yet it is an integral part of everything."

Alan said, "Let Dr. 'Gemo figure it out."

CHAPTER 22

The Conversation

Perry and Michael were going over the reports of signal variances with Jo James at the Johannesburg SETI and with Honrí Foster at the upgraded VLA (Very Large Array) Commensal Open-Source Multimode Interferometer Cluster Search for Extraterrestrial Intelligence (COSMIC SETI) in Socorro, New Mexico.

Honrí pulled up the latest data on the low-frequency signal variances on his screen.

"I'm still curious as to how Dominique, there at Hat Creek, came across this amazing data."

Michael asked Perry, "Did you go over her data with Amir before he verified it?"

Perry said, "Michael, have we ever doubted Amir or Dominique when they presented anything?"

Michael replied, "Point taken."

Jo added, "Really! That would have been totally unnecessary since we all immediately verified the data."

Perry suggested, "Honrí, I can have both Amir and Dominique explain how she discovered the source of the signal data, if you'd like."

Honrí said, "Yes please."

Perry asked Michael, "Why don't you go see if Amir and Dominique are available, and I'll transfer the call to their COMs?"

Michael said, "I'll go check. I'm sure they would like that discussion."

Michael stood up and walked around the tables in the direction of Dominique's station. Amir's station was on the way to her station. Michael went to Amir and, from behind, tapped him on the shoulder.

Amir took off his headset to listen to Michael.

"Perry and I were wondering if you and Dominique would like to talk to Honrí, in Socorro, about how she discovered the low-frequency signal variance from Alpha?"

Amir nodded. "I, for one, would like to find out more about that also. I'm certain she would appreciate that opportunity."

Michael said, "Well, get your ass up and let's go see."

Amir smiled and got out of his chair.

They walked a short distance around the left end of the stations and then to Dominique's, seated, watching a monitor.

Amir got her attention, and she noticed Michael also. She took off her headset.

"Amir, Michael, is there a problem?"

Michael smiled. "Yes, you are too good at your job."

Amir added, "Actually we would like your help. Would you like to talk to Honrí, at Socorro, and me about how you discovered the low-frequency variance from Alpha?"

Dominique smiled wryly. "Surly, I'd love to."

Michael said, "Great. I'll get Perry to transfer Honrí to your COM here, then you and Amir can talk with less chance of interruptions."

Dominique said, "That would be fine with me."

Michael nodded and touched his earpiece and spoke, "Perry, you can transfer the call to COM…" He looked for the station number on the console.

Dominique interrupted and said, "332."

Michael repeated, "332."

Momentarily the monitor lit up with the image of Honrí.

Michael said, "Okay, Perry, we got it."

"I'll leave you guys to it," Michael said and left.

Honrí started, "Dominique, I'm Honrí at Socorro."

Dominique nodded. "It's a pleasure to meet you, Honrí."

She added, looking at Amir, "This is—"

Honrí broke in, "Amir. Hi, Amir, good to talk to you again."

Amir replied, "It's good to talk to you also."

Amir offered to Dominique, "Honrí, as I am, is curious as to how you discovered the data signal."

Dominique nodded slightly and began, "As you know, Amir, we were working on the translation of the data signals, separating the different languages."

Amir nodded and she continued, "I noticed a subfrequency, dialogue, streaming in real time. That prompted me to document and record the data, and that was the same Array 14, 1,500 MHz that you asked about."

Amir also explained, "That's the verification we needed for confirmation for contact with Alpha."

Honrí had a question on his face. "Dominique, what was so intriguing about the translation of the data?"

Dominique paused and replied, "What made it stand out initially was that I needed no translation."

Amir became perplexed. "What do you mean you didn't have to translate the data?"

She continued to explain, "I'll back up a bit. I was talking to my sister, Elsa, on my headset when I noticed there was a data stream on a subfrequency in the Array 14, 1,500 MHz. At first, it was in the same format as the 1,500 MHz, but the signal data seemed to repeat while I was speaking to my sister. I hung up with my sister, and the data stream signature was like an audio stream that normally appeared in the data streams, but those appeared only 'within' the data signals. This was a distinctly separate signal."

Amir said, "What made you think the signal wasn't a bleed from standard radio waves?"

She replied, "The collector switch was not activated. So it wasn't possible to get any other signals not sent directly to my location."

Honrí asked, "Are you saying the signal was sent only to you at your station?"

"Yes. That's when I decided to not only record the digital signature but also any possible audio file also," she stated.

Amir said, "That was a smart option to choose."

Dominique continued, "Eventually I realized that it possibly was an Alpha talking to me, in English, and answering me in real time."

Honrí sat back in his seat in disbelief. "Dominique, you know how incredible that sounds?"

Amir added, "That would be so amazing. To actually talk to an Alpha and ask questions."

Dominique took a very long pause and finally announced, "Yes, it was *so* amazing and unbelievable to actually talk to an alien."

Honrí replied skeptically, "Dominique, are you saying you actually had a conversation with the aliens?"

Amir said, "I'm so envious of you, Dominique. Do you know what an honor that would be to actually talk to aliens?"

She paused again. "Actually I think it was only one alien. He or she used the name Adam."

Honrí shook his head. "Whoa, Dominique, don't destroy your credibility."

Dominique became defensive. "My credibility? You saying you don't believe me?"

Amir interjected, "No, Dominique, that's not what he's saying."

Honrí broke in, "Yes, Dominique, that is what I'm saying."

Amir tried to bring calm to the conversation, "Dominique, you have to admit that to say these things after—"

She held up her hand to silence Amir. She took a long deep breath and sat in silence.

Honrí said, "Amir, I don't know what to make of this. It's very difficult—"

Dominique held up her hand, interrupting again, and spoke calmly, "I'm sorry, but I realize that making such a claim is incredulous."

Honrí sighed. "I'm glad you admit that—"

Dominique smiled and interrupted yet again, "You want to hear it?"

Honrí's brows drooped. "Here what, the data stream? How would that help?"

Dominique dropped the bombshell, "No, I recorded the conversation. You can verify the data stream, date and time, and matrices. So…do you want the hear it?"

Honrí's mouth dropped and Amir was stunned.

Dominique typed on her keyboard and said, "Here it is."

The voice of the alien was decidedly electronically generated.

A—Hello…hello…hello.

D—Hello?

    Dominique's demeanor was lighthearted.

A—Yes, hello.

D—Who do you want to talk to?

A—I want to talk to you.

    Dominique became receptive.

D—Okay. Go ahead and talk.

A—This is Adam. What is your name?

D—Hello! This is funny. Who is this?

    Dominique continued lightheartedly.

A—I'm sorry you didn't hear me. This is Adam.

D—Adam who?

A—I wish to speak to someone from Earth.

    She laughed again.

D—I live on Earth, will that do?

A—Yes, what is your name?

    She was heard huffing a short breath.

D—Okay, I'll play along. My name is Dominique.

    There was a short pause.

A—Hello, Dominque—of the Lord. Is that correct?

    Again a short chuckle was heard.

D—That's funny. Who is this?

A—I will explain. I am what you call an alien, and I'll call
    myself Adam. This is so you will have a human reference.

D—Really?

    She replied skeptically.

A—Do you speak for Earth?

D—No, I speak for only me.

She answered as a matter of fact.

A—Do you have a Deity?

Adam's voice yet sounded digitally dry with little inflection.

D—What you mean?

A—Your name, I see that it refers to the Lord. Is that you?

She stated with a curious tone.

D—These are strange questions. Who is this?

A—I am Adam. Are you the Lord?

D—No.

A—Do you have a lord?

She was heard laughing.

D—Really? How about you, do you have a lord?

She replied in banter.

There was a short pause.

A—We are, as you are, without a, what you call, a living Lord.

The vocal tone seemed to change to less of a digital tone.

Dominique's demeanor, again, was playful.

D—Okay, I'll play along. Let me ask this. Do you have a creator?

A—I don't know.

D—Well, then do you believe in a creator?

A—I don't understand your word *believe*. Is it a physical word?

D—Are we waxing philosophically?

It seemed that it was a game of twenty questions.

There was a long pause.

A—I am still learning your language. Is the wax in melted form?

D—Okay, Adam, where are you from?

There was another long pause.

A—My location is what you call the Alpha Centauri A system and your understanding of the second exoplanet.

Once again there was a noticeable change in the voice pattern.

There was another pause.

D—Really?

Dominique answered incredulously.

She continued in a factual tone.

D—We calculate that distance as 4.3 light-years from Earth.

There was another pause.

A—We calculate the distance between us as .62847 wave A .032292 depression at C sub 2.

D—I'm not familiar with that formula.

She answered tentatively.

A—No, you would not be.

Dominique was heard sighing. She took a different tact.

D—If you are who you say you are, then why are you contacting Earth?

A—We have noted what you might call a civilization anomaly on your planet.

D—Really? Again sounding skeptical. When we say anomaly, it often means something bad. What is the anomaly?

Another really long pause.

D—Adam, are you still there?

The pause ended.

The alien's voice pattern became more light and warm.

A—Our reference is based on a noticeable change of the use of resources that will affect your species' survivability.

She paused, possibly to assimilate the statement.

D—Hmm, can you give me any specifics?

A—The enhancement process was delivered to Earth with the dissention.

There was another pause.

D—Are you referring to the electromagnetic surge that affected our moon and planet in September?

Another long pause.

A—I calculate that you mean six moon cycles past?

D—That would be approximately correct.

A—That's affirmative.

Dominique's tone seemed to relay concern.

D—That was you that caused those effects? That attack?

There was a long pause.

The vocal tone and pattern returned with a touch of empathy.

A—It was not intended as an attack. It was delivered to enhance your planet. It's unfortunate that you perceived it so.

D—Will that delivery do harm to Earth?

A—No. The delivery was a mistake. It will do no harm.

> She replied in an irritated tone.

D—I don't understand. You send a "delivery" by mistake, without warning, and expect us to not see it as an attack?

> There was another pause.

A—I understand your position. We are confident that your technology will do the proper assessment of the delivery and mitigate any perceived threat.

> Dominique was heard taking a deep sigh.
> There was another pause.
> She seemed to have calmed down.

D—Okay, Adam, or whoever you are...

> She paused.

D—How about this...Why are we using English in this conversation when there were several of our languages used in other communications?

A—The different languages are used to secure a positive reception of my message. I use English here as it is your preferred language.

D—How do you know what my preferred language is?

A—I was listening to your conversation to Elsa and deemed it to be in English.

> She became curious and concerned.

D—How did you know who I was...Okay, who is this?

A—This is Adam.

> Dominique was once again the reason for a long pause.

D—I'm having a hard time believing that you are who you say you are.

A—It's understandable for your species to be cautious. I am pleased that you are responding to me.

D—Why would I not respond?

> The voice tone and meter became more fluid and much less digitally created.

A—This is the first successful attempt to have a conversation with someone on Earth.

D—You've made other attempts?

A—Yes, but the attempts were with what you call data streams. This is my first attempt to use a vocal medium. It was difficult to ascribe the correct translation form from our language to yours.

D—What does your language sound like?

A—It is difficult to describe. We communicate with what you would call…

There was a long pause; she seemed concerned.

D—Hey, did I lose you?

Another long pause.

A—I apologize. I'm updating my database of your language and its idioms to enable a smoother translation.

There was even a more noticeable change in the voice from an electronic-generated voice to a more human-sounding voice.

D—Your voice sounds different.

A—Yes, this is an enhanced mode of speech. Is it more acceptable?

D—Yes, it is more pleasing to my ears.

A—I comprehend that observation. I had to physically modify my receptors, in order to communicate with earthlings, to hear you.

D—You modified your ears?

The conversation evolved into more of a discourse between friends.

A—It would be difficult to explain that physical modification in an acceptable time frame that we have available. I would rather learn more from you.

D—If you don't use ears, how do you communicate?

A—We normally communicate by sending neuron impulses.

D—Telepathy?

A—That's one way you might explain it. That modification has created an amusing and pleasing effect for us to experience between our kind.

D—You don't have ears?

A—We have ears, but they weren't used as much for vocal communication, nor was our voice.

D—Because you stopped talking to one another?

A—It became less important. It is becoming more enjoyable for us.

There was another pause.

D—Adam, why did you make references to various religions.

A—Again to secure a positive reception of my message.

D—Okay, what is your message?

She asked as a factual request.

A—You have nothing to fear from our kind.

D—Why didn't you say that in the first contact?

A—The delivery of the enhancement process preceded the primary message. It was sent in error.

D—You mean you shouldn't have sent it?

A—It was proper to send, but not in that sequence.

D—We understand that there is possibly another, what you call a "resource," delivery to come?

A—Affirmative.

D—What will be the content of the next delivery?

A—That content will enhance and correct the previous delivery.

D—What needs correcting?

A—There are some processes that must be accomplished in a precise order to ensure its efficiency.

D—It is possible that delivery may cause harm to Earth?

A—It's possible.

D—How can we avoid the harm?

A—It will be corrected.

Honrí and Amir had listened intently.

Honrí asked, "Dominique, could we pause the recording for a moment?"

Dominique paused the recording.

Honrí asked, "Dominique, why have you not brought this to Michael, Perry, or even Amir before this?"

Dominique thought for a moment. "I've pondered that also. Actually I've listened to this several times, trying to convince myself that it did happen. I've checked and rechecked the matrices of the data in an attempt to disprove that the conversation occurred with an alien. All of my calculations came back and reaffirmed that I was, in fact, conversing with an Alpha. It's only now that I felt confident, or brave enough, to subject it to scrutiny."

Amir related, "So that's why you had me verify that specific data signal stream?"

Dominique stated, "Amir, I'm sorry that I didn't tell you why, but I wanted to be certain it would pass the smell test."

Honrí asked, "How long was this conversation?"

"Twenty-five minutes and two seconds."

Amir chuckled. "I hope you reversed the charges?"

Dominique stifled a laugh. "Very funny, Amir."

Honrí said, "I want—no, I need—to hear this whole thing, but we need to bring someone up the chain in on this."

Honrí added, "You have made copies of this, yes?" Dominique nodded. "Good, keep it in a safe place. Amir, can you stay with Dominique until I check with Lucas Makiev?"

Amir nodded. "Of course, wouldn't think of abandoning her now."

Honrí added, "Okay, hang tight."

Honrí stopped and said apologetically, "Dominique, I'm so sorry that I came down on you like I did, but you should understand that being skeptical is part of being a scientist. So now I'm off to get ostracized myself."

Honrí disappeared from the monitor.

CHAPTER 23

The Conversation: Part Deux

Lucas activated his COM monitor as he was finished putting clothes into his suitcase. He sat on the bed and waited.

The monitor lit up, and Sal's image appeared on the screen.

"Good morning, Lucas, how's it going?"

"Sal, pack a bag. We're leaving in ninety minutes."

Sal shrugged his shoulders and asked, "Leaving as in leaving the city, the country, Earth?"

Lucas replied, "We're going to see if we can talk to an Alpha."

Sal shrugged again. "Should I take a toothbrush and extra underwear?"

Lucas smiled. "Sal, pack a bag. We're going to Hat Creek."

Sal quipped. "I know there are strange people in northern California, but usually the substances they ingest enables them to talk to a god, not aliens."

Lucas explained, "I'll try to make this short. Dominique, at Hat Creek, talked to an alien named Adam, and she recorded the conversation. The recording of that conversation should be in your buffer."

Sal's brows furrowed. "She what?"

Lucas said, "I'll tell you details on the plane. Meet me at Reagan, private airport."

Lucas hung up.

Sal checked the status indicator on his COM and noticed the buffer was activated. Sal stood for a moment, then walked quickly over to his closet and pulled out a suitcase.

*****

The private jet was idling, awaiting its passengers.

Sal hurried up the stairway and funneled through the fuselage and sat across from Lucas, who was working on his COM.

Sal asked, "Who else is coming?"

The attendants closed the doors, and the engine began to rev.

Sal heard the engine revving and answered his own question. "Guess we're all that are going."

Lucas said, "Buckle up. We're in for a ride."

Sal mumbled to himself, "And what a ride it might be."

Lucas stood up and swiveled a large monitor away from the side of the plane and positioned it between the two so they both could see it. He typed on the keyboard, and the monitor lit up.

Lucas began, "This is the conversation between Dominique and the Alpha, Adam. All matrices and time line signatures have been verified.

Lucas touched the keyboard, and the audio began to play.

Sal listened extremely close to the audio. He paused the audio several times and took notes in his personal journal.

Sal sat thinking as he, again, paused the audio.

"Lucas, is it me or does it sound like this Adam is the lone participant in this contact?"

Lucas mulled over Sal's observation. "Perhaps, but you could make that case only so far, though. If the scenario was reversed had we had that level of technology, it would be almost impossible for one person to use all of those resources on their own."

Sal pondered his observation. "Yeah, I guess you're right, but he or she yet would be at the top of the command structure."

Lucas nodded. "With that, we are in agreement."

Sal recounted, "Adam said that 'some processes must be accomplished in a precise order to ensure efficiency.' That implies that if the order is not precise, the processes will be less efficient?"

Lucas said, "I don't quite follow. It seems like you are splitting hairs."

Sal restated, "Maybe we, I, have been following the wrong order in our approach to solving the microbe conundrum."

Sal, feverishly, wrote in his journal.

He rewound the audio and continued listening.

D—It is possible that delivery may cause harm to Earth?

A—It's possible.

D—How can we avoid the harm?

A—It will be corrected.

D—When should we expect the next delivery?

A—It should coincide with your next season, at the meridian mark on your planet.

    There was another long pause.

D—That would be March 20. Why on that date?

A—That is the optimal incubation period to correct the previous dissemination at the precise inclination.

D—Incubation of what?

A—Are you familiar with the material that was delivered in the previous dissemination?

D—No, I am not.

A—That answer would be for someone else to comprehend."

    There was another pause.

D—So there is no danger to Earth?

    There was a slight pause.

A—It would be preferable if there were no humans subjected to any possible effects.

D—So it is dangerous?

A—I am not totally familiar with human physiology, but the possible effects could be, what you call, a loss of short-term memory.

D—Memory loss?

A—I must emphasize *short-term*. Those subjected may not recall that event.

There was a short pause.

D—Why don't you send this voice signal to all of Earth instead of just me?

A—I am working on that issue. I did send the data stream delineating the future dissemination, but this was the first voice medium that became available that my time spectrum could access.

D—How are you able to communicate with me on such an intellectual level. Uh, how did you learn our languages?

A—We have been processing signal streams from your origin for a period of time. We maintained the past signals in our data storage containers. Even now, I am acquiring more knowledge by accessing your storage containers. You call them databases.

Dominique paused and seemed to take a step back.

D—This is all very interesting. Yet I am not convinced that you are what you say you are. My logic presents doubt.

There was a short pause, and a brief electronic glitch was heard.

A—Perhaps I can reduce your doubt. I recalled a question you asked earlier, about waxing philosophically. I assimilated more of your database, and I now understand that inquiry.

D—I recall my question. Is that an exercise that you are familiar with?

A—I am able to rationalize and present logic and hypotheticals.

There was another pause.

A—There is one question I have for you.

D—About time you asked a question. Shoot!

There was a pause.

A—I understood your humor. *Shoot* was a slang imperative to elicit a response.

D—Very good.

There was a long pause.

A—What is god?

There was another pause.

Dominique answered in the same tone that any scholar would answer.

D—The answer to that question has eluded humanity since our beginning.

Yet another pause.

D—Do you have an answer?

There was an even longer pause.

A—It seems that we are in the same proverbial boat, and if I may add, without oars. However, I can share one of our observations.

D—That I would like to hear.

A—Life is relatively short and comes quickly. So live as you believe.

D—So...words to live by? Can I quote you on that?

A—That is an appropriated idiom. Yes, you should do so.

There was a long pause that was broken by the sound of a deep breath.

She had excitement in her voice.

D—Okay, this question will determine if you are telling me the truth.

A—Shoot!

She mustered a short laugh.

D—Very funny.

She continued deliberately.

D—If you are from Alpha Centauri A, exoplanet 2, how can you interact with me as if we are in the same place? There is no time delay of 4.3 light-years.

There was a very long delay.

Sal paused the audio and leaned back in the recliner.

Lucas looked at him and asked, "Sal, buddy. I would think that you, of all the people, would want to know that answer."

Sal smiled and said, "I'm trying to imagine the answer. And I can't."

Sal resumed the audio.

A—The answer has to do with the physicality of time itself.
Dominique seemed to pause introspectively. The curiosity of a scientist was showing through.

D—I'm not aware that time had physicality.

A—Yes, you probably know time as what you call the "constant."

D—Yes, we do.

A—We are relatively new to the concept, but we have been able to see time as a wave.

D—Not sure I can follow that.

A—Imagine time as a liquid.

D—Okay.

A—Now imagine time as a wave of liquid.

D—I can see that.

A—If you find a way to jump from each crest of the wave and avoid the depression, that would be a time jump.
There was another pause.

D—I follow the logic, but how do you jump to the next crest?

A—We use what we call *quantum-mechanics acceleration*, but there are dangers to that process. There must be a buffer.
Dominique paused and her yawn was heard.

D—This is such an interesting exercise at this time of the morning, but I still don't believe you are Adam, an alien.
There was another pause.

A—I will prove it to you, Dominique.

D—How?

A—I will send you the location on your COM device, and you will see me at three of your minutes postmeridian at that location, on your change of season.

D—Okay, Adam, I'll talk to you then.

A—Not talk. See me.

The audio became silent.

Sal stopped the audio and leaned back in his chair and rocked patiently to the rhythm of his mind.

Lucas also sat in thought. He swiveled toward the window on the transport and gazed at the horizon, then looked up at an imagined view of space.

Sal looked at Lucas, reached over, and swiveled Lucas's chair toward him. Lucas had a perplexed smile fixed on his face.

They both sat, looking at each other. Lucas finally broke the silence. "What 'cha think, O Great Mind?"

Sal paused and reported, "Thinking…that IF this was an actual conversation with an Alpha, then…THIS mind isn't so great."

Lucas stated, "In deference to all great minds…imagine how I feel."

Sal said, "Lucas, you cannot play that card with me, four-time graduate summa cum laude."

Lucas replied, "This mind feels like summa cum dumb."

Lucas thought for a second, then spoke somewhat excitedly, "You think Adam was an actual alien?"

Sal shook his head slightly. "You know what I'm impressed by?"

"Pray tell," Lucas entreated.

"I'm hella impressed by Dominique. She wasn't awestruck. She used amazing construct of thought."

Sal paused, then continued, "She was right to question the validity of Adam's claim as being an alien."

Lucas questioned, "So you DON'T think she was talking to an Alpha?"

Sal interjected, "It was questionable at the outset, but as the voice began to sound more human and not digitally processed, that lent more credibility that, as he explained, he was basically learning on the fly."

Sal paused. "Did you notice that his discourse became more thoughtful and deliberate yet acquiescent. He began to make a connection with Dominique."

Lucas offered, "Wouldn't that be what a scam artist would do?"

Sal countered, "But there was no bravado or superiority in his words, and his demeanor became…almost empathetic."

Sal continued, "He didn't try to convince her that he was an alien. He genuinely embraced the simple satisfaction of making contact."

Lucas asked, "What did you make of the second diffusion explanation?"

Sal replied, "That was intriguing, but I'm more concerned with the time line. That comes in only four days."

Lucas said, "Yes. I'm certain that this recording has been sent to everyone to analyze, including the president and Richard. They are probably listening to it as we are and probably frantic over the possibility that this is real."

Sal stated, "There is no time to question its validity. It must be presumed to be real, and preparations should me made immediately."

Lucas stated, "I agree but where do we start?"

Sal replied, "Exactly, Lucas. Where do we start?"

CHAPTER 24

Welcome to Hat Creek

As the helicopter maneuvered onto the landing site, Sal took a longing look at Mount Lassen glistening in the early morning sun. He wondered if Alphas had any beautiful sites compared to those on Earth. Surely beauty is in the eye of the beholder, but having seen Earth from the moon, as Sal has, would attract the attention of any being.

Lucas was talking to Richard on his headset as the chopper settled down. The engine began winding down, and the pilots gave a thumbs-up to their passengers, and they unbuckled their restraints.

Sal slid up in his seat and grabbed a hanger strap above the door and swung to the ground. He grabbed a suitcase and walked toward a waiting car.

Lucas moved over into Sal's empty seat and finished talking on the headset and handed it to a crew member. He clutched his suitcase and jumped out to the ground. He saw Sal getting into the car and walked over to join him.

Ari greeted Lucas as he got in and closed the car door.

"Good morning, sexy, I'm Ari, I'll be your tour guide."

Lucas looked surprised and smiled a knowing smile. "Ari, weren't you Miss Universe two years ago?"

She raised her head slightly to look in the rearview mirror at Lucas and laughed. "Only in my dreams."

Lucas replied in his best sexy voice, "You're always in my dreams, my love."

Sal shook his head. "You guys get a room?"

Ari grinned as she replied, "We already have one for tonight with a single bed."

Lucas said excitedly, "When did you get here? Are the girls here too?"

Ari started the car and began to drive. "I was going to meet you in Sac, but Mom said she would watch the girls. So I dropped them off there. Sal sent a chopper for me this morning and brought me here an hour ago."

Lucas looked at Sal and said, "Sal, when did you have time to do that?"

Sal replied, "I asked Susan to set it up. I know you haven't been home for over a week."

Lucas replied, "Well, thanks, buddy. I really appreciate this."

Ari added, "WE appreciate this."

Ari drove down a short gravel road, then turned left onto a semipaved road. She continued past a short stand of trees on the left and five arrays on the right. She pulled up the driveway to the SETI site off to the right and stopped.

Sal opened his door and stepped out of the car.

Ari bailed out of the car and rushed to open Lucas's door.

His door barely had opened when Ari grabbed Lucas by the hand and pulled him out. They immediately wrapped their bodies together in a passionate embrace and even more passionate kiss.

Sal retrieved his suitcase, closed the car door, and walked toward the SETI entrance. He opened the door and saw Perry coming toward him. They enthusiastically shook hands.

Perry said, "Sal, you ole bird, good to see you."

Sal smiled and said, "Great to see you too. Haven't been here for a while…probably a year or so."

Perry replied, "Wow, has it been that long?" Perry shook his head and added, "Yeah, I guess it has."

Perry looked toward the door and asked, "I guess Lucas and Ari are still outside."

Sal smiled and said, "Yeah, it may be a while before they cool down."

Perry added, "I wouldn't expect anything less."

Perry looked at Sal's suitcase and said, "Here, let me take that."

Perry reached for the suitcase.

Sal looked at a table a few steps away and shook his head. "That's okay, I'll just set it on the table here."

Sal eased the suitcase on the table.

Perry said, "Okay."

Sal looked around the room and noticed new stations had been added. "Hey, got some new stations in?"

Perry said, "Yeah, they arrived two weeks ago. We've been asking for more stations and staff for two years. It's strange how there was no budget for more staff or stations until the discovery of possible contact caught someone's attention."

Sal agreed, "Yep, we were an ugly stepchild until they needed someone to handle a biological crisis."

Perry added, "We'll see what happens when this settles down."

Sal asked, "Speaking of crisis, where are the star players?"

Perry smiled. "Dominique and Amir are tuning up the arrays with the new sensors and diodes that magically appeared in our budget."

Sal smiled.

Finally the door opened, and the entwined couple found their way into the building.

Lucas, with Ari hanging on his shoulder, walked over to Perry and shook his hand. "How's the premier SETI site operations codirector doing?"

Perry said, looking at the smile on Lucas's face, "Alas, apparently not as well as you two are."

Ari interjected, "Sorry, Perry. I'll try not to distract Lucas from his tasks."

Perry said, "Ari, my dear, he would be less focused without you here. Besides, I need your computer expertise dealing with the servers."

"Whatever I can do to help speed things along so I can spend more time with this guy," she explained, smiling at Lucas.

Lucas nodded at Ari. "Okay, woman, we'll have plenty of time later."

The side door to the station opened, and Amir and Dominique stepped in. They saw Lucas and Sal and headed toward them.

Lucas held out his hand and shook Amir's hand. "Amir, good to see you in the flesh."

Amir replied, "It's a pleasure for me also."

Amir turned to Dominique and said to Lucas, "Lucas, this is Dominique, our astrophysics and linguistics expert."

Lucas smiled and offered his hand. "It seems that you are more than that, Dominique. So very glad to meet you," Lucas said, shaking her hand.

Dominique replied, "Mr. Makiev, the pleasure is mine. I've followed your worldly journeys with envy."

Lucas replied with a smile, "Please, it's Lucas. Not sure it should be envy you feel. It's exhausting just remembering the places I've been."

Amir went up to Sal and shook his hand. "Dr. Uschin, uh, Sal, I've looked forward to meet you in person. It's such a pleasure."

Sal smiled and laughed. "Amir, you've got to expand your social circle if I'm a highlight of your day."

Amir laughed. "Not at all, sir."

Sal took a step toward Dominique; she smiled and excitedly scurried over to him and held out her hand. "And you are Dr. Uschin. I'm honored to meet you."

Sal met her one hand and reached and grabbed her other hand and clasped them tightly in front of him.

Sal spoke with reverence in his voice, "Dominique, I submit to your presence. I've had many honors bestowed upon me, but the honor of meeting you far outshines all that have come before. You, my dear, are a treasure."

Dominique was taken aback. "I don't really know what to say, Dr. Uschin."

Sal explained, "It's Sal, and although I am given to dramatic tendencies at times, this is one instance that the words are heartfelt."

Sal continued holding her hands. "You really don't comprehend your place in history, do you?"

She looked at Sal quizzically. "Sir, I'm not quite sure what you mean."

Sal sighed. "Of course not, you have yet to be tainted."

She was trying to follow Sal. Eventually she absorbed his words. "It was just a conversation."

Sal smiled. "Yes, and I realize that you are not convinced that you did, in fact, talk to an alien. However, should that be found to be true, you, my dear, will have to accept it and all that it may bring."

Dominique's eyes blinked several times, and she deeply sighed. She spoke slowly, "I...I really haven't taken the time to process that possibility."

Sal added more, "Lucas and I were reviewing the audio and would like to reconstruct the specific data matrices and subfrequency of the conversation."

She said, "Of course, I'll have to get my files and notes."

Lucas suggested, "Why don't we go over to your station so you can feel more comfortable."

Sal turned to Amir and asked, "Amir, we'd like you to join us."

Amir smiled. "Okay, I'd like that. I'll get my notes."

Amir got his notes, and they all followed Dominique to her station. They gathered extra seats from nearby and sat around Dominique's station.

Sal started, "Before we get to the technical aspects, I'd like to know what your impression was of the sincerity of the Alpha, Adam."

One of her brows sagged slightly as she thought. "Thinking back, I felt uneasy and suspicious at first, but as we spoke, those feelings subsided. The conversation developed into something like a friendly sparring match. The odd thing is that as we spoke, it seemed that he was more aware of my changing feelings. I thought about... would it be possible for an AI computer to sense changes in feelings using inflections and phrasing. My assessment was that, only a person would have that ability. The other part of that question is, would that person have to be human?"

Sal asked, "So…you think that you had a conversation with an alien?"

Dominique paused. "I believe so…but I regret not asking more questions about them."

Sal interjected, "After listening to the audio, I don't think you realize how much information you really got out of them. I was so impressed with your questions and your drawing out the issue of time travel, which I am yet in a quandary. Their limited use of speaking and hearing, their questions about faith, their attempt to correct an error, their faith in our ability to understand and use the content of the diffusion, that is only some of what YOU gathered in your innocuous conversation. So, Dominique, don't sell yourself short."

Dominique smiled.

Sal continued, "So…let's go over what we need to address now. If we are to believe the streaming data and the conversation is accurate, then a second diffusion is coming. We don't know what may be in the diffusion. Even if we did, we don't have time to defend against any possible effects. The effects will not cause any harm to humans, save possible short-term memory loss."

Sal stopped and asked, "Other than informing the public and dealing with that fallout, am I missing anything?"

Dominique added, "There's the meeting with Adam on the twentieth."

Sal agreed, "Yes, but that is probably going to be a positive event."

Dominique nodded, raised her brows, and wrinkled her upper lip.

Lucas listened to Sal and Dominique's interactions and made an observation, "So…the ball is in the air, and the president and or Richard have to catch it."

Sal said, "That's about it. So…let's dig into the data streams and audio matrices."

CHAPTER 25

Dinner at Fall River Hotel

Sal decided to play chauffer to Ari and Lucas for the twenty-minute drive to the Fall River Hotel. The hotel had withstood numerous fire threats and economic downturns to evolve into a pleasant retreat with historic-landmark status.

Sal pulled into a parking space, turned off the power, and opened the car door, got out and closed the door. He walked around the vehicle and opened the passenger door and retrieved his suitcase from the front seat. He bent down to see the lovebirds cuddled up, half-asleep.

Lucas opened his eyes a little wider and stirred his shoulders against Ari's arm tucked under his arm.

"Sal, buddy, thanks for driving. It was good to nap a little after today."

Sal stretched out his shoulders and said, "No problem. Let's see if the dining room is open, I'm hungry."

Ari leaned off Lucas and said, "Yeah, I could use some sustenance too."

Lucas gave Ari a kiss and opened the car door. He rolled out, with Ari following. She closed the door and followed Lucas around to the trunk. Lucas opened the trunk, and they pulled out two suitcases and closed the trunk lid.

The trio ambled toward the entrance, and Sal opened the door. He waved Ari in first, then Lucas, then took his turn.

They walked between dinner tables and booths, seating a few diners, to the desk at the end. A waiter saw them approaching and called to someone in the next room, "Carson, our guests have arrived!"

The waiter moved to greet his guests. "Good evening, welcome. I'm Jerry, I believe you are our guests for the night?"

Ari replied, "Yes, sir, Makiev for two and—"

He nodded to Sal. "Uschin for one."

Jerry looked at their luggage and asked, "I can take these to your rooms if that's okay?"

Lucas said, "That would be great, thanks."

Sal asked, "Is it too late for dinner?"

Jerry replied, "No, Glenda thought you would be late arrivals and held the cook for you."

Jerry set the luggage aside and reached for Sal's COM, and Sal declined, "That's okay, buddy, I'll hold on to this."

Jerry said, "Very well, sir. Can I show you to a table or booth?"

Ari said, "How about a booth?"

Jerry replied, "Certainly."

He grabbed some menus and led them around the corner to a secluded booth and offered it, "Will this do, ma'am?"

Ari smiled and said, swaying her shoulders in banter, "This will be great for this ma'am."

Lucas smiled and shook his head as she slid into the booth.

Lucas looked at Sal and said, as he slid in beside her, "We're in trouble now, she's got her second wind."

Sal said, "That's YOUR problem, pal."

Sal sat down and put his COM next to him on the seat.

Jerry placed the menus appropriately and asked, "Beverages?"

Ari responded, "Coffee, cream and sugar."

Lucas said, "Iced tea with lemon."

Sal said, "Iced tea with lemon also."

Jerry said, "Thank you." And he left.

Sal opened his menu and searched the choices.

Ari and Lucas sat holding hands and with their heads together.

They breathed a sigh together and began to peruse their menus.

After a few minutes, the manager came up to the booth with the drinks and asked, "Who gets the coffee?"

Ari raised her hand. The manager distributed the beverages to the proper patrons and sorted napkins and dinnerware on the table.

"Good evening, I'm Glenda, or Gee as some call me. I want to welcome you to our hotel and restaurant. I noticed you made the reservation from Hat Creek, SETI. We have had several scientists from there, as customers. I've been interested radio-signal research for years, and I have more than passing interest in biochemistry. I've seen all of your faces on the Vision Network. It's a pleasure to have the Makievs"—nodding to them and then to Sal—"and you, Dr. Uschin, as our guests. Just to let you know, I've heard the not-so-secret rumors that contact has been made and I, for one, am *so* excited."

Gee paused and said, "I apologize for interrupting your dinner." Gee gestured a bow and started to leave.

Sal held up his hand to stop her from leaving. "Gee, is it?"

She nodded. "Yes, sir."

Sal said, "Call me Sal. I'm interested as to why you are excited about the rumors of alien contact?"

Gee smiled. "Sir—"

Sal said, "It's Sal, Gee."

Gee continued, "Sal"—she seemed embarrassed—"I don't want to interfere with your evening."

Sal countered, "Gee, I'm interested in what you think…your thoughts on possible alien contact."

She replied, starting slowly and becoming more excited, "For me, realizing that there is other intelligent life out there invigorates my thirst for knowledge. What do they look like? How do they live? What kind of environment do they live in? I have so many questions."

Sal listened intensely and smiled. "Gee, we are of the same mind. So many questions."

She changed course. "I'm sorry, I just came to see if you were ready to order, but it seems that you probably need more time."

Lucas replied, "Thank you. We will need a little more time."

Gee smiled. "Of course, I'll give you a few minutes." She turned and left.

As Lucas continued to look over the menu and, without looking up at Sal, said, "Sal, I can't take you anywhere without you getting in a conversation."

Sal replied, "People are so interesting, especially the passionate and intelligent."

Ari smiled and said factually, "I agree, and she was that."

They sat in silence for several minutes, scanning their menus.

Ari sat back and said, "I'm gonna have brisket with broccoli."

Sal decided, "I'll try the salmon in green beans almandine."

Lucas sighed. "I spy the braised trout with hollandaise sauce and red potatoes."

Lucas looked quizzically at Ari. "I thought for sure you'd want the rib eye."

Ari smiled and squirmed. "Lucas, stop that."

Lucas grinned. Ari backhanded his shoulder.

Almost on cue, Jerry returned. "Are we ready?"

Sal and Lucas presented their selections, and Ari introduced her choice quietly, "I'll have the rib eye, medium well, mashed, gravy, and the corncob."

Lucas chuckled. Ari smiled broadly and backhanded Lucas again.

Sal shook his head, smiling.

Jerry said, "Thank you." He collected the menus and left.

Sal leaned forward and rested his arms on the table and clasped his hands. His thoughts raised his head slightly, and he took a slow deep breath and exhaled slowly. He looked at Ari and asked, "So you locked in the server codes and all of the signal data? You didn't find any signs of braiding in any server connections?"

Ari replied, "Yes, and that left the isolated audio file that linked only to the 1,500 MHz subfrequency."

Lucas added, "So we are agreed that this anomaly was NOT an anomaly. It was an inextricably directed stream!"

Sal polled the thinking. "Have either of you found a nexus between the different languages and different religious factions?"

Ari observed, "It was rather obvious to me."

Sal asked, "How so?"

Ari continued, "Adam stated that using the various languages and religious references was intended to lend comfort and unity to their message."

Lucas thought for a moment and offered, "You know, maybe it's just that simple."

Sal added, "Perhaps so. I keep looking for a hidden nefarious agenda."

Ari offered a reality explanation, "So…let's examine this. What would Alpha gain by being disingenuous. They've sent us tons of data that, so far, seems to only enhance our livelihood. You yourself, Sal, extrapolated that some of the formulas could lead to arresting or even curing cancer and heart disease. And you, Lucas, said that understanding the signal transmission methods could enhance our interstellar communication capabilities."

Sal nodded, "All that may be true, but we are yet at a disadvantage. We have no knowledge of any mal-intent nor even time to come up with a plan to counter it, even if we knew what it might be."

Lucas agreed, "Yeah, and that's what we told Richard and the president. Unless we find out something new, it's out of our hands."

They sat in combined silence.

Jerry and Gee arrived with their meals on a serving cart.

The two busied themselves arranging the meals to suit the guests.

They placed condiments in the center and scanned the table one last time. Jerry refilled the beverages.

Glenda asked, "Is there anything else you would like?"

The trio glanced at their meals. It seemed to be an acceptable fare.

Ari stated, "I don't see anything missing, this looks really good." She eyed back at her rib eye.

Glenda said, "Jerry or I are available if you need anything."

Lucas replied, "Thank you."

Jerry grabbed the serving cart handle and pushed it with him as they left.

They began arranging their plates in their desired positions and proceeded to satisfy their appetites.

Sal generally concentrated on keeping portions of his trout on his fork. Ari and Lucas also meted out their meal while engaged in conversation about their children.

Lucas noted, "It was so nice of your mom to watch the girls."

Ari laughed and said sarcastically, "You know she had to be bribed to watch them."

Lucas smirked. "Yeah right, she would never try to spoil them."

Ari added, "No, she lets my dad do that."

Lucas nodded in agreement.

Sal took a break from his meal. Is Angela still trying to play big sister to Nicole?"

Lucas answered, "Two minutes older and forever the big sister. It's good that Nicole lets her think she is in charge, but Nicole manipulates that to her advantage. We're fortunate that there is no resentment between them."

Sal nodded. "Let's hope that stays that way as they grow. But eventually, they will find their own ways in life."

Ari observed, "Actually we look forward to that dichotomy. It would be nice to have two independent girls with different goals in life."

Lucas added with scrunched brows, "Of course, I will have to get used to having THREE independent females to deal with."

Ari batted her eyes at Lucas and asked, "Aw, honeybun, I'm not too much for you, am I?"

Lucas smiled and shook his head slowly, said nothing, and continued to eat.

*****

The diners rested in silence for a short while.

Jerry came by several times to check on the status of the meal.

Sal finished first, pushed his plates aside to accommodate his COM.

His fingers tapped often on the keyboard, and Sal would gaze at the screen.

Ari finished her steak and was sopping up the juice with her mashed potatoes and homemade bread. Lucas was savoring the last of his green beans.

Sal looked up from his COM and asked, "Ari, I'd like to revisit your thoughts about the religious phrases used in the data stream."

She leaned back in the booth and listened.

Sal paused and thought, "Have we translated all of the phrases that addressed religion?"

Ari replied, "Yes, so far. But it's interesting that each of the phrases is linked to the language normally used in that religion."

Lucas tried to clarify, "So...the intent of the separate data streams is to vocalize the phrase in that language?"

Ari further explained, "Alpha hadn't been able to sync up the words and add voice to the words until the conversation with Dominique."

Sal followed with the process, "It seems that Alpha was working on the process to combine the two into a single audio file. And... they finally were able to match a voice with the words."

Lucas tried to uncomplicate the thoughts, "I can imagine the difficulty in learning the language phonetically and then trying to match the intonation of the subtitled words with it."

Ari tried to anticipate the next step, "You recall Commander Yost saying that the hologram seemed to be talking, but there was no audio?"

She paused. "What if Alpha was an attempt to add voice to that video or hologram file?"

Sal added, "They are learning to send audio with a hologram. That's why 'Gemo didn't describe his hologram as talking."

Lucas stated the obvious, "Well, we may have solved what their communication obstacles may be, but it doesn't get us any closer to understanding what their intentions are."

Sal nodded and shook the cobwebs out of his head. "Well, my intentions are to pile into bed."

Lucas saw Jerry clearing a table and got his attention.

Jerry walked quickly to the booth. "May I get you anything else, dessert, wine?"

Lucas declined, "No thank you, Jerry. I believe we are ready to retire for the evening."

Jerry offered, "Shall I put the meal on your bill?"

Lucas replied, "That would be fine."

Sal took issue, "Put it on my tab, Jerry."

Jerry nodded. "Certainly, sir. I'll wait at the desk to show you to your rooms."

Jerry left.

Lucas eased his way out of the booth, and Ari followed. Sal retrieved his COM and slid out of his side of the booth.

"Thank you, Sal, for the meal. I'll leave the tip."

Sal waved his hand. "Naw, I got it."

Ari said sweetly, "Sal, I'll have Johnny deal with YOUR TIP."

Lucas smiled, shook his head, and grabbed her shoulders from behind and said, "Come on, evil woman…leave Sal and Johnny alone."

Lucas guided her out of the dining room to the desk where Jerry was waiting.

"This way." Jerry stepped around the desk and walked a few steps and started up the stairs. The entourage followed him.

The stairs turned to the left, and then at the top of the stairs, Jerry walked to room 202, unlocked the door with a keycard, and gave it Sal. Sal stepped in and closed the door. Jerry unlocked 201, and Ari took the keycard, eased the door open with her shoulder, and said, "Thank you, Jerry, I've got it from here."

Jerry smiled and walked away and mumbled to himself, "Of course you do."

Ari led Lucas into her lair and closed the door. She tossed the keycard aimlessly across the room. Lucas, being a willing prey, grabbed both of her hands, raised them above her shoulders, and released them. His arms wrapped around her back and waist. Her hands draped across his shoulders to the back of his neck. The passionate embrace was punctuated by the passionate longing kiss of lovers. The kiss continued softly while his hands gently unbuttoned her blouse. Her hands reached to his back and lifted his shirt above his shoulders. His hands temporarily left their assignment to allow his shirt to be removed. His shirt fell to the floor. His hands promptly finished their task, and he rolled the blouse off her shoulders, along with her bra straps, and her bra rested below her breasts. Both delivered gentle kisses to each other's neck and shoulders. His lips found her wanting breasts. His wandering hands found all the right places as they eased down to the bed.

*****

Sal noticed his suitcase against the closet door. He picked it up and set it on the bed and unzipped it. He sorted through it and put his underwear, socks, and T-shirts in a drawer. He hung his pants and shirts in the closet. He got undressed and headed toward the bathroom with his toiletries. After a brief shower, Sal propped up several pillows and settled into the bed. He opened up his COM and searched the screen for files. His eyes found its target. Sal thought out loud, "*Quantum Mechanics Acceleration.*"

He checked the status of Mark's COM and found it active.

He took a chance and sent a COM request.

Mark's image appeared on screen. "Yes, Sal, I'm awake. Can't sleep either?"

Sal replied, "Just got into bed, and no, probably won't be able to sleep for a little bit."

Mark offered, "I've been fielding questions from Richard, Silver, Marilyn, and even Paul Le Cross."

Sal questioned, "Paul? What did he want?"

Mark said, "The guy actually asked some impressive questions about the composition of the diffusion particles."

Sal said, "Guess that was scary?"

Mark replied, "The scary thing was that I think he actually understood what I was saying."

Sal said, "Well, good for Paul, guess he's not just a smooth talker."

Mark asked, "So, Sal, what's up?"

Sal began, "I've been going over the ad-hoc symposium to research and define what Alpha called *Quantum Mechanics Acceleration* relative to time jumping. I see they are using the acronym QMA for it. I don't find any one scientist that is heading it. Have you heard who might be collecting the research?"

Mark shook his head. "No, no one has stepped up to put their name on it yet. However, I saw an offshoot of theoretical discussion trying to use the Schrödinger equation to explain the possibility."

Sal said, "I saw that discussion also. A time/wave theory is such a radical concept it has everyone in a tailspin."

Sal looked at more conversations on his screen. "We have to build a theory block by block to move anything forward. The problem is that using our established concept of time, the wave theory of time doesn't hold water."

Mark laughed. "I hear what you did there, Sal."

Sal chuckled. "Sorry, couldn't help but using that pun, didn't want it to slip through my fingers."

Mark smiled. "That was even worse. Give up!"

Sal stepped back. "We've all alluded to the various constructs of time and its being a wave one of them. However, no one has been able to present that as an acceptable theory, using the physics of quantum mechanics."

Mark sighed. "At the moment, the elements of QMA are unknowable."

Sal added his sigh. "Yes, Mark, but you know how I hate not knowing."

Make yawned. "Good night, Sal."

Sal replied, "Good night, Mark."

Sal shut down his COM and floated off into his cyber dreamland.

*****

Next door, the evening activities were in a lull but only temporarily.

Hands began to move over both bodies, searching for prime targets. Several targets were being assaulted softly, and just as a detonation was about to occur, Lucas stopped. The lack of movement made Ari take note.

"What's wrong?" she asked softly.

Lucas said, "I can't do this."

Ari said concerned, "What?"

Lucas said with a fake whimper, "I can't do this...I miss my girls."

Ari could visualize, in the dark, the grin on his face. She rolled over on top of Lucas and countered sexily, "Well, luv, maybe I can help ease your suffering."

She pulled the sheets over her shoulders and began sliding down under the sheets to her designated target.

CHAPTER 26

Getting to Know You

Richard took a breath and raised his shoulders off the floor, completing one last sit-up. He looked at the COM monitor and noted the time displayed. He rolled to his feet and headed for the shower, discarding his workout clothes in a hamper. Fortunately he showered quickly, as the COM notification flashed and beeped a soft tone.

He continued drying off and was finishing with drying his hair, when the COM voice stated, "Evelyn Walker on COM standby."

Richard replied, "COM 2, hold five minutes."

The voice replied, "Five minutes."

Richard quickly dressed and tended to his hair. He checked the mirror for disarray and saw none. He sat on the edge of the bed and directed, "COM 2, Baker 2. Activate VC."

Evelyn Walker's image appeared on the screen.

Richard greeted with a smile, "Good morning, Eve."

Eve noticed Richard sitting on a partially made bed and eked out, "Good morning, sir, uh, Richard. Did I catch you at a bad time?"

Richard had a curious look on his face and scanned the room. Finally it dawned on him.

"I'm sorry, Eve, I didn't realize where I was. Let me move into another room." He started to stand up.

Eve smiled appreciatively. "No need…Richard, I know you are a man of routine of sorts."

Richard chuckled and smiled. "Rather presumptuous of me, huh?"

He noticed she was in her car. "I assume you called to say you were on your way here."

She nodded and smiled. "Just wanted to give you fair warning. From the looks of it, perhaps you need more time."

Richard chuckled. "No, Eve, you're not interrupting ANYTHING. I'll see you in—"

She completed the thought, "Twenty?"

He replied, "Breakfast awaits."

She laughed. "Bye, Mr.—Richard, bye."

Her image disappeared.

"COM 2. Baker 2. Disengage," Richard directed.

"Disengaged."

*****

Shari saw Eve, on camera, drive up to the residence and met her at the door.

"Good morning, Ms. Walker."

Eve replied, "Good morning, Shari. How are you today?"

"I'm doing well, Ms. Walker. Just concerned about the vice president. So much confusion."

Eve allayed Shari's concerns as she walked in, "Shari, you should trust that the president and the vice president are doing their best to keep the nation safe."

Shari replied, "I know they are good men. The vice president is waiting for you in the study."

Eve said, "Thank you, Shari."

When Eve came into the study, Richard was walking over to another door. He noticed her and asked, "Good, you're here. I'm going to get some breakfast. You want to come with me?"

She nodded, put her briefcase down on a chair, and followed Richard.

As they got to the kitchen, Richard asked, "Good morning, Eve, how are you this morning?"

174

She replied, "Actually I feel a little out of my element."

Richard was gathering his breakfast choices on a plate.

He pointed to the spread on the table. "You may select whatever your pleasure is."

Eve scanned the menu on the table, smiled, and followed Richard with her eyes, then finished scanning the table. She started picking out her supplements.

Richard spoke as he continued collecting his choices, "Eve, I wasn't aware that your element had limits."

She picked up a tray and put her choices on it. "Thank you for your confidence, Mr. Vice—" She stopped in midsentence when she noticed Richard's glance, then continued apologetically, "Richard... I'm sorry, it's hard to call you Richard."

He smiled and said, "Say Richard."

She looked at him curiously, and he prodded, "Say Richard."

She complied, "Richard."

He smiled and asked, "What?"

She smiled and repeated, "Richard."

He prodded with continuing hand gestures.

"Richard! Richard! Okay enough, Richard."

The last Richard was a more natural Richard.

"Very good...Ms. Walker," he said with a chuckle.

He put his breakfast choices on a tray and set the tray on a serving cart. He watched her minor embarrassment as she poured a mug of coffee. He continued to take in the view as she put her tray on the serving cart.

He pushed the cart down a hallway into the study.

There was a table placed between two chairs. She took her tray and set it on the table. Richard chose not to sit on his desk chair but opted for the chair next to Eve. He set his tray on the table also. Eve noticed the choice of seating.

They busied themselves arranging their food. They began their meal.

Richard spoke as he ate, "Eve, I realize that much of the scientific discourse may be difficult to follow, but you should know that it is difficult for all of us to digest. We are all out of our element. Rest assured that I am in no way patronizing or diminishing your ability to comprehend the discussions. You have exceptional intelligence."

Eve looked at Richard with a skeptical leer. "Really? Exceptional intelligence?"

He smiled, with his hand in the cookie jar. "Went a little too far with that, huh?"

She smirked. "You think?"

Richard backed off and regained his composure.

He leaned his elbows on the arms of his chair. He tilted his head slightly to absorb her intelligent reply, "So...explain to me the principles of *Quantum Mechanics Acceleration*?"

She laughed and tossed a napkin at him.

He fended off her assault, and they laughed together.

Eventually he gathered his serious face. "So...I have a face-to-face with the president, and I want you as my second."

She thought carefully, "You want me as your second? You want me to supply the dueling pistols?"

He smiled and she continued in banter, "Are they muskets or revolvers? You may need more than one shot?"

She suddenly realized that she was implying the shooting of the president.

"Oh god...I hope we aren't being recorded, I am *so* screwed."

Richard shook his head and said, "No, of course this isn't being recorded."

She was yet in distress. "I can't believe I said those things, even as a joke."

He spoke with sincerity, "I don't record conversations."

He added with a devilish look, "I only use livestreaming worldwide."

She smiled and countered, "If that were, true we should both be drawn and quartered, shot, and tortured to death, in that order."

Richard replied, "I'm not really into that much pain. I prefer dying in my sleep."

She slowly continued to eat and took a gulp of her coffee. "Seriously, you want ME there? Who else will be there, Peter, his cabinet, the AG?"

He replied, "I believe only Marilyn Richter and us."

She said in surprise, "That's it? Is it a livestream?"

Richard shook his head and swallowed some food. "Eve, listen. This is going to be just the four of us talking."

She yet questioned, "Who set this up?"

"Richard called me personally, and we agreed that it was time we talked this out."

She took a bite of a scone and sipped some coffee.

She put down the scone and took another sip of coffee. She leaned back in her chair with the mug still in her hand.

She said emphatically, "This is big. This is a really big moment."

She thought for a long moment and said in earnest, Okay. I'm in."

CHAPTER 27

The Talk

There were several small press tents at the front of the White House. Only one group took note of the nondescript three-car caravan as it approached the White House. The cars were mingled with normal traffic, but at the last moment, they turned quickly into the security entrance. The press reacted fairly quickly to capture a video and snapshot of the vehicles' occupants, but the major actors were unexpectedly in the first vehicle, against the normal security protocol.

After the entourage passed, a press member looked at the images that were captured and exclaimed, "I didn't get anyone I recognized."

She turned to another press member and asked, "How about you? You get anything?"

Her partner checked his display and offered, "All I got was shots of Secret Service."

She stated, "Gotta be someone up the chain to be that sneaky."

He added, "Yeah, something's going on."

She agreed, "Yes, but they'd knock out our drone with EMF and arrest us if we tried to get another peek."

He watched for a moment and saw the lead vehicle going around to the rear of the White House.

He exclaimed, "Yes! I knew it, something big is going down."

The lead vehicle stopped at the rear of the residence. Two agents scanned the area as Richard stepped out of the car, and he assisted Eve out also. They walked up some steps, and a door opened. They entered the short entryway, and staff greeted them, "Good morning, Mr. Vice President, good morning, Ms. Walker."

Both replied, "Good morning."

Philip came around the corner and said, "Good morning, Mr. Vice President"—and nodded to Eve—"Ms. Walker."

"Good morning, Philip," Richard replied and shook his offered hand.

Eve smiled and also shook his hand. "Good morning, Philip."

Philip stated, "Follow me. The president is waiting in the study."

Philip led the way down the hallway to the study. Philip opened the door and nodded for the two to enter.

Tsirch and Marilyn were sitting behind a table with two chairs on either side.

Tsirch and Marilyn both stood, and Marilyn came around her side of the table, and Tsirch followed her.

Tsirch waited as the ladies secured their greetings.

Marilyn walked directly up to Eve and, smiling, offered her hand. "Good morning, Ms. Walker, it's good to see you again."

Eve also smiled and shook the offered hand. "And I you, Madam Secretary."

Marilyn half-nodded. "Let's make this easy. I've known you too long, it's Marilyn."

Eve replied with a nod of her own. "Yes, Marilyn, Eve agrees."

Marilyn stepped around Eve and over to Richard.

Richard offered his hand and spoke first, "Let's make it Richard, if that's all right with you, Marilyn?"

She smiled and replied with intended faux magnanimity, while gesturing a bow, "Well of course, SIR Richard."

Richard chuckled as they shook hands.

Eve walked up to Tsirch and smiled with restraint, "Good morning, Mr. President."

Tsirch opened a big smile and spoke purposefully, "Well, good morning to you, Ms. Walker, I am pleased that we are here in a less-formal setting, rather than challenging my intellect during a press conference."

He offered his hand, and she accepted.

Marilyn advised, "I hope, Mr. President, that you only meet her as a journalist and not as a counselor."

He replied, "Yes, I understand she is a formidable barrister."

Eve took the foray in stride, "Mr. President, I was not, as you were, second in your class at Harvard Law."

Tsirch countered, "But Ms. Walker, YOU were first in your class, although it was at 'lowly' Yale Law School."

She replied with emphasis, "Objection!"

Marilyn lamented to Richard, "I would not want to be the jurist in that courtroom."

Richard stood mildly laughing at the exchange. He raised his head and straightened his posture, as he approached the president.

The president also stood tall and half-smiled.

Richard spoke first, "*Como va la guerre?*"

Tsirch slowly nodded, smiled, and replied, "*No hay guerre aqui, solamente amor.*"

They looked closely into each other's eyes.

They both offered their hands to shake. Slowly their hands bonded.

The metered handshake stopped. Years of emotional bonding resurfaced as they drew each other together in a strong brotherly embrace.

Slowly each took a step back.

Richard nodded and spoke in formality, "Mr. President."

Tsirch returned the respect, "Mr. Vice President."

Eve and Marilyn both fell into the role of historic witnesses.

The president took a breath and said, "Let's sit and talk."

He offered the accommodations, and Eve sat across from Marilyn, and Richard sat across from Tsirch.

Richard reached over to his desk and pushed a button. A voice answered, "Yes, Mr. President."

"Kevin, will you bring in the beverage cart?"

"Right away, sir."

Tsirch said, "Thought we could use something to wet our whistles."

Richard nodded. "We'll need something to moisten the conversation."

Tsirch replied, "I think that the dialogues will be anything but dry."

There was a knock at the door.

"Come in," Tsirch said.

The door opened, and Kevin pushed the serving cart over to the table on the side nearest the president.

"You want me to serve, sir?"

"No thank you, Kevin, we'll handle it."

"Very well, sir." Kevin turned and left, closing the door.

Tsirch opened the choice to the quartet. "Who wants what?"

Richard looked over the beverage selection. "Well, I think I'll have the OJ."

He looked at Eve as a question.

"I'll take the iced tea, please?"

Richard poured the iced tea and handed it to Eve.

"Marilyn?" he queried.

She requested, "How about the tea also?"

"Tea for two," he quipped.

He poured another glass for Marilyn and handed it across the table.

Tsirch assisted the delivery of her drink so Marilyn wouldn't have to reach for it.

She smiled, noting the joint assistance. "Thank you, kind sirs."

Richard poured a glass of juice, paused, and held the pitcher up, looking at Tsirch.

Tsirch stifled a laugh and picked up an empty glass. He pushed the glass toward Richard and said, "Yes, please."

Richard filled his glass and said, "Just like old times."

Neither of the ladies decided to ask.

The party was patiently waiting.

Tsirch broke the ice with a big grin. "So what do we talk about?"

Eve answered, "I thought you would have an agenda."

She immediately retracted, "I don't mean that in a negative sense, I thought—"

Tsirch laughed. "Ms. Walker…may I address you as Eve?"

Eve nodded. "Yes, sir, you may."

He smiled. "Eve, I know what you meant. As the host, I should have topics of discussion, but I think we should have a free for all. I've found that the more open a discussion is, the more productive is becomes."

Eve replied, "Thank you, Mr. President."

Tsirch sighed and said, "Eve, if, for our purpose here, you prefer to call me—"

Eve held up her hand to delay further commentary. "Mr. President, if you are going to ask me to address you by other than Mr. President, I must respectfully decline. The office is sacred to me, my oath, and my upbringing."

The president was in awe. "Ms. Walker, I almost think I should stand up and salute the flag."

Eve, though somewhat embarrassed, continued, "Mr. President, I honestly don't mean any disrespect—"

He interjected quickly, "I'm sure you don't."

She continued without missing her meter, "But I've always seen this office as above reproach, and it's difficult to dishonor it's stature."

Tsirch took a long pause in thought. "Ms. Walker, I totally understand and admire your view of this office. It's an absolute that, as a nation, there should be a focal point that represents the aspirations of the constitution, and to diminish those aspirations by downgrading its standard bearer, a la the president, would be unacceptable."

He continued, "But, Ms. Walker, isn't the mantra of this great nation, all of us are equal?"

Eve listened and was compelled to answer, "Yes, it is."

He continued, "I believe that this nation is a work in progress, as implied in the preamble 'in order to form a more perfect union.'"

He offered his summary, "So why shouldn't the president be seen as a work in progress? After all, I am just a man and worthy of being your equal."

Richard slapped his thigh loudly and exclaimed, "Now that's the Renny I know."

Eve and Marilyn were taken by speechless surprise.

Tsirch gave Richard the you-had-to-say-that look. He shook his head, smiled, and said sternly, "Richard!"

Richard laughed, and Eve and Marilyn stifled their laughs.

Tsirch took a breath but said nothing.

Eve began, "I totally enjoyed your soliloquy, Mr. President. I am yet not ready to address you by anything but Mr. President."

Tsirch nodded an *I understand*. "Perhaps, Ms. Walker, when you get to know me better?"

She replied acceptingly, "Perhaps." She paused. "And…it's Eve…Mr. President."

Richard decided it was time to get down to business.

"So, Mr. President, what are we going to do, and what are you going to say at your press conference?"

Tsirch replied, "That I'll have to figure out, but I mostly have questions."

Richard sighed. "Well, I'm here to help any way I can. I can tell you what I've been told and what my band of brothers and sisters have done and are doing."

Tsirch thought, "What can you tell me about that audio I listened to with the alleged alien?"

Richard relayed, "It all seems legit that the Alpha called itself Adam, and it/he/she/they has scientists everywhere going crazy."

Marilyn and Eve leaned off to their side of the table and Marilyn said quietly, "Renny?"

They both smiled quietly.

Tsirch asked, "How concerned are you about the twentieth deadline?"

Richard suggested, "I'd rather not see it as a deadline but as an opportunity."

Tsirch was curious. "That I'd like to hear about. The DOD, media, and the people are catching wind of the contact, and now, with the audio surfacing, I've got to allay their concerns and take out the fearmongers."

Richard stated, "Yeah, there are always those that create their own message simply to cause dissention. Who do you have to oversee those naysayers?"

Tsirch smiled and said, "Van Hook and General Porter recruited Edward Narkiewicz."

Richard replied, "Wow, that's a catch. He and his brother will work well together."

Richard asked, "What are you going to say about the conversation and the possible second diffusion on the twentieth?"

Tsirch sat back in his chair and said, "The only thing I can do. Tell the truth."

CHAPTER 28

Cat's Out of the Bag

January Yee walked out of the prep room in the side of the conference room and stepped up to the dais. All of the cameras and COMs were trained on every person, movement, and word that may transpire. He placed a single paper of the agenda on the podium, looked around, and began.

"Ladies and gentlemen and members of the press, thank you for being here."

Yee smiled and paused. "I guess, you, members of the press, should also be included as ladies and gentlemen. Sorry if you feel slighted."

There was a smattering of laughter around the room.

Yee smiled and continued, "Didn't expect that much laughter." He paused. "While I'm on a roll..." Yee took a casual stance and said, "A horse walked into a bar..."

There was a temporary lull, but a little more laughter ensued.

Yee smiled, regained his formal composure. "Okay, I'll quit while I'm ahead. The president will be addressing you, along with the DHS Secretary Julia Van Hook, Secretary of Defense General Walter Porter, and a newly appointed Domestic Security Commander Colonel Edward Narkiewicz."

There was a mumble registering in the crowd. One of them asked, "Can you spell that name?"

Yee paused and restated, "Yes, that's Narkiewicz. It's spelled just as it sounds."

A little more laughter was heard.

"Okay, that's *N-A-R-K-I-E-W-I-C-Z*, Edward. If you prefer it militarily, that's November, alpha, Romeo, kilo…"

Yee stopped and chuckled along with the crowd. "Okay, I'll keep my day job."

Yee continued in a serious tone, "Also available to answer questions will be various scientific experts. There will be a surprise addition to the agenda."

Yee picked up his agenda and started to leave but heard a question from the crowd. He turned to the podium microphones and repeated the question, "What is the surprise?"

Yee smiled, looked around at the gathering, and said slowly, "If I told you, it wouldn't be a surprise."

There were a few chuckles. Yee stepped to his right of the stage and waited.

In short order, the lead Secret Service agent opened the door.

That was the cue for Yee to step back to the podium.

"Ladies and gentlemen…the president of the United States, Tsirch Ren Lang."

The president entered the room and looked around the room as he made his way to the dais and stood at the podium. Every camera flashed and recorded his journey.

Tsirch put his notes on the podium smiled and perused the gathering. He nodded to Yee and began, "Thank you, Mr. Yee, for warming up the crowd."

A few chuckles were heard. He leaned slightly on the podium with both hands.

"The world, this nation, and you, the people, are living in the most unusual and exciting period of time ever witnessed. There is no historic comparison. We are facing a challenge of our understanding, our character, and our intellectual resolve."

He raised his right hand at shoulder height and punctuated, with his voice and hand, "Make no mistake, I know we are up to that challenge."

He softened his tone. "Mankind has looked at the stars, the heavens, and questioned our part in the universe." He spread out his hands, then placed them back on the podium.

"We have tried to imagine"—he pointed above the crowd and increased his volume slightly—"what is out there, and we've questioned, is there anyone else out there? Are we truly alone?"

He softened his tone at the start, then increased the volume somewhat. "We now have an unequivocal resounding answer."

He paused and said in a subdued matter-of-fact tone, "We are NOT alone."

He increased the volume one level. "We have made contact with another intelligence. Our radio telescopes and signal-gathering antennae arrays across the globe, known as SETI, have been responding to signals from the Alpha Centauri A system. The increase in signal interaction was punctuated in September of last year, when an overwhelming signal burst was felt by all of Earth, that caused the temporary disruption of electronic devices that you all know as the Lunar Fall."

Dozens of hands went up and "Mr. President" entreaties engulfed the crowd.

Tsirch held his hands up to hold that in abeyance. "Hold on, hold on. As Mr. Yee would say, wait for the punch line! I'm still in my first act, there is more."

The crowd settled down amid some chuckles.

He continued, "As you know that disturbance was short-lived and resulted in a minor inconvenience for us on Earth. However, scientists began to translate the signal patterns into several of Earth languages, among those, English, French, Italian, Hebrew, and others. The ongoing translations were found to be relative to the signals we had sent and received by those we call the ALPHAS. That discovery led to the realization that the communication was being sent and received in real time, as though we were talking on a COM device."

He paused and again held up his hands to hold questions. "We yet do not know or understand how it's possible to talk to someone 4.3 light-years away and get an immediate response. The world's scientists are dumbfounded and in disarray over that possibility or, I should say, that reality."

The crowd became active again, and he held up his hands once again. "Now I'm still not done."

He looked down at his notes. "Now as a matter of transparency, I must relate the latest development. Recently a possible—and I emphasize *possible*—secondary contact was made in the form an actual audio conversation with a staff member at the Hat Creek SETI in California."

More hands and questions started to foment.

He quelled that foray also but with an added smile. "No, no. Hold on, I'll tell you when I'm done.

He paused one last time. "For the staff member's privacy, I will not reveal their name. But there is one last relative item to cover, at least, as far as we know. The signal data stream translation indicated that a second disturbance would be occurring, and that was possibly confirmed during the audio conversation."

He put his hands back on the podium and leaned forward. "I must strongly impress upon you that Alpha assured us in both the data stream translation and the audio conversation, that the disturbance may possibly present a benign and temporary effect."

He took a breath. "I've been as transparent as I can be, and I am trusting you, the people, with the truth."

He added, "Now I'm done."

The expected flood of hands and entreaties erupted.

Uri Dahl was the first selection.

"Thank you, Mr. President, Uri Dahl, *Daily News*. You said there was an audio conversation with a SETI staff member. Is that audio available and what was the content of that conversation?"

Tsirch replied, "The audio is in the process of being verified by several SETI stations to determine if, in fact, it was an Alpha and not someone from Earth attempting to deceive the SETI program. To answer the second part of your question, Mr. Dahl, if the audio is verified as actual contact, I expect that it will be made available."

Uri tried to follow up, but Joshua McGarr secured the next spot.

"Joshua McGarr, *Science Daily*. Mr. President, I can't help but wonder that the audio would not be an issue unless there was something relevant to the signal data streams that makes it credible."

Tsirch smiled. "You just cut right through to the heart, huh, Joshua?"

Tsirch turned to Yee and said, "Mr. Yee, you might give this guy a job application."

He paused amid some laughter. "You are correct. Some of the audio content does align with the data streams and that lends to credibility, but we must be certain that the data stream translation wasn't leaked."

The press selection sequence continued.

"Barry Martin, the *Times*. You said that the coming event may result in a 'benign and temporary effect.' Can you elaborate on what benign effect might represent?"

Tsirch winced somewhat. "I hesitate to answer, since the possible effect was not identified in the data stream translation but only stated in the unverified audio conversation. I can say that due to the urgency in verification of the audio file, I will make the conversation available at that time."

Barry jumped in with the follow up, "Will that conversation be edited?"

Tsirch thought for a moment, then scanned the wings of the dais and saw a familiar face. "You know, I see someone that can help me answer that."

He motioned to Lucas to come to him. "Lucas Makiev, could you assist me?"

Lucas was standing near the entrance door and took a breath. He stepped around some dignitaries and proceeded to the president's side. Tsirch stepped several steps away and leaned to Lucas's ear, and they engaged in a private conversation.

"Lucas, is there anything that would need to be edited out of the audio?"

Lucas paused and mentally recounted the conversation. "I believe that only the two names, Dominique and Elsa, her sister, would need to be edited."

Tsirch said, "Thanks, Lucas."

Lucas stepped away, back into the wings.

Tsirch stepped back to the podium. "I'm sorry for the delay. So as for editing the audio, as far as I can recall, only the names of two people mentioned in the conversation would be edited for privacy."

Evelyn Walker was the next selected.

Tsirch saw her stand and take the microphone. He knew she would have to be the one to test the lock on Pandora's box. He smiled as she spoke.

"Evelyn Walker, *Independent Services*. Mr. President, you spoke of a possible second disturbance, do you know when that event is to occur?"

Tsirch took an easy breath. "That possible specific date was mentioned only in the unverified audio conversation, and since at this time, it cannot be corroborated by signal data stream translation, it would be premature to divulge that date."

She continued with a follow up, "Do you know when that specific date might be revealed?"

Tsirch nodded. "We expect the date and the audio conversation should be available tomorrow some time, perhaps in the morning."

Once again, there was a deluge of hands and questions.

Tsirch again held up his hands to abate the throng. "Ladies and gentlemen, I need for you to indulge me. I need to step back, and the present dignitaries Mr. Yee mentioned at the outset, they will able to supply you with more relevant information and answer your questions."

Tsirch paused. "They will be addressing the plans dealing with and mitigating any possible effects regarding the possible alien-disturbance event similar to the Lunar Fall we experienced last September."

He turned to his right, nodded to General Porter and said, "I have Department of Defense, General Walter Porter. General, please."

Tsirch offered the podium to the general and stepped away to his right.

The general took his place at the lectern and took an easy posture. "Thank you, Mr. President, it's an honor to be here. I've been asked by the president to bring you up to speed with the unusual circumstances relative to our discovery of alien intelligence we have called Alpha. On 19 September of last year, Earth and the moon were subjected to what has been called a diffusion, possibly sent by the Alphas. That was, what you know now as, the Lunar Fall. At the time, we theorized that event was an anomaly of our solar system and planetary alignment, drawing a rogue electromagnetic field. The analysis of the remnants of the diffusion revealed it contained unusual compounds and microbes. Our biochemical scientists, along with those from other nations, embarked on a joint effort to determine the source and possible ill effects of the diffusion. That effort was called Operation Haystack, and the president tapped Vice President Natás as its director. Over the past year, new data stream translation technology was developed, and we reanalyzed the translation of data streams that we had been receiving for years. Subsequently it was discovered that data contained evidence of systematic intelligent signals. Further translation of the data found that it was indeed from an alien source. That discovery caused the president to direct the military to oversee the possibility of an alien threat."

The general took a breath and continued, "Our military involvement reached across the globe, and soon our resources were stretched too thin. That's when I suggested to the president that the Department of Homeland Security assume the domestic portion of guarding against a possible alien threat. That's when DHS secretary Julia Van Hook accepted the challenge."

Porter turned and looked toward Van Hook and said, "Madam Secretary, would you please?" He offered her the podium.

Julia nodded and proceeded to the podium. "Thank you, General Porter."

She looked around the venue and began, "When I was given the opportunity to join Operation Haystack as a protector from possible alien threats, I eventually realized the scope of that protection would require coordination with the National Guard and the US Coast Guard under the purview of the Department of Defense. After a few months, Secretary Porter and I found it was a challenge to coordinate both services and maintain the efficiency of our individual mandates. We asked the president for direction in solving our coordination dilemma. He came up with a solution by creating a position of Domestic Security Commander."

She paused. "The list of candidates to fill the position was extensive, but soon the perfect candidate was selected, and after much strong-arming and persuasion, he relented."

She rested her hands on the lectern. "I now introduce to you the Domestic Security commander, Colonel Edward Narkiewicz." She turned to the wings and said, "Commander, will you join me?" She stepped aside.

Edward sighed and took the walk. He stood at the lectern, took off his hat, and tucked it under his arm.

"Thank you for the introduction, Secretary Van Hook."

He nodded to her and looked around the crowd.

"It is true...that I did not seek this position nor was I aware that there was such a position. However, when the need and importance of its operational directives were explained to me, I accepted the challenge."

He paused. "My task is twofold—coordinate the courageous women and men of the Coast Guard and the National Guard in identifying and preventing possible alien threats, and protecting against domestic unrest. I will be working closely with scientists at SETI installations to keep abreast of the developing interactions with Alpha. Additionally I will be engaging with biochemistry experts to determine that, if a biological threat develops, we can decide how best to counter such threat. Relative to domestic unrest, I realize that there are those who have only one agenda—to be subversive and create unrest, often through violence. To those I pledge my unwavering perseverance to protect life and property and root out all those that would do harm."

Edward finished and took two military steps back from the podium, put on his hat, pivoted to his right, and stepped lively back to his previous spot.

As he left the dais, the president stepped back to the podium.

Tsirch rested his left hand on the lectern and looked to the wings on the right.

"I want to thank Defense Secretary Porter, Homeland Secretary Van Hook, and Domestic Security Commander Narkiewicz for bringing us up to speed with the overall plans to protect our nation and the world."

He took a preparatory breath. "I want to apologize"—he paused; the room buzzed softly—"to you, the people, and most of all to my friend, Vice President Natás."

The crowd's buzz increased.

He continued in a remorseful tone, "For the past months, I have misinterpreted his actions and intentions as subversive and counter to the safety and security of our nation."

He paused and sighed. "I ignored something that I believe is the key to resolving almost every disagreement or roadblock."

His tone became livelier as he gestured with his hands. "Yesterday we decided to use that magical key to unlock the door between us. Something that I truly believe we, as a nation and as a world, have forgotten to do."

He stopped and looked at the crowd, gestured, and said emphatically, "We talked and listened!"

He continued, "While I've known the vice president since law school, I somehow forgot that we have always been of the same mind. We have the same passions for the truth."

He paused again. "We...actually, I, let the very minor division of political direction blind me from seeing his integrity and moral resolve."

He leaned on the lectern with both hands. "I no longer seek the resignation of Vice President Natás."

He spoke as if at a political rally. "I give you, Vice President Natás."

He turned and applauded to the wing at the right. The crowd was taken by surprise. As Richard stepped out of the door, the buzz grew noticeably, and the applause was light but gracious. Richard continued toward the dais and shook the outstretched hand of the president, and both patted each other on their shoulders. They separated, and Richard settled in at the lectern and took a deep breath.

He looked over to Tsirch and said, "Mr. President, you have my vote."

There was a small wave of laughter. He smiled and put his hands on the lectern and perused the audience.

"While I am moved by the president's words of praise and acceptance of blame for the misjudgment of intent, with that, I take issue. I became wrapped in my singular purpose and abandoned my obligation to keep the lines of communication open with my boss. My quest for gathering the best possible minds to take part in Operation Haystack became more about ME and my goals than the operation itself. By the time I was made aware of my egotistical stance...by no other than my great friend Lucas Makiev, I had missed the opportunity to correct my mistake."

He turned to Lucas in the wing. "Thank you, Lucas." Lucas nodded.

Richard continued, "I am impressed with the accurate description of Operation Haystack by the president, the secretaries, and the commander. Also their assessment of the current status was extremely accurate. I doubt that there was anything I could add."

A hand went up and was recognized by Richard.

"Thank you, Mr. Vice President. Martin Singh, *Toronto Star*, I was tipped off with a couple of morsels you could verify for me."

Richard said, "Okay, Martin, let's chew on your morsels."

Martin's chuckle was supported by many more. "Well, one was Dr. 'Gemo's notes were found on the moon and brought back to Earth. What was in them, and will they be released?"

Richard smiled and quipped, "Damn, Martin, the FBI and the CIA may want to talk to you."

The crowd laughed lightly. Richard added quickly with a big smile, "Martin, I guess you can't give me your source..."

Richard paused. "Actually, Martin, that's true. The notes were found, and Dr. Sal Uschin has been tasked with reviewing them, and I would think it would be up to the president to decide about the release of their content."

Richard gave a sideways head nod toward the president.

He put his hands firmly on the lectern as if to brace himself. "Okay, Martin from Canada, what else you got?"

Martin smiled and looked at his notes.

"I was told there were two sightings of what was described as holograms, one in space during an EVA and another on the surface of the moon? Can you comment?"

There were mumbles among the crowd.

Richard thought for a moment. "Martin, are you an alien?" Richard quipped again.

Richard took a deep breath and held it for a moment. "You know, I'm not sure how to answer that, as that is probably classified information." Richard looked over at the president.

"I would like to answer you but—" Tsirch nodded to Richard. Richard was surprised and asked Tsirch, "Really?"

Tsirch nodded in affirmative.

Richard took a breath. "Your source is 100 percent accurate."

The crowd had interspersed gasps and moans.

"While the sightings have NOT been verified, they were witnessed by credible sources. I must stress that we have no idea how those sightings were generated. Other than that, I have no further comment on the sightings."

Richard looked up to the ceiling. "Are you listening, Canada?"

The president walked over next to Richard and put his hand on his shoulder and said, "I'll have to talk to my booking agent about being upstaged by the closing act."

Several hands went up, and Tsirch held up his hands to quell the throng, and he and Richard walked off the dais together.

CHAPTER 29

The Colonel and Lieutenant Fast-Fingers

The staff at the nation's SETI sites were surprised at the new security implemented practically overnight. New encoded picture ID badges were issued to all staff. Gated entrance structures were built and manned with armed National Guard 24-7. Two additional armed guards, with night vision, were tasked with roving the grounds. Two drones were deployed in rotation for added security. Personal COMs were given to all staff for security and communication. Various hourly check-in logs were maintained for security and documentation. Aside from lethal weapons, the guards were directed to use less lethal means as the primary method to stop or control any dissidents. Each location had a National Guard unit, ready to deploy at a thirty-minute notice, as backup if needed.

The cost of the national SETI sites security implementation was a blank-check authorization given to Commander Narkiewicz by the president. That was only part of the commander's security design. The nation's biolabs were secured in similar manner. A central command office space was made available at Cheyenne Mountain in Colorado Springs.

The newly minted Domestic Security commander Colonel Edward Narkiewicz was acclimating himself to his new position in his new office. He recruited his reliable lieutenant Brie Smithey, from Camp Lejeune, as his assistant. Brie stood behind Edward, watching the screen on the computer as Edward typed. She pointed to the screen.

"Is that the code you wanted?" she asked.

Edward replied, "That's perfect, Brie, good job."

"Thank you, sir," she replied.

She spun to the right and walked over to the desk and sat down at her COM.

Edward looked up at the large monitor on the wall. A digital map of the United States and insets of the nearest border, biolab, and SETI sites were displayed with blue or red status markers.

Blue identified the site as active and secure; red was a designation of offline or attention required.

Most of the markers were lit blue and more had become active as the morning dragged on.

Brie asked, "Still waiting for Lucas for an update about the public release of the date of the second diffusion?"

"Yes, hopefully we get most of the stations online before then," he stated.

She looked at the map. "At least we have the obvious targets online, but who knows which soft targets disruptors might attack."

He leaned back in his seat and swiveled toward Brie.

"I yet wonder what is the rationale behind attacking those whose only goal is to deliver the truth?"

Brie smiled. "Sir, we've been over this before. It's the fear of the truth."

He offered, "Whatever happened to, 'The Truth Will Set You Free'?"

"I'm sure Dr. King wonders the same thing, as racial injustice yet exists," she suggested.

A flashing image of Lucas Makiev appeared on second large monitor.

Brie's fingers flashed on the COM to answer the call.

Lucas was a little surprised at the quick connection. He saw Edward and the lieutenant.

"Wow, that was a quick connection," he expressed.

Edward said, "Get used to it, Lucas. I'd like to introduce you to my fast-fingered lieutenant, Lieutenant Brie Smithey."

Lucas smiled and replied, "It's a pleasure to meet you, Ms. Lieutenant Fast-Fingers."

She smiled and offered, "I am pleased to meet you also, sir."

He corrected, "Lieutenant, we are probably going to have a lot of conversations, so just call me Lucas."

She accepted and returned, "Thank you, sir…Lucas, you may call me Brie."

Edward inserted with a smile, "Okay, we're all friends. So, Lucas, what do I owe the pleasure of your company?"

Lucas advised, "I just got off the COM with Carl Browning, and he is mirroring your setup across the pond and requested a coordinated link of some sort."

Edward looked at Brie and said, "I think we can add another link on our monitor. How about it, Brie?"

She nodded quickly and said, "All I need is his secured COM address, the name of his director, and I'll set it up."

Lucas chuckled and said, "I can hear Browning now saying, 'Jolly good.'"

Edward asked, "Still no heads up on the publication of the twentieth?"

Lucas responded, "Not yet. I'm at Hat Creek now, and it should happen within an hour or two. You are my second call."

Edward said, "Roger that. I await your call."

Lucas smiled and said, "10-4, 10-8, I'm out."

Edward laughed as Lucas's image disappeared.

CHAPTER 30

Authentication

Lucas sat for a moment after talking to Edward and Brie. He thought about what repercussions there may be with the release of the date of the second *diffusion* and also the audio conversation to the general public as promised. With less than three days left before the potential *diffusion*, it was both a danger and a blessing. Hopefully the three-day notice would catch any subversive group off guard and delay any organized effort to plan a coordinated attack. On the downside, the ability to analyze the microbe data and develop any defense to mitigate any possible biological threat, in that time frame, was practically impossible. In any case, it would all be moot in less than three days.

Lucas got up and walked over to a large table where the primary minds were entangled in several approaches in solving unwanted scenarios. He leaned over Perry's shoulder and asked, "Are we any closer to authenticating the Alpha audio?"

Perry thought for a moment and said, "Yes, we only need to isolate two more signal arrays."

He stopped and stared at the monitor and said excitedly, "Yes! Now only one more signal array, and the audio stream will be cleared."

Lucas stepped over a few steps where Michael, Amir, and Dominique sat, going over COM data and monitor frequencies.

Amir asked Dominique, "What if we use the subchannel and double the frequency?"

She studied for a moment and said, "But that could cancel out the sending array."

She paused and exclaimed, "Wait, I was calculating with a direct array and not alternating arrays."

Amir looked and observed, "I think you found the key. Maybe Michael can verify this simulation."

Dominique nudged a very much focused Michael. "Michael?" She nudged him again. "Michael?"

Michael was slow to respond, "Uh, yes?"

"We'd like you to verify this simulation," she said.

He looked at their screen for a moment and said, "Okay, send it over."

She entered a few keystrokes and sent the simulation to Michael's COM.

Lucas had been listening to Amir and Dominique's exchange and asked, "What are you trying to do?"

Amir sighed. "Dominique had a brainstorm. She was using a workaround to send an audio message to Adam to initiate another conversation rather than waiting for him to contact us. We tried duplicating the exact circumstances of the prior conversation but have yet to get a response."

Dominique added, "I even tried calling my sister and talking to her like I did at the first contact, but to no avail."

Lucas sighed. "I guess we'll have to wait for Michael to run the simulation."

Lucas stepped away and touched the keypad on his COM.

He waited for an answer.

Sal answered, "Lucas, any progress?"

Lucas replied, "Yes, won't be long. How about you?"

Sal said, "Michael sent more translated signal arrays, and now things make more sense. It's a major breakthrough, but even if we decode the specific microbial sequence, we still can't decode a spectrum that hasn't been sent yet."

Lucas offered, "Well, Amir and Dominique might help you out if they can make contact with Adam."

Sal asked, "They're actually working on that?"

Lucas said, "Yes, they are having Michael run a simulation as we speak, but not sure if it will pan out."

"That would be incredible, regardless of when that happened. Imagine what we could learn?" Sal exclaimed.

Lucas looked back over at the crew. "Okay, Sal, I'll go see if there's any progress."

Sal replied, "Okay, Luke, later."

Lucas put his COM away and went back over to Perry, who sat with his eyes closed and head tilted up against the headrest.

Lucas studied Perry for a moment and touched his shoulder.

Perry rallied around and smiled. "It's done."

Lucas was semishocked. "What? It's done? It's been authenticated?"

Perry nodded several times. "Just exhausted, taking a breather before we make the call."

Lucas sat down easily next to Perry and swiveled his chair around one complete turn, then swiveled toward the trio at the table.

He picked up the all-call COM and stood up and announced, "We now have authentication of the audio array. Great job, everyone."

Applause was heard across the room. The trio smiled and congratulated one another and summarily went back to work.

Lucas looked at Perry and asked, "You want the honor of making the call?"

Perry smiled and looked down toward the trio's table.

Lucas followed his gaze and recognized his thoughts. "Yes, I agree, who else?"

Lucas walked over to the table where Dominique sat talking to Amir. "Excuse me, Dominique, could you help Perry and me for a moment?"

She smiled and accepted. She stood up and followed Lucas over to Perry's station.

She asked Perry, "How can I help?"

Perry picked up the COM pad and punched in a code, and the president's image displayed on the monitor. She saw the image and seemed confused.

Lucas spoke with pride, "We have to let someone know the conversation you had with Adam has been authenticated and would like to extend you that honor. Would you do that for us?"

She asked, "Why me?"

Perry replied, "It was YOUR conversation, who else?"

She shrugged her shoulders. "Well okay, what do I say?"

Lucas directed, "When I activate the COM, I'll introduce you, and all you have to say is, 'Mr. President, the audio has been authenticated.'"

She backed away a step. "I can't do that. I've never talked to someone that important before."

Perry said, "Really, Dominique? Do you know anyone else on Earth that has talked to someone more important than an alien named Adam?"

She hesitated. "No but—"

Perry said reassuringly, "Dominique…you can do this."

She reluctantly nodded.

Lucas activated the COM. The president's image converted to a live video.

Lucas spoke, "Mr. President, I have someone to give you an important message."

Tsirch replied, "I'd love some good news."

Lucas replied, "Then you shall have it."

Lucas stepped to the side to give Dominique the entire video feed. "Mr. President, I introduce to you, Ms. Dominique Soul."

"Good morning, Ms. Dominique Soul, it's a pleasure to meet you."

She hesitated but replied, "It is totally my pleasure, Mr. President. Thank you."

He offered, "Lucas said that you have good news for me."

She glanced at Lucas, who prodded her, and she replied, "Mr. President, the audio conversation has been authenticated."

The president smiled. "Ms. Soul, you are a *National Treasure*, and all of humanity will forever see you as the beginning of a new era for mankind."

She was humbled. "Thank you, Mr. President."

Tsirch replied, "You are welcome, Ms. Soul. Lucas, thank you."
Lucas stepped back into view. "Of course, Mr. President."
The image vanished.

CHAPTER 31

Talking to Neighbors
Across the Fence

Tsirch sat silently in the Oval Office, looking out the window after the COM with Dominique. He sighed slightly and turned toward Richard sitting across from him.

Richard leaned up in his chair. "So…it's been authenticated?"

Tsirch nodded slowly. "Yes, it seems that we have neighbors talking to us across the fence, in our own backyard."

Richard redirected, "Sure, if you call someone 4.3 light-years away, a neighbor. However, I guess time and distance are truly relative."

"That's a fact," Tsirch stated.

Richard questioned, "You want me to make the calls before you let, what some may see as, Pandora out of the box?"

Tsirch pondered, "You know, I have faith that the majority of the people will take the news as a positive step forward, but it only takes a relative few reacting on the dark side to portray this as that proverbial Pandora's box, you alluded to."

Richard agreed, "So…my first calls will be to DOD, Homeland, and Domestic Security?"

Tsirch sighed. "Actually call Domestic first. They'll need time to notify his contingent and law enforcement agencies."

Richard asked, "Shall we call from the Situation Room?"

Tsirch nodded and stood. "Guess we'll have to get moving. Time waits for no man."

He paused and questioned, "I'm not sure that adage applies anymore. We're not even sure what *time* is."

Richard quipped as he stood, "You'll have to come up with some *Rennyisms*."

Tsirch shook his head, laughed, and started walking. "Careful, Mr. VP, I may have to fire you."

Richard made it to the door first, opened it, and waved Tsirch through. "After you, Mr. President."

Tsirch said as he walked out, "I detect a note of sarcasm."

Richard replied as they left, "Not at all, Mr. President...not at all."

CHAPTER 32

Circling the Wagons

Richard's image appeared on the monitor. As usual Brie answered with haste.

"Good morning, Mr. Vice President, are we to assume that our mission is a go?"

Richard replied with a smile, "Good morning to you, too, Lieutenant Fast-Fingers."

She replied while collecting herself, "I apologize, sir. Good morning, Mr. Vice President, how are you this morning?"

Edward walked into Richard's view. "Mr. Vice President, good morning, I assume you have news?"

Richard sighed. "I see I don't have to worry about Domestic Security falling asleep at the wheel."

Edward looked puzzled. "No, sir, why is that, sir?"

Richard smiled and reported, "The president has given you the green light. I believe he will wait for your operation to circle the wagons."

Edward observed, "That's rather an appropriate figure of speech, sir. We should be a go by 0905 hours."

Richard grimaced. "I was hoping for 0904 hours."

Edward looked at Richard curiously. "Sir?"

Richard replied, "Commander, you and Lieutenant Fast-Fingers should take a breath once in a while. All work and no play?"

Edward got his message and regrouped, "I'm sorry, sir, we have been a little busy getting the system online. We'll take two chill pills each during our fifteen-minute union break."

Richard smiled. "Now that's the Narkiewicz brothers I know. Carry on, soldiers." Richard gave them a faux salute and exited the monitor.

Brie observed, "I assume he knows you and your brother?"

He replied with a drawn out, "Yeah…"

Edward looked at the map monitor and continued, "Okay, where're we at?"

He noticed that all but three status lights were blue.

He said to himself, "Okay, I can deal with that."

Brie was on COM with Sal at the BSL-4 in Fort Detrick.

"So I expect that since your BSL-4 is the most recognized, it is more of a likely target. Sal, remember we are only one touch of the COM away."

Sal replied, "Thank you, Brie."

Sal left the monitor.

Brie looked at the map monitor and stated, "Okay, I sent a group message to all the stations. How do you want to handle state and local agencies?"

Edward said, "We'll go with plan A, group message to each agency's central office. We are here for backup and for them to strongly advise the local agencies to take all threats seriously."

Brie entered the proper keystrokes and sent the message. She looked at the time display: 0900 hours.

*****

Tsirch and Richard sat silently in the Situation Room, in individual thought, after making all their notifications.

Tsirch broke the silence, "Guess I have a joint session of Congress to address."

Richard asked, "I assume the Secretary of State is the designated survivor?"

Tsirch nodded. "Safely tucked away."

Richard asked with a smile, "Shall I bring the car around, sir?"
Tsirch bantered, "Yeah, but I get to drive this time."
Richard stood and bowed. "But of course, my liege."
They walked toward the door.

CHAPTER 33

Joint Session

Richard walked through the rotunda of the capitol on the way to the House Chamber. As he encountered various representatives and staff, he received pats on the back, handshakes, and well-wishes. He made his way up the steps to a seat next to where the House Speaker, Indira Fernell, was seated. She stood and he shook her outstretched hand.

"Madam Speaker, good to see you," Richard offered.

Fernell leaned in to Richard and said, "Great to have you back, Richard."

Richard smiled and said, "Thank you, Indira."

They both sat down.

The Chamber was abuzz and filled to capacity. Dozens of media took aim at the repatriated son. Richard understood the process of newsworthy people and events. His presence was notable.

It seemed like an eternity for Richard since he had graced the Hill. It was pleasing.

When most of the participants had made their way to their seats, the sergeant at arms made the highly anticipated announcement, "Madam Speaker, the president of the United States."

Tsirch entered the Chamber, shaking hands and patting shoulders and backs and pausing to impart an occasional comment. He continued around to the speaker's podium. He waved his hands several times, waiting for the applause to subside. Eventually he was ready to begin. He looked around the room and said, "Ladies and gentlemen, members of Congress." He turned to acknowledge the vice president and speaker. "Madam Speaker, Mr. Vice President, I thank you for the opportunity to address this esteemed joint session of Congress, the great people of the United States of America, and, by extension, the people of the world."

He put his left hand on the lectern and then raised his right hand to chest height.

"These are unprecedented times in the history of mankind. Yesterday I came to you and told you of amazing scientific accomplishments that have led to contact with those from another world we now call Alphas. I choose not to call them aliens, as that designation implies distrust and ill will."

He paused and continued, "I submit to you that in all of our contacts with the Alphas, there has only been a desire to enhance the well-being of human endeavors and promote scientific efficiency. Today I fulfill my promise to make available the actual authenticated audio recording between a SETI scientist and an Alpha, self-named as Adam. As you listen to the recording, you will hear a sincere desire of Adam to exchange trust for trust. The scientist involved in the conversation remained skeptical throughout their interaction. It was not until the conversation was authenticated by the worldwide scientific community that the scientist came to the realization that they, in fact, did converse with an Alpha."

He paused and raised both hands slightly off the lectern. "You will also hear some dialogue concerning religion that presents no conclusions of any particular religious conviction."

Tsirch leaned both hands on the lectern and took a more serious tone. "As I said yesterday, you will also hear that the Lunar Fall event was not intended to occur until contact was made to explain its meaning. We now know that a second event will occur to supplement the Lunar Fall event."

He shifted his weight, removed his hands, and replaced his hands on the lectern. He continued deliberately, "I need to preface the last segment with the following. The conversation will be delivered to the media and the public in all media formats—digital, audio, hearing impaired, and in all available languages. There are military and local safeguards in place to protect the public and governmental sites. Safety of the people is my major concern."

He stopped and continued with concern, "You will hear the date and possible minor effects of the coming event. The possible effects on those subjected to the event may be a temporary loss of short-term memory, and the date of the scheduled occurrence is about three days from now, March 20, at around noon on each time zone."

He continued amid highly elevated gasps and moans and vocalizations, "Again we are prepared for any negative effects. I thank you for your patience and support during these unfamiliar times."

CHAPTER 34

Prepping for Pandora

FBI director John "Pepper" Martin was more often found in the field, where he felt more effective, rather than at the headquarters in DC. His alias, "Pepper," followed him from Quantico, where he insisted on being the guinea pig to receive sprays or be gassed with new formulas of less-lethal chemicals, always without a mask. He rationalized that he wanted to know the effects, as an aggressor, on their ability to fight back and overcome its effects.

His latest field trip was to Janco Industries. He and his team were investigating the theft of a cargo container of reflective coatings.

It became of interest to the FBI when Abby Gonzales, CEO of the social media platform Flashcom, notified the FBI regarding suspicious posts from a newly formed dissident group called Anti-Adam. The group was espousing that the effects of the pending "alien rays" of the Alpha *diffusion* could be stopped by using reflective paints and coatings. The group used their illogic to encourage people to coat their houses and property as preventive measures. By extension of thought, the followers encouraged, the covering of heads and bodies with aluminum foil to deflect the rays. Those machinations seemed benign, until more aggressive posts appeared. The group was planning to coat or paint the SETI arrays to stop communications with the Alphas. That was when Gonzales and the FBI took notice. The scheme was further complicated when fringe dissidents, called Hi-Hanger and the British counterparts, the Silk-mates, intended to make their parachuting skills available to help deliver the coatings.

The threats did not end with the SETI assault. Other factions were suggesting that chemical compounds of bleach and caustic substances be infused with alien samples kept in biolabs in an effort to kill the aliens when they come to retrieve them from Earth.

*****

Martin was on COM with Edward and Brie at Domestic Security.

"Thank you, Martin, for keeping me updated," Edward said.

Martin replied, "We think we know where the container is headed. They will have to stop somewhere and split the shipment to make it harder to track. Satellite tracking last had it in Springfield, Missouri. I have an agent embedded with the Hi-Hangers, so if they try to move it with them, we'll know about it. We've secured the local airports, and we're monitoring the private airstrips."

Edward looked at his map monitor. "I have an Air National Guard unit available in St. Louis if you need it."

Martin replied, "That's good to know, but hopefully we can stop it here."

Edward stated, "Yes, but it probably won't be the only threat out there."

Martin replied, "No, but first things first, let's contain this one."

Edward affirmed, "We got this, Martin." He paused. "Okay, gotta update the SETI sites, talk to you later, and thank you."

Martin replied, "No problem." And he disconnected the COM.

*****

Brie was sending the update from Martin to the various sites. Edward scanned the map monitor once again and selected Hat Creek on his COM. Lucas appeared on his monitor.

Edward connected the COMs. "Lucas, just got an update."

Lucas said, "Okay, I got Richard on my COM also."

Edward replied, "Okay, cut me in."

Richard appeared on the monitor also.

Lucas said, "I was asking Richard what size of tinfoil hat he wears."

Edward asked, "Why is that?"

Lucas replied, "There is a run on aluminum foil and reflective sheets in the stores."

Edward was still clueless.

Lucas explained, "Sorry, I forgot you have been busy protecting the world. There are people out there that believe that aluminum foil will protect them from the alien rays from space, and they're making aluminum hats."

"Haven't heard that. Maybe we can get the Anti-Adams and the hate group Segr8 to wear that as a uniform and make our job easier."

Brie slid over in view of the monitor and added, "I just ordered the last tin hat in stock for you from Walco, sir."

Edward looked at Brie. "You know about this tinfoil stuff?"

She replied, "Certainly. I don't want my brain scrambled by alien rays."

Lucas stepped away out of view.

Edward shook his head and looked at Richard. "The FBI update from Director Martin seems promising. Has Browning had any similar incidents in England?"

Richard shook his head. "Not there. He locked down all of his potential targets when Germany had their attempted theft."

Edward sat down. "I am concerned that the biolabs in city areas may be subject to the Hi-Hangers using tall buildings to base jump to the tops of the labs. Director Martin advised he will use our National Guard troops to help secure possible breaches."

Richard asked, "I spoke to the Canadian PM, Carl Stillman, about his sites, and he said the weather is helping keep the remote sites inaccessible for attacks."

Lucas came back into view wearing a makeshift foil hat.

Edward looked at Lucas shook his head and said, "At least our leaders are taking this crisis seriously."

Lucas replied, "We are totally serious, Commander."

Edward replied sarcastically, "Of course you are." And he added, "Good day, Lucas, and to you, Mr. Vice President."

Richard replied, "And to you, Commander." Richard reached down and donned a tinfoil hat and disappeared from the monitor.

CHAPTER 35

Managing Chaos

Shasta County sheriff Edgar Wright, along with two FBI agents, Frank Knox and Robin Lane, sat in his patrol unit, watching a few dozen would-be protestors readying signs and forming a vehicle convoy. Edgar was watching the news feeds on his COM of media interviewing various protestors in Johnson Park, near Burney. He had a contingent of his deputies and Lassen County deputies waiting to escort the protestors to a designated area near the entrance of the Hat Creek SETI station. A few Lassen County deputies were tasked with monitoring the highways to the south.

Two squads of a National Guard unit were stationed in a secluded area, about five minutes from the Hat Creek station as backup.

Most of the actors were self-identifying as part of the new Anti-Adam protest group. The FBI had identified at least three members of a potentially violent faction, Segr8, infused in the group. The organizer of the group, Parker Heiser, walked up to a deputy and talked to him. The deputy nodded and keyed up his radio.

"Sheriff Wright, the caravan is a go."

Wright keyed his radio. "Wright copies, all units to your positions and advise."

Agents Knox and Lane got out of Wright's cruiser and got into their vehicle and drove off to the north.

When most of the units had checked in on the radio, Wright started his car and drove to the lead and stopped.

As the caravan formed, he heard the final unit check-in. He began to lead the procession at a moderate pace. He continued up to Four Corners, and as he made a sharp right turn toward Hat Creek, he noticed the FBI vehicle parked across the intersection.

Several minutes passed, and Wright made a left turn on the road toward the SETI Institute. The caravan wound around and came to the designated rally point for the protest. Wright pulled his vehicle past the rally point, slightly off the road, and parked.

The protestors began exiting their vehicles and setting up several speaker cabinets. Dozens of signs and megaphones were handed out.

A van appeared, driving slowly, coming from the direction of the SETI Institute. Atop the van was a long oval metal cage-like structure, with several rotating disks and a large dish. Inside the van, two SETI technicians viewed monitors and scopes that detected various electronic devices, occupants in structures and vehicles. They began a 360-degree sweep of from behind the van across the field, through the protest group, and across the field on the other side of the van. The technicians replayed the results of the scan that identified the content and occupants at the SETI station and each individual and content of all the vehicles. The images of the two National Guard security troops stationed five hundred yards away and the drone flying above were also captured.

Sherriff Wright's COM received a screen capture of two suspicious individuals and their location. He studied the screen and keyed his radio.

"Atnip, Shaw, the two individuals standing next to the pickup to your right, possible CCW."

"Atnip copies."

"Shaw copies," were the replies.

Deputy Atnip unsnapped his weapon, walked slowly toward the pickup, and Shaw walked around the backside of the pickup. Two other deputies surreptitiously meandered toward the pickup and stopped, pretending to talk to each other. When Shaw reached the right front bumper of the pickup, she stopped, unsnapped her weapon, and waited. Atnip finally approached the two suspects; he smiled and said, "Afternoon, gentlemen."

The two returned, "Afternoon."

Atnip continued, "I believe you understood that Mr. Heiser's permit for the protest restricts the possession of firearms within three miles of the protest."

The two said nothing.

Atnip continued, "It's come to my attention that a scan revealed that you are possibly in possession of a firearm."

Again they said nothing.

Atnip advised, "You, sirs, have not one but three choices—submit to a search of your person, surrender your firearms, or leave the protest peacefully."

Shaw watched intently.

The two suspects whispered a few words to each other and looked at Atnip. One of the suspects answered, "We're getting bored anyway. We'll take off."

They paused for a few seconds, looked at Atnip, and then separated slowly, one toward the driver's side and the other toward the rear of the pickup.

Shaw moved to the front of the pickup. Atnip carefully watched the movements of the driver as he entered the pickup. The other two deputies separated and eased toward potential cover. Shaw watched the other suspect as he rounded the back of the pickup and opened the passenger door. As he got in, Shaw moved carefully past the passenger door toward the rear of the pickup.

The pickup was started, and the two suspects drove back up the road, toward the town of Hat Creek.

The SETI technicians in the van continued checking their monitor and saw a radiation spike in one of the larger vans parked near the front of the protest group. The driver of the van started it up and pulled to the other side of the road so the rear of the van faced toward the complex. A scan of the protestor's van showed two figures inside moving a large electronic device.

The SETI van COMed Michael in Hat Creek.

Michael answered, "We're sending a scan and scope readout from a protestor's van."

Michael opened his COM and looked over the scope data and the scan.

The SETI techs asked, "Is that what we think it is?"

Michael checked the scan again and said, "It conforms with the profile of an electromagnetic radiation generation device."

The techs asked, "It's your call…you want us to take it out?"

Michael called Perry over to look at the monitor. They conferenced for a minute, and Michael said, "Affirmative, disable it."

The dish on top of the SETI van rotated toward the protestor's van. The disk in the cage atop the van began spinning. The SETI tech pressed a button. The device in the protestor's van suffered an electronic spark, and smoke filled the van. The two figures exited the van rather quickly. Two minutes later, another SETI van came up the road and parked near the protestor's van. Three techs in hazmat suits came out of the van carrying a sensor device and waved it in the door of the back of the van. The techs returned to the SETI van.

Michael received a COM.

"Neutralized, minimal radiation threat."

Michael replied, "Base copies. Return to base."

The second SETI van turned around and headed back toward the SETI complex.

CHAPTER 36

Happy Campers

The Hereford RV Park in Hat Creek was experiencing an unusual uptick in business for this time of year. The owner, Kyle Arlitz, was busy emptying the trash bins with his four-wheeler and cart along the RV sites. He noticed the four toy-haulers that arrived earlier that morning—without reservations—were hooking up over-sized box trailers to several four-wheelers. He was curious about where the tenants were planning to go. The grounds were somewhat soggy from the recent rains and any off-road ventures with those box trailers could be hazardous. He parked his four-wheeler and walked over to talk to one of the tenants.

"I'm Kyle, the owner/manager. I don't remember your name, but you guys look like you're out for some fun."

The camper smiled, shook Kyle's hand, and replied, "I'm Arlin. Yeah, we thought we'd drive through the woods and pick up trash and debris left by the irresponsible off-roaders."

Kyle thought for a moment. "I've been all over those woods and don't recall a lot of trash in there."

Arlin replied, "We do a lot of off-road four-wheeling all over the county, and we are planning to make this one of our stops this summer. We always make a pretrip to scout the routes and pick out campsites."

Kyle explained, "If you guys are planning any camping, you have to clear it with the county sheriff and get a BLM permit."

Arlin replied, "Yeah, we know. We already cleared it with the sheriff."

Kyle grew suspicious. "Oh, okay, you already talked to Sheriff Miller?"

Arlin nodded. "Yeah, Miller gave us the green light."

Kyle replied, "Well, I guess you got your ducks in a row. Have a good one."

Kyle got back on his four-wheeler and drove past the line of box trailers and noticed that several campers were crumpling aluminum foil into balls and tossing them into the box trailer. He continued around a shortcut road back to his office. He went into his office and called the sheriff's office on his COM. He told the dispatcher about his encounter with the campers.

CHAPTER 37

Welcome to Walco

The clerk at the Walco home improvement store scanned the three five-gallon pails of reflective coating and asked, "Will this be all?"

The woman replied, "Yes, thank you."

The clerk confirmed the total on the computer and said, "Your total is $567.45."

The woman scanned her payment in the pay station.

The female clerk said, "Thank you for shopping Walco. Would you like some help loading this?"

The slight-statured woman looked at the sixty-five-pound pails and said, "Yes, please."

The clerk called to another clerk, "Richard, service out, please."

The clerk pushed the cart with the pails to the side of the exit. The woman followed the cart and waited for assistance.

The female clerk flagged down Richard before he went to help the woman with the cart. She talked to him softly, "Richard, take a picture of her license plate on the sly."

Richard asked, "Why?"

She replied, "There's an alert for anyone buying that coating."

Richard replied, "Really?"

She nodded. "Just sneak a pic."

Richard nodded and went to help the customer.

She reprinted the sales receipt.

The Redding Airport Air Traffic Controller looked over the flight logs and noticed an arrival manifest and flight plan that matched an FBI alert. He called the number on the alert notice.

CHAPTER 38

Having a Ball

Sheriff Wright's COM buzzed and flashed. He recognized the sender's image, Jerry in dispatch. He pressed a key and answered, "Hey, Jerry, what 'cha got?"

Jerry replied, "Hey, Edgar, just got a call from Kyle at the RV Park. He said he has some suspicious characters down there planning a trip into the woods down your way. They have six or eight four-wheelers pulling big box trailers filled with balls made of aluminum foil. They told Kyle that they had talked to Sheriff Miller, so he knew they were up to something."

Edgar listened closely. "Okay, Jerry, thanks."

Edgar ended the COM and called the SETI station.

Perry answered the COM, "Morning, Sheriff."

Edgar replied, "Good morning, Perry. I have a potential problem that may affect your station."

Perry replied, "Well, let's have it. You're handling the protest really smoothly. I'm sure we can deal with whatever comes up."

Edgar offered, "Kyle at the RV Park across the tree stands said a group of four-wheelers may be heading in your direction towing big box trailers with aluminum foil balls. He thinks they are up to no good."

Perry replied, "Yeah, seems that some weirdoes think that reflective materials could block the aliens from communicating or landing on Earth. I'll let security know."

Edgar replied, "I could send some deputies to cut them off, but I doubt they would get there quick enough."

Perry said, "Thanks, Edgar but, I've got the Guard as a backup. Don't want to spread your guys too thin."

Edgar said, "Okay, Perry, you take care. Talk to you later."

Perry replied, "Thanks, Sheriff."

CHAPTER 39

Alert

Perry disconnected the COM and picked up another COM and sent an alert. Perry walked over to a security monitor and entered some keystrokes.

"Security 1, base."

The roving security replied, "Security 1."

"Be advised, there may be several four-wheelers coming from the RV Park through the trees and brush to your west and southwest. I've sent the Alpha drone for a visual."

Security 1 replied, "One copies. I'll pick up the feed on my monitor."

Perry replied, "10-4, base, out."

Perry ended the call and walked over to the main monitor, entered some keystrokes, and sent a call to Edward at DS command.

Edward saw Perry's image and connected the COM. "Perry, what's up?"

Perry replied, "Protestors are under control, but there may be some interlopers on four-wheelers coming from the southwest. I have security checking it out."

Edward added, "Good, they'll know how to handle it. They have one NG squad at their disposal. But, Perry, just to advise you, there is another possible threat in the offing I'm dealing with."

Perry asked, "How's that?"

Edward relayed, "The FBI received a call from the Redding Airport that three Segr8 actors landed in Redding and booked a private twin engine to Fall River Mills Airport. Earlier that morning, another Segr8, Lynne Barker, bought three five-gallon pails of reflective coating at the Walco in Redding. They are tracking the coating, but there wouldn't be enough time to drive to Hat Creek or the Fall River Airport if they wanted to use the protest as a distraction. So the FBI thinks that it probably will be taken to the airport in Redding. They are surveilling the area to determine if there are any aerial delivery methods available other than those at the airport. In any case, it's 98 percent under control."

Perry replied, "Just FYI for you and the FBI, there are several farmers around here with crop dusters and choppers."

Edward said, "Thanks, Perry I'll let them know."

CHAPTER 40

Handling Business

Edward ended the COM and immediately COMed Agent Lane near Hat Creek. As Edward talked to Agent Lane, Brie was scanning the map monitor and the news feed monitor, keeping abreast of worldwide incidents. Numerous minor incidents of foil being dropped from planes or thrown from the ground on SETI arrays were registered in Great Britain, Germany, New Mexico, Texas, and even the UC campus in Berkeley, where foil was thrown on the telescope when someone climbed on top of the dome. The more serious attempts of coating or painting arrays were limited to two arrays partially sprayed in Maryland and Boston.

Fortunately only one attack was attempted on a biolab was on a level 1 at the UC Berkeley, where the perpetrators were prevented entry by students.

Command noted that the frequency of incidents was waning as little more than twenty-four hours remained on the clock. Mostly the public on the fringe that followed the Anti-Adam cult seemed to be preparing self-protection by painting houses with reflective coating and making and/or wearing foil coats or hats. Some even put reflective sheeting on their houses and even vehicles. An entrepreneur in southern California was selling shielded doghouses.

Edward finished his COM to Agent Lane and returned to watch the map monitor with Brie.

Edward sat down and leaned back, looked at Brie, and chuckled. "Well, Lieutenant, it looks like you have everything under control."

Brie replied, laughing, "The only thing I have under control is my appetite."

She growled and took a vicious bite of a sandwich.

CHAPTER 41

Not-So-Happy Campers

The Alpha drone was flying over the trees near the RV Park and hovered above the four-wheelers' camp.

The leader, Arlin Harper, finished checking the last hitch on the box trailers. He walked over to the lead four-wheeler and started it up. He gave a hand-signal motion—*forward*.

The group began their journey in accordion style. As they reached their following separation, they moved slowly across the RV boundary and around the left edge of the tree line.

The Chinook hovered near the SETI arrays. After the last of the National Guard squad rappelled to the ground, the chopper bladed away to the northeast. The unit went to work, driving metal posts into the ground and threading heavy rope through eyes in the posts.

They tied yellow flags on the rope in between the posts.

Security 1 drove up to the squad on an ATV. He pulled out his drone monitor and guided it to follow the line of four-wheelers. The second four-wheeler began to slow down and stopped. The trailer had bogged down in the soggy earth. Arlin heard the riders yell to him that the trailer was stuck in the mud. Arlin stopped and walked back to the rider. The other riders came over to the trailer, and they all pushed the trailer out of the mud to more-solid ground. The caravan began to move again. It wasn't long before another trailer got stuck, as the farther they went along the perimeter of the tree stand, the softer the ground became. Arlin led the group into the trees where there was more stable ground. That mistake was soon realized as the trailers were too tall and wide to navigate the random height and separation of the trees. Eventually they found their way back out of the tree stand into the open field. After several incidents of a trailer getting stuck and then being pushed out, they decided to disconnect two stuck trailers and continue with two trailers pulled by two four-wheelers, one towing another with a rope tied between them.

Eventually the caravan caught site of the arrays and also the perimeter of posts, ropes, and, more problematic, the squad of National Guard. Arlin stopped his four-wheeler and thought for a moment. He got off his ride and went back and talked to his friends. They assessed the situation and decided to turn around and go back. Arlin got back on his four-wheeler and made a wide turn around, and his trailer wheel sunk to one side, and the momentum of the turn caused the trailer to fall on its side. There were many expletives heard as the crew discussed the problem. The decision was made. The one trailer on its side was unhooked, and they left it. They turned around and went back the way they came with only one trailer in tow.

Security 1 rode his ATV up to the dumped trailer and inspected its cargo. As reported, the cargo was foil crushed into balls.

Security 1 opened his COM.

Perry answered the COM, chuckling. "Perry," he said.

Security 1 reported, "Perry, Security 1. Looks like the four-wheelers group ran into too many obstacles and decided to abort their mission. They left one of their trailers that fell on its side. What do you want to do with it?"

Perry replied, still chuckling, "Yeah, I was watching the show on the Alpha drone camera. I couldn't quite see what was in the trailer. What is it?"

Security 1 replied, "It was what we thought, aluminum foil squeezed into balls. What you want me to do with it?"

Perry said, "I don't know what they intended to do with the foil. It wouldn't affect the arrays unless they piled them up on top. Actually that might increase the signal strength."

Security 1 asked again, "Yes, sir, but what you want me to do with it?"

Perry said, "Sorry, go ahead and leave it there. I'll keep an eye on it and check on the riders every once in a while with a drone. Maybe the Alphas might want the balls."

Security 1 said, "Copy that." And he ended the COM.

CHAPTER 42

Gotcha

Agents Knox and Lane were parked near a hangar at the Fall River Mills Airport. They were waiting for the expected arrival of a twin-engine Cessna. The other squad of National Guard waited in the Chinook on the far end of the runway. Fortunately radar had the Cessna on a flight path consistent with arriving at Fall River. The Guard squad in the Chinook was on standby should the plane change course. The other NG squad remained at the SETI arrays in case the plane diverted its course to drop anything on to the arrays. As a third option, Air National Guard air support was available at Beale AFB to the south. At this point, it was yet a waiting game.

Except for three protestors wanting to edge closer to the arrays, the protest was yet peaceful. Sheriff Wright sent a COM message of A-okay to Perry and to Agents Lane and Knox.

Lane checked the COM message and said, "The sheriff messaged the protest is going well."

Knox nodded and stated, "So your daughter scored a goal yesterday? She must have been elated."

Robin replied, "I was the one jumping up and down and yelling. She just took it in stride and ran back down the field."

Frank responded, "So much for reserved mom on the sidelines."

Robin countered, "You're one to talk, didn't you almost get kicked out of your daughter's basketball game?"

Frank replied, "Well, how can you not call a foul when an elbow takes the defender down?"

Robin said, "Face it, Frank, we both have our passions for our kids."

The COM buzzed and flashed. Frank answered, "Knox."

The tower controller, Jed, stated, "The plane is one mile out and on course."

Frank replied, "Thanks, Jed."

Frank said, "Showtime."

Robin sent a message to the corporal in the Chinook.

"Okay, it's about time our buddy in the van makes his move."

The Cessna came into view and landed softly and taxied around into a hangar. The agents watched as a van, which had been parked in the parking lot, drove up to the hangar.

Lane said, "And Allen Landry makes his appearance."

Knox watched through his binoculars, as did Lane. The cabin door opened, and a known Segr8 member, David Poole, stepped out of the plane.

Frank said, "We got David too."

They continued to watch as the two met with a brotherhood greeting. They talked for a moment, and David got into the plane and came out and set a five-gallon pail on the ground. He retrieved another pail from the plane and set it on the ground. They loaded the pails into the back of the van and closed the doors.

They talked for a moment, and David got on his COM. He spoke for several minutes and wrote something down. He ended his COM and spoke to Allen. They got into the van and drove toward the exit.

Lane and Knox watched the van drive off.

Lane wondered, "Okay, where is the third pail?"

Frank replied, "Yeah, what's up with that?"

Lane COMed Sheriff Wright. Wright answered, "Sheriff Wright."

Lane asked, "Edgar, this is Agent Lane. Do you have a deputy free?"

Edgar replied, "Sure, what do you need?"

"I need someone to follow a van from the Fall River Mills Airport."

Frank started the vehicle and slowly followed the van.

Edgar said, "I have a deputy in town. Give me the info, and I'll have her keep tabs on them."

Robin sent the van info to the sheriff's COM.

Frank said, "Okay, hold on, let me see which way the van goes."

He followed the van to the highway and saw it turn toward town.

"Okay, Sheriff. Tell her the van is heading toward town."

Edgar replied, "Okay, I'll let her know."

Frank said, "Thanks, Sheriff."

He ended the COM and made a U-turn. He drove back into the airport and up to the hangar where the plane was. They stopped the car and stepped out of their vehicle and walked up to a man standing by the plane.

Lane asked, "Good morning, sir, are you the pilot of this plane?"

The man replied, "Yes, I'm the owner and pilot. Can I help you?"

Lane said, "I was supposed to meet David Poole here to pick up a pail of coating."

The pilot said, "Wow, you just missed him and Allen."

Lane said, "Damn, did he leave a pail for me?" She looked back at the pilot pleadingly.

The pilot said, "Naw, they took both pails with them."

Lane said, "I guess he didn't need the $500 I was going to pay him."

She paused and asked, "You don't happen to know where I could get another pail, do you?"

He replied, "No, wish I did, if that's what they're going for."

She exclaimed, "Darn!"

She looked at Frank and back at the pilot and exclaimed, "Now where am I gonna get another pail?"

The pilot said, "Don't know…that's all Dave had."

She said, "Thanks anyway." And she started to leave but turned and asked, "You don't happen to know which way they went, do you?"

He replied, "Naw, he was just saying something about Hat Creek."

She said, "Okay, you take care."

He replied, "You too."

She and Frank went back over to their car, and they both got in.

Frank smiled and said, "Wow, Robin, that was one of the smoothest interrogations I've heard. Way to go."

Robin replied, "I thought it went well, just went with the flow."

Frank said, "Don't know what else you could have gotten out of him without causing suspicion. Just would like to know where the other pail is."

He picked up his COM.

Robin reasoned, "It's likely that Lynne Barker still has it in Redding. Have to check with the Redding office."

Frank said, "I'm COMing them now."

He waited for an answer and spoke, "This is Knox. You have a location on the other pail of coating? I have two accounted for."

He listened for a minute, then smiled and hung up.

"Good news, it seems that Barker is using the coating on her house. And we wonder where some people get their brains."

Robin added, "Well, I have an idea where HER brains are located."

Frank replied, "Yeah, but now we gotta catch up with the other two pails."

Frank backed the car out and drove toward the exit. He turned toward town, and Robin COMed the sheriff.

"Sheriff, Lane here. You have a twenty on the target vehicle?"

Edgar responded, "My deputy said they turned south on Cassel Road."

Lane said, "Can you give me her COM?"

Edgar said, "Better yet I can patch you through, hold on."

Lane prepared to wait, but she heard a voice on the COM, "This is Deputy Ariza."

Lane replied, "Ariza, this is Agent Lane, FBI. I understand you are following the suspects' blue van."

Ariza said, "10-4, south on Cassel Road, headed toward a logging company."

"We're about two miles to that turnoff. Should be on your six in about four minutes."

"No hurry, the road is pretty rough for that old van."

"Copy that, if they stop, do not engage, only surveil."

"Okay, I'll just hold my position."

"Thanks, Ariza, can I keep this channel open?"

"10-4 Lane. We can go 10-8."

"Copy that, Ariza. We're 10-8."

The van went down the dirt road for about a mile, then turned into an old logging company. Ariza anticipated the turn and had stopped back out of view.

"Agent Lane?"

"Yes, Ariza?

"The van pulled into the logging company as expected. There is a crop duster parked there also. It looks like Josh Frazier's plane from Burney."

"Thanks, Ariza, stand by. We're two away."

"10-4."

The van pulled up close to the plane, and Landry and Poole got out and opened the back doors of the van. They carried the pails over to the plane. Josh Frazier was indeed there with his plane.

They talked for a minute, and Frazier went over to the plane and opened up the cap to the sprayer tank. Landry carried a pail over to it and began to pour its contents into the tank.

Agents Lane and Knox pulled behind Ariza's cruiser and got out.

Ariza got out and met them. They shook hands.

Ariza explained, "So far they are pouring the pails' contents into the sprayer tank. The plane does belong to Josh Frazier."

Lane replied, "Excellent work, Ariza, we're going to make contact. Do you have a rifle?"

Ariza smiled and said, "Hold on." She went to her trunk and came back with a scoped .30-06.

She smiled. "Yep, I got a rifle."

Frank said, "I assume you can shoot it."

Ariza said, "Piece of cake…anything within two hundred yards."

Lane smiled and said, "We got cover. I guess we're a go."

Frank nodded, and they got back in their car. They drove down the road and turned into the logging area and up to the plane.

They stopped and got out. He told Lane, "Okay, smooth talker, you got this."

Landry and Poole saw them drive up and stood by the plane.

Lane walked over to Landry and Poole and said, "Good morning, gentlemen. Nice day for a plane ride."

Poole asked, "Who's asking?"

She put her cards on the table. She took out her ID, as did Frank, and showed them to Poole.

"I am Special Agent Lane of the FBI, and this is my partner, Special Agent Knox. We'd like to ask you some questions."

Poole replied, "Well, Special Agents, I don't care to answer any questions."

Frank joined in, "Thank you, gentlemen."

He walked over to the plane and looked into the sprayer tank. He looked at the label on the pails and took a pitcher and pressed some buttons. He went over to Frazier and asked, "Josh Frazier, right?"

Frazier was surprised. "Yes, sir, do I know you?"

Frank continued, "You operate a crop dusting business, hereabouts, correct?"

Frazier was still perplexed. "Yes."

Frank continued, "I know you have all the necessary licenses, permits, and FAA documentations, so I'm not going to have you show them to me."

Frazier said, "Don't matter. I have all of my documents in the plane, I'm completely legit."

Frank said, "I respect a man who works hard to build a business and live the American dream."

Frazier was still wondering where this was going. "Thank you, I'm proud of what I've done."

Frank asked, "I guess you know these two gentlemen, David Poole and Allen Landry, known members of the Segr8 group on the FBI terrorist list."

Frazier looked at Landry, who shook his head.

Frazier said, "I'm done talking."

Frank said, "I appreciate your courage and devotion, but I see that you are preparing to take off and possibly dust some crops."

Frazier said, "Yes...so what of it?"

Frank asked Lane, "Agent Lane, did you get a reply back from the FDA and FAA on the picture of the label I took of the pails over there?"

Lane nodded. "Yes, I did."

Frank asked, "And what did you find out?"

Lane explained, "It was determined that the coating in those pails are a class-B carcinogen prohibited for use in aerial dispersal or in contact with livestock or vegetation."

Frank added, "I'm sorry, Mr. Frazier. I will have to confiscate your plane and charge you with intent to illegally disperse a known carcinogen, a class-C felony."

Frank leaned toward Frazier and added, "And between you and me, you better ask for more money, the coating will probably clog up your spray rig and seize the pump."

Lane walked over to Frazier and pulled out her handcuffs.

"Can you turn around and put your hands behind you?"

Frazier said, "But what if I was forced to do it?"

Frank said, "That might help. Who's forcing you?"

Frazier said, pointing to Landry and Poole, "These guys."

Lane looked at Poole and Landry with a big grin and said, "Gotcha!"

CHAPTER 43

You...Talking to Me?

Maryland Representative Johnny Walsh stepped out of the elevator and several media correspondents stretched microphones and cameras toward her. A cacophony of questions was thrown at her.

She smiled and asked, "Hold on, please. Can you all settle down? I'm not going anywhere. Let me take a breath."

She walked a few steps to the side of the elevator and stopped. The gaggle followed her.

She sighed. "Okay, go."

A female reporter asked, "Are you satisfied with the vote on shutting down SETI?"

"What do you mean satisfied?"

"You must enjoy doing your boyfriend's bidding."

"Excuse me! Are you referring to Dr. Uschin?"

"Do you have another boyfriend?"

Another reporter began to ask a question, but Johnny stopped him, "Hold on, I'm going back to her first."

She pushed other mics aside and faced the first reporter.

"What exactly are you trying to say? I mean exactly!"

The reported stalled and continued, "We know your boyfriend makes you say and vote the way he tells you."

Johnny saw red but took the high road. "I'm sorry, MA'AM. You obviously know nothing about me. I have never and will never be controlled, manipulated, or ordered by anyone to do anything I don't want to do or say."

She continued, "Dr. Uschin has his own mind, and I have mine. I voted against shutting down funding for SETI because it was an asinine and fruitless attempt, by idiots, to stop our ongoing contact with the Alphas. You can hide your head up your ass and not listen, but not listening will not prevent their efforts in contacting us. Why would you not want to listen to new ideas or possibilities of a better future? Like we've done a great job as a human race so far—ravaging the earth, starving people, killing people in personal vendettas or wars, hating and abusing those of a different faith, race, gender, or opinion. Do I think the Alphas are a threat? No! Do I know they don't want to harm us? No! What I do know is if I don't listen, I can't hear what they want with or from us. When we do get together and talk, only then can we take a next step. Oh, I'm sorry. I forgot where your head was stuck, so you can't hear me."

She paused. "But thank you for your question."

She said, "Next!"

The next reporter took a less-confrontational tact. "In listening to the audio, there seemed to be an implication by Adam that they believe there is no God. Is there more audio that has been withheld from the people?"

Johnny sighed and spoke somewhat exasperatedly, "Sir, perhaps there is no way to make you, the people, believe that the time for lies is past. The president spoke of transparency, and that idea seems to have fallen on deaf ears or, in some cases, ears that are up their own asses. I was privileged to have heard the unedited audio before it was released to the public during our congressional session and the same audio that was offered to the public. There are no other versions or unedited formats of the audio. I can tell you that every effort is being made to make further contact by whatever means."

Johnny took a breath. "To answer your first question… What I got from the audio was that the Alphas are as we are, without a physical god. Now for me, it seems that they are yet searching for such an answer. Perhaps there is no universal necessity for god but more of an individual necessity for God. I would like to see a universal acceptance of choice of belief or nonbelief. If either gives one comfort and peace, shouldn't that be enough?"

Another question was delivered, "How are you preparing for tomorrow's possible event?"

Johnny thought, "Some are preparing as if it's the end of the world...and I have to laugh. Get real, people...if the Alphas meant us harm, why would they contact us...why would they warn us...to scare us? Enough people are scared just by the thought of there being actual ETs. Think about it, if they had the capability of destroying us and wanted to, would it make any difference in how we prepare for it? The result would be the same, save any divine intervention. And...if there were a divine intervention, then you have nothing to fear anyway.

"So...How am I preparing? I'm gonna live like I always do—try my best to enjoy each day and look forward to the next one...hopefully with my boyfriend, Sal."

CHAPTER 44

In-Flight Movies

Eve looked out of the window of the C-40 Clipper as it made its way to Beale AFB. Several military commanders and assorted brass were spread out among the comfortable seats in the craft. Although she was accustomed to flying, it was her first trip on a military plane. She took note that as a civilian, she garnered more than her share of glances. Admiral Scott, of the Lunar Fall event, sat across the aisle from her. He seemed to be a pleasant man but was engulfed in conversation on his COM.

The deluxe COM, supplied by Richard, buzzed and flashed. She saw Richard's picture, put on the headset, and accepted the COM.

Richard opened the dialogue, "Good morning, Eve, how is your flight?"

She looked at her watch, showing 12:15 p.m.; her error dawned on her.

"That's right, it's still morning here. I forgot to reset my watch."

He replied, "Yes, that's a dilemma for you jet-setters."

She retorted, as she changed the time back three hours, "I'd hardly think two trips a year would qualify me as a jet-setter."

He replied, "You might have to get used to it."

She asked, "You know something I don't know?"

He smiled and went past an answer and asked, "Okay, are you ready for your documentary segment?"

She responded smugly, "Yes, it's not my first interview?"

He reasserted, "That's true, but this may be your most relevant interview from a historical perspective."

She replied, "I realize its importance, but I've prepared my mind to record the humanity of the moment for posterity."

He smiled. "That's why I..." he mumbled and continued, "think you are perfect for this."

She noticed his stumble but continued, "Thank you for your encouragement."

He replied, "Always, Evelyn Walker, journalist."

She replied with a grin, "Are you mocking me?"

He smiled and changed the subject, "I assume your flight is enjoyable."

She countered, "Oh yes, I love the in-flight movie."

He chuckled. "Yeah, but I fall asleep and miss the ending."

She replied with a pleasing sigh, "Well, I want to be awake for this ending."

He replied pensively, "Perhaps we can catch the ending together sometime?"

She smiled and took a long pause and said under her breath, "I'd like that."

But in her speaking voice, she replied, "Yeah, I'll bring the popcorn."

The plane banked to port, and the notice came on the cabin speakers, "Touchdown in ten."

She said, "Okay, gotta get ready to put my parachute on and hook up. Do they still say Geronimo?"

He smiled. "They'll probably change that jump yell to Alpha."

He smiled and said, "Okay, break a leg."

She replied, smiling, "That's not funny."

Richard laughed and said, "Later!"

He disappeared from the COM.

CHAPTER 45

The Interview

Eve looked out at the mountain range, appreciating its beauty and taking pictures. Even the noise from the engine of the Huey didn't detract from her view.

As she prepared to land, she watched the protesters that had gathered on the road to Hat Creek SETI, her destination.

She hadn't seen a SETI array in person before and documented also that with her camera.

A temporary landing zone brought her safely to rest near a stand of trees where a Jeep was waiting. She waited for a moment and the guardsman opened the door and helped her out. She grabbed her valise and was escorted to the Jeep. They drove only a matter of yards to the main SETI building.

The driver escorted her to the building and opened the door.

*****

If you were to summarize Dominique Soul, you would have to begin and end with HOPE. Certainly there were days of despair, disappointment, despondency, and discouragement as part of every life. However, at the end of every day, she had hope. The positive always won over the negative.

Family life in Walnut Creek was rather normal: mother and father, older brother and younger sister, and an occasional dog or cat. School was fairly enjoyable, friends and sports activities rounded out her social life. Of course there were trips to the malls and school dances and a couple of young romantic interludes. She developed interest in computer technology and enjoyed weekend hikes on Mount Diablo. Her interest was piqued by more and more trips to the Lick Observatory on Mount Hamilton. She began attending Science and Technology Workshops and cherished her visits to SETI at Hat Creek. Eventually her PhDs in Planetary Sciences, Astrophysics, and Space Physics and Scientific Computing prepared her for her current destination.

Her passion for the unexplored and unexplained set her on the path to her logical destiny she now submitted to. Her unassuming status of being the first contact with alien intelligence was overshadowed by being the first to converse with an alien. She understood her renown, but she would not let it consume her.

She met Amir Hadad at Berkeley early on in her studies, but they went separate ways in educational disciplines. They kept in touch and were pleasantly surprised when they both landed at Hat Creek SETI a year ago.

Amir, although he himself had a place in history, instead of being jealous of Dominique's notoriety, embraced her with respect and support that defined the personal bond between them.

Amir and Dominique were deep into their effort to replicate the audio contact she enjoyed a few days earlier. Perry stepped over to Dominique's station that was now in between Perry and Amir.

He spoke to both of them, "You realize that you two are obsessed with reconnecting with Adam? You need to take a break for a while."

Amir looked up at Perry and nudged Dominique. "Hello, Dom, Perry's talking to us."

She looked at Amir and took a breath, gathered her awareness, and smiled. "Yes?"

Amir said, "Time for a break!"

She nodded. "Okay."

They both stood up and walked toward the end of the building where a few tables were, that served as a makeshift café. They found some drinks and snacks and sat down at a table.

*****

Michael was sitting at his desk when he saw Evelyn Walker walking toward the door. He got up to meet her as she stepped in.

He extended his hand. "Ms. Walker, welcome to SETI, Hat Creek. I remember you from our COM meeting."

She shook his hand and replied, "Yes, Michael, isn't it? It's a pleasure to meet you in person."

She scanned the complex and noted the large number of stations and monitors. "Wow, I didn't realize there were so many workstations here."

Michael replied, "Well, there were only five before the Alpha event last September. We went from stepchild status to front street. Don't know where they found the money, but looking the gift horse in the mouth was never my thing. We'll take what we can get."

She nodded. "I don't blame you, but it looks good."

He said, "We're so glad you're here. We are anxious for the positive exposure rather than having protesters at the gate."

She explained, "You realize that the protesters only represent perhaps 5 percent of the population. The overwhelming majority of the public is in support and anxiously awaits a positive outcome."

Perry walked up to Eve and offered his hand.

Eve shook it and said, "Morning, Perry, I recognize you from the COM meeting."

Perry replied, "Of course, it's great to meet you in person, Ms. Walker."

She set her valise down on the floor. "If you address me as Eve, I'd feel better."

They both nodded and Perry said, "Can we offer you something to drink and snacks?"

She nodded picked up her valise and said, "Sure, I can go for that."

They walked toward the end of the unit, where Dominique and Amir sat.

Michael went back to his desk, and Perry led the way. Eve smiled as she approached Amir and Dominique. Perry stopped when they got to the table.

He introduced Eve. "Eve, this is Dominique and Amir." He added, "This is Evelyn Walker."

Eve extended her hand.

Amir and Dominique both stood; Dominique shook her hand.

Eve smiled and said, "It's truly a pleasure to meet you.

Dominique replied, "It's totally my pleasure, Ms. Walker. I've read and heard so much about you."

Eve replied, "Me? You are quite the hidden star as of late."

Dominique replied, "Yes, and if it was my choice, I'd stay hidden."

Eve added, "You'll eventually find that your star will shine around what you might choose."

Eve extended her hand to a seemingly excited Amir.

Amir shook her hand and hugged her awkwardly. "I'm so glad to meet you."

Eve accepted the hug. "Glad to meet you too."

Amir said, "I've looked forward to meeting you since the video conference."

She replied, "Well thank you. I didn't realize I was so impressive."

Dominique said, "Ms. Walker, as you see, Amir is the hugging type."

Eve replied, "That's fine, but please, call me Eve."

Perry asked, "Eve, can I get you something?" He pointed to the food and beverage selection.

She said, "Thank you, I can help myself."

She set her valise down and went to a shelf and selected a glass and poured herself iced tea from a pitcher. She came back over to Amir and Dominique and asked, "May I join you two?"

Dominique answered, "Please do."

They all sat down and Perry said, "I'll leave you to get acquainted."

Eve said, "Thank you, Perry."

Eve began, "I'm sure you are aware that I've been asked to interview you both."

Dominique replied, "Yes, Perry told us you were coming, but we are not sure what else we can tell you."

Eve smiled and replied, "I'm sorry, but I'm not here to get more information about the Alpha contact. I'm here so you can tell your stories."

Amir asked, "What story?"

Eve began to explain, "I'm here to record your roles in what is now the single most-significant event ever witnessed by mankind."

Amir shrugged his shoulders.

"I didn't talk to the alien, Adam, Dom did."

Eve smiled and broke it down for Amir, "You understand the general reasoning of a domino theory?"

Amir nodded.

Eve continued, "I've interviewed almost all the players in the recent events, from the president, vice president, Sal Uschin, other SETI stations on down the chain. I plan to interview Perry, Michael, and hell, even the janitor. I even need to interview protestors and the man on the street. Those are figuratively all dominos. You follow, Amir?"

Amir nodded.

She continued, "But...without you and Dominique, there would be no last domino to fall, the most important domino. But the bigger picture, yet to come, starts with your domino falling on whatever the next domino might be."

She continued with passion, "Don't you see how important it is to chronicle these events?"

She hesitated and continued, "Do we know how the use of the wheel came about?"

Amir said, "Not really. We can only guess."

She ended the search, "We have the chance to not only document the search for extraterrestrial intelligence but also to document how the first contact with extraterrestrial intelligence came about."

Amir's brows furrowed, and then he chuckled. "So...who invented the wheel?"

Dominique backhanded Amir on the shoulder and said, "Really, Amir?"

Eve smiled and answered, "That information is highly classified."

She leaned forward in the chair. "First of all, please, you two, call me Eve."

Dominique partially nodded and said, "You can call me Dom if you wish."

Eve said, "Thank you, Dom."

Amir said, smiling, "I'm still Amir."

Eve smiled and reached into her valise and took out a COM.

"May I record our conversations?"

Dom and Amir nodded.

Eve said, "Thank you."

She paused and set the COM across the table to get all three of them in the picture. She turned on the COM.

She went through her automatic interview process of identifying all the participants and explaining standard video agreement and disclaimers. When she was finished, she paused and asked, "Okay, are you two ready?"

They both said yes.

Eve began, "First of all, although you are both being videoed, for privacy and security purposes, the background, audio, and your faces may be altered in some formats, depending on the classification level for release. You both have full control over the content you present. You understand?"

They both said yes.

"I have all the audio and COM of your SETI interactions prior to today. But what I'd like each of you to do for me is to describe your thoughts and feelings as you realized that you were actually in contact with the Alphas."

She turned to Amir. "Amir, when you discovered that the contact was authenticated, what went through you mind?"

Amir reflected for a moment. "My first thoughts were that of excitement that Dom had just given the key to verify the actual contact, and I just wanted to let Perry and Michael know what she had given me and that the printouts verified the source."

Eve asked, "When they asked you to announce to all of SETI, your now-famous 'We are not alone' statement, what did you think and feel?"

Amir thought, "Of course I was nervous and anxious at the same time. I didn't want to do it, but I also wanted to do it. Does that make sense?"

Dom added, "It does to me."

Eve also added, "How did it make you feel when you announced it?"

He thought and said, "Actually it was like a weight was lifted off my chest. I reflected on what this actually meant to me...the satisfaction of realizing all of my goals and also what it meant to humanity. It's hard to describe."

He continued, "I felt pride...but not self-pride. I saw the faces of all those whose hope was finally fulfilled."

Eve smiled. "At some point, when you finally found yourself alone, and you had time to process the experience, what about then?"

Amir said, "I felt anxious, maybe of the unknown...of what may lie ahead."

Eve asked, "And now?"

Amir responded, "Now I feel exuberant, refreshed, and ready for what may lie ahead."

Eve smiled and watched Amir, resting in his thoughts.

She looked over at Dominique, who had been absorbing Amir's experience.

After a moment, Eve focused on Dominique. "Dom as you look back on the morning of the day of your conversation with Adam, was there anything different than any other morning?"

Dom shrugged and thought, "Not really. I thought about the SETI project and was looking forward to catching up with my sister, Elsa."

Eve asked, "Do you see her often?"

Dom replied, "Not often enough. She moved away a few months ago and started a new job. I was anxious to hear her voice."

Eve asked, "So...would you say you were upbeat and focused, another normal morning?"

Dom nodded. "Yes, but more so looking forward to talking to Elsa."

Eve asked, "So…as you were talking to Elsa, what caused you to notice the change in the signal data stream array's substream frequencies?"

Dom thought and scrunched her eyebrows. "Actually there was something different other than just the change in the frequencies."

Eve prodded, "What was that difference?"

Dom explained, "I noticed that as we spoke, the signal data stream repeated, but also the substream appeared to mirror each word we spoke in length and intensity, much like a scope of a voice track. It was as if it was recording our conversation. That was when I disconnected the call from Elsa, but the COM stayed open, as does a keyed microphone uses a carrier to clear the frequency. That indicated that the collector switch was not activated. Then I heard a voice say, 'Hello, hello.' I answered with my own hello."

Eve tried to summarize, "So…you are saying that it was like you were getting an incoming call, and your current conversation was being recorded?"

Dom replied, "That's a good analogy to make."

Eve stated, "So…you answered the COM and began the conversation."

Dom nodded.

Eve continued, "I know you said that the voice appeared computer generated, but gradually the vocal pattern and intonation became more humanlike. But at what point did you think that Adam could actually be an alien?"

Dom replied, "I went over the audio numerous times before Honrí and Amir had me reveal the audio, and I became intrigued when Adam began to relate specific information about the data stream translation process. Very few people would have had access to that data. Soon I dismissed the COM as an ordinary prank, but it could have been generated from a SETI worker. As we spoke, I isolated the data stream and found that the source was indeed from Alpha Centauri A."

Eve asked, "You were checking the sources while you were talking to Adam?"

Dom replied competently, "Yes, I do have three PhDs."

Eve smiled and conceded, "Forgive me, I know not of what I speak."

Dom smiled. "The most telling point was that Adam appeared to have no agenda, especially with our discussion of the existence of god. An earthling would have not missed the opportunity to espouse their personal belief."

Eve brought a subjective question, "Do I get the sense that you yet have some doubt about the Alphas?"

Dom replied, "Yes, but not about their existence. They are real, and I did talk to one—the science is unequivocal."

Eve asked, "Then where does doubt lie?"

Dom chuckled. "I guess I should explain this so as not to seem arrogant."

Eve smiled. "Please do."

She continued, "We as humans have, for the most part, have postulated that if there were aliens, they would be all-knowing. I find that the Alphas are rather humanlike in that they are prone to errors and don't have all the answers. I don't see that as a negative. I actually find it endearing and comforting. To me, that breeds trust in their intent but doubt in their efficacy."

Eve replied, "Now that, I understand and agree with. What's that old proverb, 'trust but verify.'"

Dom said, "Exactly."

CHAPTER 46

The Situation Room

Tsirch sat in the Situation Room watching the various COMs attached to the walls around the room. There were two temporary monitors stationed at one end of the table. The largest main monitor on the wall, at the near end of the room, had his main focus. DOD secretary General Porter sat two seats away from Tsirch, switching his focus between monitors and several documents in front of him.

Tsirch was on a COM with Great Britain's president, Carl Browning.

"Aside from the two accidental deaths in the London protest, were there any incidents in Ireland or Scotland?"

Carl replied, "No deaths or serious injuries were reported. It appears that the Islanders have a more rational outlook than us Brits."

Tsirch asked, "So the Chunnel is without incident?"

Carl replied, "So far, the French president and I are on the same page, searching all suspicious vehicles and scanning trains. The traffic has slowed drastically, but it hasn't been shut down."

Tsirch stated, "I just touched base with the presidents of Germany and Iceland, and they said you and Norway have synced up your military COMs."

Carl replied, "We secured that early this morning, and the eastern Europe countries between the Adriatic and Black Seas were synced last night."

Tsirch stated, "Sounds like the CO-OP plan is coming together. Richard is working on the rest of Europe and cultivating a unity solution between Russia and China."

Carl looked at one of his monitors and sighed. "Sorry, Tsirch, have to cut this short. I have to take another COM."

Tsirch said, "Okay, Carl. Good luck."

Carl nodded and disappeared from the monitor.

General Porter looked over at Tsirch and said, "Well, Mr. President, it seems like the chess pieces are moving into position. I'm working on the last of the Oceania agreement with Australia and Indonesia. The Japanese prime minister, Yoshida, has engaged with Asia and eastern Africa and is working through various linguistics problems. She has them at the table as we speak."

Tsirch replied, "You're doing a great job, General, I might even buy you lunch."

Porter replied, "I'll have to negotiate a deal to get apple cobbler with that. But I'll leave the tip."

Tsirch replied, "You always were a big tipper."

Porter asked, "Speaking of big tippers, where is your vice president?"

Tsirch replied, "He's finishing up the Central/South American collective agreement. He should be coming over fairly soon."

Tsirch pushed a service button on the table.

"Yes, Mr. President."

"Kevin, could you come and take a lunch order?"

"Yes, sir."

Tsirch asked Porter, "I guess there have been no incidents reported in China and Russia?"

Porter replied, "That was an easy guess, sir."

Tsirch said, "Are you implying I have a simple mind?"

Porter replied, "No comment."

Kevin entered the room.

Tsirch said, "Kevin, charge this lunch to the general's account."

Vicki entered the room behind Kevin, carrying a glass of OJ.

Kevin smiled and added, "So...should I charge the First Lady's lunch order on that also?"

Vicki said, "Kevin, is my cheapskate husband at it again?"

Kevin rolled his eyes and avoided further comment. "What is your pleasure, sir?"

Tsirch said, "Et tu, Kevin?"

Kevin stood in stoic silence.

Tsirch scowled at Kevin but quickly smiled at Vicki. "Okay, dear, I trust you have already placed your order."

She replied, "Yes, I'm having the grilled tuna sandwich with avocado on the side."

Tsirch said, "General, your turn."

Porter said, "How about fried chicken with potato salad."

Kevin said, "Of course, will that be with Dijon on the side, sir?"

Porter nodded and replied, "Thanks for reminding me, Kevin."

Kevin nodded and asked, "And you, sir? The chef made your favorite clam chowder, and may I suggest the shrimp tacos?"

Tsirch sighed. "Kevin, you know my weaknesses too well, but add some turnip fries."

Kevin replied, "Of course, sir."

Vicki said, "Kevin, I'll have some turnip fries also, please."

Kevin replied, "Yes, madam. Anything else…anyone?"

There were no takers. Tsirch said, "I guess we're covered, Kevin, thanks."

Kevin said, "Thank you, sir." And he left.

Porter refocused on the document in front of him.

Vicki sat down next to Tsirch and smiled at him; he returned the smile and put his hand on hers.

She asked, "You okay?"

Tsirch nodded and looked back at the main monitor.

He saw an image on the monitor of the president of the Peoples Caucus, Charea Dixon, appear. He accepted the COM.

"Ms. Dixon, good afternoon, how are you?"

She smiled and said, "Good afternoon, Mr. President"—and, noticing the First Lady, added—"and, Madam First Lady Victoria, afternoon to you also."

Vicki smiled. "I'm doing well, Charea, and I'll try to keep the president on his best behavior."

Charea replied, "So sorry for you, a difficult task, I'm sure."

Tsirch said, "You two realize that I'm right here…you know, the commander in chief!"

Charea smiled. "Yes, Mr. President, forgive my lack of manners."

Tsirch said, "Okay, Dixon, let me have it."

She smiled and said, "It's all good news, Mr. President. Although there are concerns with the protests against the Alpha's pending incursion, there is widespread support of your plan. The inclusion of the vice president in the military coordination of DOD, DHS, and the new DS Commander secured an 87 percent vote."

Tsirch expanded the view with the remote pad to include General Porter. "And here is General Porter to accept his accolades."

She saw the general on her monitor. "Yes, General, you also are to be congratulated."

Porter smiled. "Thank you, Ms. Dixon, but there are 'miles to go before I sleep.'"

She replied, "You like poetry, General?"

He replied, "Not really, Ms. Dixon. I save a few quotes and adages to impress people, and Frost and Sun Tzu's *Art of War* makes me seem smart."

She responded, "Your secret is safe with me."

Porter replied, "You know what they say about those keeping secrets."

She replied, "Two can keep a secret IF…"

Porter replied, "Exactly."

She changed her tact. "I hear, General, the results of the microbe composition data indicate they contain no military benefit."

Porter nodded. "Nor do they require a military solution."

Tsirch added, "However, Dr. Uschin and European biochemists are still following the potential of using a combined formulation of the algae and archaea microbes with nonearth microbes indicated by the revised translation older data streams."

Porter replied, "That's what Lucas and the vice president have been scrutinizing."

Tsirch's personal COM bussed an alert. "Actually the vice president is five minutes, out and it's almost time for the tactical COM meeting."

Kevin knocked on the door and waited to enter.

Tsirch checked a monitor and said, "Enter."

Kevin came into the room with a lunch cart. He pushed it around to the end of the room near the president. He effortlessly portioned out the meal selections and turned to leave.

Tsirch and Vicki said, "Thank you, Kevin," almost in unison.

Vicki addressed Charea, "How rude of us to eat in front of you."

Charea smiled and picked up a sandwich and said, "Bon appétit."

The diners prepared their choices and started to eat.

Tsirch kept an eye on the main COM monitor that began to populate with images.

There was another knock on the door, and Tsirch looked at the door monitor and said, "Yes, Mr. Vice President, come in."

Richard came through the door with Lucas Makiev following him in.

They each had a briefcase in one hand and a bowl of clam chowder in the other hand.

Richard said, "Sorry to barge in during lunch, but we figured it was lunchtime and came through the kitchen and borrowed some chowder."

Vicki said, "My dear, we have to change the code on the kitchen entry."

Richard said, "Then I'd just send Lucas through the doggie door."

Lucas responded, "So I've been relegated to lapdog status?"

Richard replied, "That's a step up for you."

Tsirch stated sternly, "Let's be a little more professional. We have guests."

Lucas replied, "Of course, Mr. President."

Tsirch added, "Richard, take his leash off and make him sit."

Vicki said, "Really?"

As Richard and Lucas found their seats, Charea spoke up, "Well, I for one am enjoying the show."

Richard saw her on the monitor and said, "Ms. Dixon, didn't see you there. These guys are reprehensible and have no decorum."

She replied, "Vicki, I feel sorry for you."

Vicki replied, "If you only knew."

Tsirch looked at the main COM monitor and said, "Two minutes till showtime."

The players in the room prepared for the living collage.

One by one, Tsirch brought the images movement: Evelyn Walker; Jack Silver, CIA; Carl Browning, British prime minister; Garrard Arneaux, Canadian prime minister; Sal Uschin; Julia Van Hook, DHS; John "Pepper" Martin, FBI; Edward Narkiewicz and Brie Smithey, Domestic Security.

Tsirch began, "Afternoon, one and all, I'm sure you all recognize the participants on your monitors. If not, let me know."

Tsirch waited for a response that was negative.

Tsirch activated the multicam and expanded the view of the Situation Room to encompass its participants.

You should now be able to see my entourage here in the Situation Room—General Porter, Lucas Makiev, Vice President Natás, and my only lady, Victoria Ren Lang."

The group seemed to be visible to those on the COM monitor.

He began, "Very well. I have good news and sad news. The sad news is that there is some worldwide unrest, a few deaths—mostly accidental—and numerous injuries. It seems that there are those that insist on spreading untruths and harmful disinformation. The use of reflective paints, coating, and sheeting and foil coverings has been touted as a prevention to either stop alien attacks, blind alien ships, cloak the earth, and or deflect alien rays. These useless attempts have resulted in destruction of government properties, larger amounts of personal property, personal injuries, and the aforementioned deaths. Subversive groups have engaged in violent attempts and conspiracies to disrupt SETI sites, biolabs, governmental structures, and military installations. Fortunately much of the possible damage has been mitigated by the accelerated time frame of the anticipated Alpha-diffusion event.

"The good news is that nations worldwide have given unprecedented coordination of their scientific and military experts in an effort to assure all our people that every precaution is being made to keep Earth as safe as possible. People are encouraged to stay under a shelter or indoors, between 1100 and 1300 hours tomorrow, the twentieth.

"After that time, they should report any ill effects to a qualified medical professional. All hospitals, urgent care, law enforcement, fire and EMT responders, in addition to military personnel, have been placed on alert. All transportation methods—air, land, and sea—have been advised to cease operations during the diffusion event and carefully and safely resume operations subsequently."

Tsirch paused. "I'll ask each of you for an update or if you have any pending situation that needs to be brought to the attention of this group."

Tsirch scanned the monitor. "Mr. Silver of the CIA, do you have any secret updates?"

Jack Silver smiled and nodded. "Thank you, Mr. President. Aside from classified operations, we have tracked international crossover dissidents from Central Europe aligning with North African Nyabinghi factions. As yet, there has been no indication of any potential attack on high-risk operations."

Tsirch moved on. "I know the FBI and Domestic Security have melded several joint operations and propped up Homeland's footprint in the west and southwest. Julia, has Homeland any overwhelming needs at the moment?"

Van Hook replied, "I can't say enough about the coordination benefits Domestic Security and the FBI have brought to DHS. Countless potential dangerous incidents have been identified and stopped or minimized. Although there are always ongoing national threats, any immediate threats related to the Alpha situation have been quelled."

Tsirch asked, "Mr. Martin, how does the FBI defend against such accolades?"

Pepper smiled and chuckled. "The FBI pleads *nolo contendere* and also to conspiring with Domestic Security." He continued, "As expected, several subversive groups have reared their ugly heads in an attempt to take advantage of fearmongering. Most of the credit in stopping serious attacks goes to the local law enforcement. Their roles were greatly expanded by their inclusion in the Domestic Security umbrella, and they exceeded all capabilities. Several new players in the Segr8 faction were uncovered with their tenacity."

Tsirch looked at Richard. "Mr. Vice President, what say you about the fledgling Domestic Security division?"

Richard smiled. "I prefer that the usual suspects speak for themselves."

He looked up at the monitor. "Commander Narkiewicz and Lieutenant Smithey, what do you have to say for yourselves?"

Edward looked at Brie and said, "Lieutenant, you're up, front and center."

Brie shrugged and trudged ahead, "Domestic has weathered through several obstacles under the direction of Commander Narkiewicz and with the support of the FBI and the aforementioned local law enforcement agencies. And may I state, for the record, that I firmly believe that the national tension was greatly dampened by the recent off-the-cuff interview of Maryland congressional representative Johnny Walsh. She spoke with logic and told the truth. And people listened."

Richard asked, "Commander, you have anything to add?"

Edward looked at Brie, shrugged. "No, sir."

Richard wrinkled his face in approval and looked at Sal. "Dr. Uschin, Sal. I guess this falls next to you."

Richard leaned back in his chair. "Are you making headway in your research?"

Sal took a short breath. "I should answer yes, but a qualified yes. I'm not sure that compiling the results of possible biological eventualities and interactions qualifies as a yes. We have yet to determine what effects of the next diffusion may have if it contains unknown microbes or antigens. So we wait."

Sal shifted in his chair and added, "Let me say this to Johnny Walsh, I am NOT your boyfriend. YOU are my girlfriend!"

Richard smiled and looked at Lucas. "Lucas, anything you would like to share?"

Lucas quipped, "Not about Sal and Johnny, but…how about an update on the SETI signals?"

Richard replied, "That would be nice."

Lucas continued, "Worldwide, scientists have been analyzing the data streams using the new technology and have uncovered new digital technology and biological formulas that have greatly advanced our understanding of atmospheric interactions that increase and stabilize the oxygen content and strengthen the ozone layer. Additionally the biological formulations can increase methods of food-supply production processes."

Tsirch asked, "Lucas, is there any progress in our effort to recontact the Alphas in real time as before?"

Lucas responded, "Not as yet, but the circumstances of that data and signal streams that existed at that time have been shared with all available resources to make that possible."

Charea Dixon added her comments, "Mr. President, if I may. The Peoples Caucus has initiated a resolution to sanction all scientific and military research to support any interaction with the Alphas."

General Porter interceded, "On behalf of all military, the Peoples Caucus resolution will greatly enhance every defensive capability. Thank you, Ms. Dixon."

Tsirch scanned the monitor and focused on Eve. "Most of you recognize Evelyn Walker as an exceptional journalist and counselor. However, she has been tasked with a special assignment. Perhaps she would like to share the nature of her assignment."

Tsirch said, "Ms. Walker."

Eve settled into her seat. "Two weeks ago, I met with Vice President Natás, and he hired me as his attorney and as a documentarian. I was conflicted by the duality of his request, but I eventually accepted his offer.

"He understood that my obligation to the courts and law took precedent over any journalistic venture, and I discovered that was exactly why he wanted my particular skills. He wanted me to document all of his actions relative to his involvement in the scientific and military activities relative to any alien interactions. I soon realized this would be no easy cause. I interviewed every contact he made, that included all of you. I documented all his COMs and COMs of his contacts. I was given near-top-level security clearance and eventually top-level clearance by the president. All the conversations, interviews, and documents I had access to, even this COM meeting, will be included in my report. I have yet to collect examples of hopes of the people, after which this segment will be completed. This endeavor was, and is, an effort to document transparency and the truth for the people and, apparently by extension, the nonhuman Alphas. My tour of duty will likely extend through the diffusion event tomorrow, unless I resign or get terminated."

She glanced at Richard. "On a personal note, this has yet been the most gratifying experience of my life. Thank you, Mr. President and Mr. Vice President, for this opportunity."

Tsirch took a breath. "Well, ladies and gentlemen, we yet have a nation to run, and I will take the last participant's interrogatory in private—my only lady, Victoria Ren Lang."

Tsirch smiled, and the COM meeting was terminated.

CHAPTER 47

What People Say

When the meeting concluded, Eve disconnected her COM and placed it in her valise. She opened the car door, grabbed her valise, and headed toward a waiting Huey. Its engine started as she stepped out of the car. She walked to the Huey, was helped inside, and she buckled her seat belt. The door was closed, and the aircraft idled for a while and eventually lifted off the ground, gained sufficient height, and banked away toward St. Louis. Eve opened her COM and put her headphones on. She selected a file from her most-recent interview of Carla Miller at her farm, in a rural area of Leland Grove, Illinois. It began to play.

"Carla, you've grown corn as fuel here for fifteen years. Are you concerned about possible changes if the technology the Alphas may have is adopted?"

She paused. "No, ma'am, I'd love to see how I can increase production, if it protects the environment. I have to rotate crops with soy, but often the rotation doesn't align with the market pricing."

Eve asked, "So are you concerned about any threats from the Alphas?"

She replied, "From what I heard from the president, he believes the Alphas only want to help us, and with what I heard on that audio, I agree."

Eve asked, "So you aren't afraid of them?"

She replied, "Heck no, I'm sorta excited to find out what they look like."

Eve closed that file and selected one from a protestor at Hat Creek, Ed Bowman.

Eve asked, "Mr. Bowman, what exactly are you protesting against?"

He replied, "Those aliens need to stay away from us. They can bring viruses and suck our oxygen out of Earth. They already took the air out of the moon last September."

Eve replied, "You realize that the Alphas aren't physically coming to Earth, and they aren't on the moon, and that the moon has never had air?"

He replied, "That's what the lyin' government wants you to believe. Hell, there might not even be any aliens, and the government just wants to scare people."

Eve tried logic, "If there aren't aliens, how does that scare people?"

Bowman replied, "They want us to think there are aliens to scare us into making us fight other countries."

Eve tiptoed around the rabbit hole. "So...the government wants you to think there are aliens to scare you into fighting other countries?"

Bowman said, "Yeah, and while we're fighting for the government, they'll take our land and homes."

Eve asked a different question, "So...what do you want the people at this SETI site to do?"

Bowman said, "They need to fire up their machines and tell the aliens not to come."

Eve realized the segment came full circle. "Thank you, Mr. Bowman."

The Huey pilot motioned to Eve, pointing to their destination. The St. Louis Arch still beckoned.

The Huey landed, and she was escorted first-class style, without a check-in process, onto her flight. She settled into her first-class seat and sipped on a glass of Chianti. The flight from St. Louis to Washington, DC, would take less than two hours. Maybe Eve could get a nap in.

More than halfway into the flight, Eve rallied from her sleep and decided to watch another interview. She opened her COM and selected her interview of a disassociated veteran, Paul Nguyen, near Stanton Park in DC.

"Mr. Nguyen, you told me you're a veteran, is that right?"

Paul replied, "Yes, ma'am. I haloed out, above the Sphinx, during the Nile War."

Eve replied, "That's amazing. That must have been exciting."

Paul replied, "Looking back, it was exciting, but at the time, I was just worried about getting shot or my O_2 running out."

"You must have been at a high altitude."

"Yeah, about thirty-four thousand feet."

"How long were you in the conflict?"

"The twenty-three days of the incursion."

Eve thought, "I forgot it lasted that long."

"That was only six days, but I stayed there to mop up."

"What do you do when you got back?"

"I worked construction for about eight years, until the economy tanked."

Eve said, "You said before that, you live day-to-day and have no regular job. Do you have any family?"

Paul explained, "They live in another state, but I choose to live as I do. I get by fine on my own. I find daywork and help out in the kitchen at the shelter."

Eve changed the subject. "Have you heard about the Alphas?"

Paul nodded. "Sure, I caught the audio, and I keep up on current events."

Eve asked, "What do you think about the Alphas?"

Paul said, "Wish they would hurry and show their cards. They can't be too advanced, though."

"Why do you say that?"

"Didn't they send the first diffusion by mistake?"

Eve was surprised. "You are paying attention."

"Not just another ugly face. I can read, I've got a BA in aeronautics."

"Then why—"

Paul interrupted, "Why do I live as I do? I don't answer to anyone, I have a place to sleep, I don't go hungry, and I can help my friends out when they need me. I get a small pension, and the VA takes care of my medical. It's like retirement."

He redirected, "Now back to the Alphas. They seem like decent neighbors. They say they want to help, then take them at their word. It's not like we can stop them anyway."

Eve asked, "Are you sure you are not CIA?"

"Ms. Walker, you know the saying 'if I told ya, then I'd have to kill ya'?"

Eve spoke the words of the last half of the saying in sync with Paul.

Then she added, "Thank you for your service."

Eve closed the COM and looked out the window at the waning daylight.

The captain uttered the standard prepare-to-land words.

Eve put her COM in her valise and prepared to disembark.

CHAPTER 48

Getting Ready for Company

Light rain fell on the DS Center at Cheyenne Mountain as Edward and Brie were walking into the main entrance. They diverted through the cafeteria to gather some extra rations as they were preparing for a twenty-four-plus-hour shift. The opened the door to the office and saw a technician finishing the installation of a new larger monitor. They set their briefcases and lunch containers down and walked over to admire the new addition.

Edward said, "Can't have too many monitors."

Brie stated, "Now we can track the diffusion ourselves."

She asked the technician, "Is that ready to go, Sergeant?"

He replied, "Affirmative, Lieutenant."

She went over to her desk and typed on the keyboard. The monitor activated, and with a few more keystrokes, the Hat Creek logo appeared.

Brie said, "Thanks, Aaron, this is great."

The sergeant said, "You're welcome, Lieutenant." And he left.

Edward picked up their lunch containers and put them in a cabinet. He opened his briefcase and took out a COM. He keyed the pad, and the Hat Creek logo began flashing. Brie opened her briefcase and took out her COM and keyed her pad, also activating the multicam. They rolled their desk chairs in front of the new appliance and sat down. Perry's face appeared live, in place of the Hat Creek logo.

Edward said, "Good evening, Perry."

Perry replied, "Good evening, Edward and Brie."

Brie replied, "Sir, we now have capability of tracking the diffusion. You only have to give us access. I sent you our location code access ID."

Perry looked at his monitor and said, "I see it." He entered some numbers on a keypad. "Okay, that should do it."

Brie entered a code, and another logo was added to the monitor.

She said, "Got it, thank you, sir."

Perry asked, "Did you see my report about the protestor's activities?"

She replied, "Yes, sir, the commander and I appreciated the details."

Edward asked, "Have they left for the day?"

Perry replied, "Yes. Guess they are getting their own places ready for tomorrow."

The Johannesburg logo flashed on the monitor.

Brie accepted the COM.

Jo and Cory appeared on the screen.

Edward said, "Good morning, guys, you getting ready for the happening?"

Jo replied, "We're ready, but I've been retranslating the prior and most-recent data streams, and we want to confirm the frequency shift with you, Perry."

Perry replied, "Michael saw that, and he is checking it now."

Cory added, "This looks like the same data Amir and Dominique sent me. They found that the direct translation is of the same three or four sentences translated into ten or so languages."

Perry said, "Here comes Michael now. We'll see if he has more details." Perry added, "Edward, you guys should be able to tap into the DOD Super-COM and analyze the data quicker."

Edward asked Brie, "What do you think, Lieutenant?"

Brie said, "I'll give it a try." She busied her fingers on a keyboard.

Michael appeared next to Perry.

"Michael, what did you make of the direct translations?"

Michael said, "I got Jo's data, and it's the same that I received and what Amir and Dominique has. There is one difference. It appears that it includes an audio stream, attached like an actual audio track in an old video file."

Cory looked at his data stream on his monitor and agreed, "Dominique and Amir are working to sync both together. But my COM isn't powerful enough to combine two different media types."

Perry said, "We may have an ace in the hole. Edward and Lieutenant Fast-Fingers are trying to tap into the DOD Super-COM."

Cory asked, "She can get clearance for that?"

Edward said, "We got A-One clearance from the boss himself."

Cory said, "Damn! Do Amir and Dominique know?"

Perry winced. "Oops, I'll go tell them now." He left the screen.

Michael advised, "If this works, why would the Alphas send it in this format? We already can read the words and hear the audio and can combine them digitally like a video?"

Brie entered back into the conversation, "I've been following your conversations, and I have one take on one possible answer."

Michael said, "Okay, let's have it."

Brie related a scenario, "The Super-COM came through and combined the two stream types into one data stream, but we don't have the capability to send the stream, only receive it."

Michael summarized, "So we can receive the combined file and hear and see it, but we can't send it in that format."

Perry came back and said, "I told Amir and Dominique, and they were listening in on your conversations."

Cory quipped, "So much for secure channels."

Perry added Amir and Dominique with a push of a button. "Guys, tell them what you think the Alphas are trying to do?"

Dominique said, "We believe the Alphas are trying to broadcast the file to all of Earth. We just have to figure out how for us to receive it."

Cory offered a devilish smile. "We need some sort of compatible speakers to receive the audio and a screen or monitor to receive the picture."

Cory asked Jo, "Jo, dear, do we have enough cable to connect to Alpha Centauri A to our SETI station?"

Jo shook her head and rolled her eyes.

Edward said, "Okay, ladies and gentlemen, I think this is out of DSC scope of capabilities. So we'll bid you good luck and adieu."

Perry said, "Okay, Commander, and thanks again, Lieutenant Fast-Fingers."

DSC disappeared from the monitor.

Dominique continued, "Seriously, that's what I believe they want to do. I don't know how, but as I watched the streams, it appeared that they were probing various audio and video options."

Amir added, "That's one of the approaches we are working on but still can't send and receive a message. We even sent all of you, Dr. Uschin, and Lucas the data streams of our attempts to make contact."

Cory said, "Yes, we've tried those simulations but haven't had any success either."

Michael relayed, "I resent your data to the other SETI stations also. We're all working on it."

Perry stated, "Dominique, don't forget, you have an appointment tomorrow."

She replied, "No, all of us have an appointment tomorrow. Eve and the vice president are coming also."

Michael added, "I understand that Adam sent you the coordinates for not only for your meeting but also several thousand coordinates on Earth and two on the moon. Still wondering how they are going to accomplish that feat."

Dominique also noted, "It's interesting that, so far, we are finding that the coordinates are not random but for specific locations that generate more viewing access."

Amir relayed, "We have sent the locations to all COMs for dissemination. However, there may be those who do not get the message and may be disturbed by the sudden appearance of an apparition."

Michael stated, "Dr. 'Gemo and Commander Yost certainly had that unnerving experience."

Cory added, looking at Jo, "We, for two, can't wait."

Dominique offered, "I've read the text of the data stream several times. It gives me pause in how I see my own life. I wonder what Commander Yost understood when he read the lips of the hologram. Was it the same as the data text?"

Michael replied, "From what I understand, he only told Sal and the president. I don't know who else knows. However, I'm sure that Sal told the vice president. The commander said that since he became aware of the possible data stream text, he wanted to see if it was the same message."

Dominique smiled. "Are we not all looking for validation of some sort? I am anxious to find what Adam has in the offing."

CHAPTER 49

Home Sweet Pizza

Angela and Nicole hurried out of the car and raced to the front door. Lucas and Ari watched the routine with pleasure as they exited the vehicle. Lucas hugged Ari as he walked and rolled his suitcase to the door. Ari unlocked the door, and the girls rushed inside.

Lucas followed Ari inside and closed and locked the door. They wound around the living room and down a hallway to their bedroom. He set the suitcase next to the dresser and sighed.

"Hopefully, these last three months of travel is the last trek until the end of summer."

Ari took off her coat and tossed it on the bed. She walked up to Lucas, and they wrapped themselves together and held on for a long moment. They leaned away from each other and smiled in sync.

Ari said, "My love, I know it's been trying, physically and emotionally, but being a part of history has its own reward. You have to admit, we couldn't resist this journey...and it's still not over."

Lucas sighed again. "Yeah, tomorrow will be the end of the beginning...of...or maybe the beginning of the end of...something."

Ari chuckled. "Lucas, dear, philosophy BEFORE dinner?"

Lucas nodded softly. "Okay, okay, I'm gonna go roust the girls."

Ari smiled. "They love that. You wanna cook or go out?"

Lucas thought, "Ya know, I should be tired, but I'm so anxious about tomorrow." He paused. "Let's let the girls decide."

Ari smiled. "Yeah, good idea, but you know the answer already!"

Lucas nodded and ran down the hall to the girls' room.

Loud scuffling noises, laughs, growls, giggles, and happy screams ruptured the quiet. Eventually there was quiet conversation and an eruption—PIZZA!

CHAPTER 50

Family Dinner

The residence was abuzz with various staff preparing seating in the garden area for a possible visit from Adam. Also in the garden area, a Faraday-type room was erected with a special glass front. It was designed to ward off possible effects of the diffusion. Tsirch chose this option to be able to view Adam in the garden rather than the safety of the bunker.

*****

Tsirch, Vicki, and their son were trying to relax in the dining room after their meal.

Thomas engaged his last few bites of fish tacos and rested his wrists on the table.

"Dad, is there anything special you want me to do tomorrow?"

Tsirch asked, "Like what, Thomas?"

He laughed. "Oh, like wash the car, mow the lawn, to make this place look presentable for our visitor?"

Vicki chimed in, "Thomas dear, you could wash the dog."

Thomas smiled. "Mom, we have a cat, and Sneakers wouldn't go for it."

Tsirch thought, stood up, and said, "Thomas, there is something I'd like you to do."

Thomas expected a smart-ass request and asked cynically, "What would that be, dear ole Dad?"

Tsirch replied seriously, "Your mom and I would like you to stand with us tomorrow and represent the youth of the world."

The unexpected request gradually soaked into Thomas. Certainly he has joined the family celebrations and state functions, but it was overwhelming to be asked, by the President, to attend this historical event and to represent the youth of the world.

Thomas stood and took a breath of pride. "Mr. President, Madam First Lady, I would be honored."

CHAPTER 51

Foreplay

Sal sat on his sofa going over data on his COM that rested on a coffee table. He saw Johnny moving toward him out of the corner of his eye. He feigned noncognizance until she came within striking distance. Sal pushed the COM away and attacked her with a double-arm wrap and pulled her on top of him. Johnny fought him with vicious acceptance. They tussled for a moment, and Sal held her shoulder with his free hand and pushed her away slightly to look in her eyes.

"Your boyfriend loved your impromptu press conference."

She smiled. "Your girlfriend didn't like what the jerk of a reporter was implying."

"Your boyfriend especially liked your take on the Alphas."

"Your girlfriend was just stating the obvious."

"How'd she get so smart? Guess she just said what her BOSS told her to say."

She pushed away slightly and said, "Really?"

She raised up and pinned his shoulders on the sofa with her hands.

"I'll show you who's BOSS of this relationship."

Sal submitted completely, smiling. "Take me, I'm yours."

She bounced him on the sofa with her hands and said, "You wimp!"

Sal laughed. "You expected me to put up a fight?"

She relaxed and rested her elbows on his chest and looked into his eyes. "Okay, what were you checking out on your COM?"

Sal shifted around and sat up with Johnny's help, and confessed, "I was checking out the various coordinates Adam sent to decide where we should go to bear witness. I asked Commander Yost if he wanted to join us."

She replied, "If you want to go to Hat Creek, we'll have to leave tonight."

Sal nodded. "Or we can catch it at the Lincoln Memorial or at the presidential residence."

Johnny stood and smiled. She grabbed his hand and tugged on it. "Either way, we should make our own appearance in the bedroom."

Sal shrugged. "What would your boyfriend say?"

She replied, "Hopefully he would say YES."

CHAPTER 52

Precursor

Dominique waited in her car outside of the apartment complex, half-listening to music on the radio. The bulk of her attention was given to her COM. The darkness was co-opted by the interior light when Amir opened the car door.

"Good morning, Dom."

Dom said eagerly, "And a good morning to you, Amir."

He asked, "Okay, have you been eating happy food?"

She replied, "No, just anxious for this day."

She fired up the engine and started to drive.

"I feel the same, Dom...So much anticipation."

"Can you believe what's happened in less than a week? It's hard to comprehend...actual contact with aliens."

"Yes, but you got to actually speak to one."

"Yes, but I realize that he could just as well have talked to any one of us."

Amir grinned. "Dom, I don't believe that. He was probably stalking you."

She laughed. "Amir, don't make it sound creepy, yuk."

He said, "Actually I think he listened to your conversation with Elsa and knew you were the perfect one to contact."

"He could tell from my conversation? That's funny." She turned on to the highway.

"Sure, you are intelligent, have family, and you were already responding to their data streams."

"All of us were responding to them. I just happened to be there at the right time."

"I still think he was stalking you."

"Sure, from 4.3 light-years away."

"Well…sure. He did ask you out on a date."

"Yeah, me and 9.2 billion other earthlings watching."

Amir continued his onslaught, "And you're on a first-name basis, and he knows where you live."

She chuckled. "Amir…that's enough."

Amir continued, "He probably wants you to meet his mother."

"Amir, stop."

She continued driving as they pursued their banter.

CHAPTER 53

Prevalidation Party

Two Chinook helicopters circled the Hat Creek SETI station.

Two Secret Service vehicles waited along the road, with five agents spread around the landing zone.

The radio crackled.

"VP LZ clear."

"VP copy."

One Chinook touched down as the other hovered. In the distance, a Huey scoured the area. The agents compressed on the Chinook, and the bay door opened. Richard and Evelyn walked down the ramp and got into one of the cars. The second Chinook landed, and Sal, Johnny, and Commander Yost walked out and got into the second car.

The vehicles drove a few hundred yards to the SETI station, and the passengers exited the vehicles and went into the station.

*****

Dominique was making the last turn toward the station and saw the remnants of the protest the day before. The protestors had vanished, and the abandoned signs and various trash bags were scattered along the road. As they neared the SETI station, Secret Service agents waved Dominique to a stop.

She said to Amir, "The VP must be here." Amir nodded.

She rolled down her window.

"Good morning, ma'am, may I see your IDs, and could you open your trunk, please."

Amir and Dominique were prepared for the ask and handed the agent their IDs, and she popped her trunk lid.

The agent compared the faces with the documents, turned to one side, and spoke to an unknown recipient. An agent inspected the trunk, and another agent walked around pointing a large multiscan device at the vehicle.

"Soul and Hadad."

She paused for a response. A response appeared to be acceptable, and the agent returned their IDs and said, "Thank you, they are expecting you."

She waved them on toward the station.

As they approached the station, they noticed a large room-like structure had been erected just past the end of the station. It had a glass-like front wall on one end.

They parked at the station and got out of the car, carrying their briefcases. The approached the entrance, and an agent with a hand-held scanner had them stop and scanned their persons and their briefcases.

He nodded. "Thank you, sir, ma'am." And he opened the door for them.

They went through the door and saw another agent near the door.

They saw the friendly faces gathered at the café setting at the end of the station. Michael, Perry, Richard, Eve, Sal, Johnny Walsh, and Commander Yost were all engaged in various conversations.

Amir and Dominique set their briefcases down at their workstations and went to join the party.

Perry saw the couple coming toward them and said aloud, "Well, there they are, the guests of honor."

Amir smiled embarrassingly, and Dominique smiled at the vice president and asked, "Shall we bow and curtsey?"

Richard smiled and offered, "No, but you can join us peons."

Dominique shook her head. "Mr. Vice President, you are hardly a peon."

He countered, "I beg to differ, Ms. Soul. Am I not but a mere servant of the people?"

Dominique responded, "You were elected by twelve million people."

Richard explained, "My very point. I was yet elected to serve."

He extended his hand. "It is an honor to meet you, and you can call me Richard."

She took his hand and smiled tentatively. "If you insist, sir. I am Dom."

He smiled. "Thank you, Dom."

Richard turned to Amir, extending his hand. "Amir, it's good to see you in person. I watched several of your COMs, and I enjoyed your exuberance and wit. Our COM meetings are so impersonal."

Amir nodded. "Yes, they are. I'm much taller in person."

Dominique nudged Amir. "Amir."

Richard laughed. "Amir, she should know you by now."

Amir replied, "It keeps her on her toes."

Dominique shook her head.

Yost stood up as Richard spoke to him.

"Commander Steven Yost, I want to introduce you to Dominique Soul and Amir Hadad. Both are integral components in our successful contact with the Alphas."

Steve shook their hands.

Dominique said, "Commander, I understand you were the first to encounter the Alphas. It must have been captivating and exhilarating to witness the unexplainable."

Steve said, "It was all those things and more. I yet have questions about my sanity. Except for the encounter documented by Dr. 'Gemo in his notes, I am still in need of validation of what I saw."

Dominique acquiesced, "I understand, Commander. Even though we have verification of data streams and the audio file, I need some kind of validation myself. I hope that, if today's diffusion and appearance come to pass, others seeing it will give both of us validation."

Yost agreed, "True. So far we only have ourselves as witnesses… and please call me Steve or Steven."

Amir interceded, "Neither of your experiences needs validation for me. I believe in you both completely."

Steve said, "I appreciate your support."

Sal and Johnny approached Amir and Dominique.

Sal said as he chuckled, "Amir, you ARE taller in person."

Amir shook his hand. "Dr. Uschin, wow, it is such an honor to meet you in person. Dom and I have followed your accomplishments with awe. The latest microbe diffusion citations were amazing."

Amir turned to Johnny, took her hand, and shook it. "Ms. Walsh, Congresswoman, your financial expertise is second to none."

Johnny was surprised at his acknowledgment. "Thank you."

Amir put his hand on Dominique's shoulder and said, "Ms. Walsh, Dr. Uschin, I want you to meet Dominique Soul, scientist extraordinaire."

Dominique shook her head and smiled.

Johnny took her hand and said, "Yes, Ms. Soul, I've heard so much about you and Amir."

Dominique responded, "But you, Ms. Walsh, are an icon for political acumen and women's rights. Your dressing down that reporter yesterday was priceless, and your logic regarding the Alphas was flawless."

Dom continued, "Wow, meeting Dr. Uschin and Johnny Walsh, what an experience."

Sal diverted the conversation, "Come now, you two. We are old news. You are the beacons of the future. You have yet to absorb your own realities."

Michael eased into the conversation, "Okay, how about we add some breakfast to the activities."

The mutual-admiration society infused itself with sustenance.

CHAPTER 54

Ante Meridiem

Lucas drove up to the rear of the residence and stopped. He got out and walked toward the rear of the car. Ari opened her door and stepped to the rear passenger door and opened it. Angela and Nicole got out of the car and waited. Lucas came around the rear of the car and took Angela's hand, and Ari took Nicole's.

They walked up the steps and through the door being held open by staff. Philip met them inside.

"How are you today, Mr. and Mrs. Makiev?"

Lucas replied, "Doing fine, Philip, thank you."

He continued, "And Angela, Nicole, are you excited?"

Angela said, "Yes, sir, we are."

Nicole added, "Maybe we'll see an alien."

Philip smiled. "We hope so."

Philip led them down the hall to the Oval Office.

Philip knocked on the door, and he heard, "Come in."

He opened the door, and the family went in. Tsirch and Vicki were sitting at a table, talking. They stood as Lucas and Ari came in.

Vicki and Ari clasped their outstretched hands and leaned together, touching their foreheads.

Lucas walked over to Tsirch and shook his hand.

"Thank you for inviting us, it means a lot to share this with you."

Tsirch replied, "Lucas, this is not a reward for you service. This is out of love and respect for a friend."

285

Lucas replied, "Sadly our schedules have kept us in different time zones for too long."

Tsirch offered, "Yes, and there may be more separation anxiety ahead. The Alphas have changed much of our directions of life."

Lucas added, "True, and we can embrace those changes with hope for the future."

Ari interrupted, clasping Tsirch's hand with both of hers. "Hey, stranger, long time no see."

Tsirch smiled. "Oh you know, croquet tournaments, book club meetings, learning to knit, running the country, dealing with aliens—busy, busy, busy."

Ari chuckled. "Oh, excuses, excuses."

Lucas hugged Vicki hello, and Vicki knelt down and hugged the girls.

Tsirch went over to the girls and reached down, held each by their shoulders against his sides.

"Young ladies, who has the most boyfriends?"

Before they could answer, Thomas came through the residence door and was promptly mugged by the girls.

Lucas watched their antics for a moment, then walked up to Thomas and shook his hand and put his other hand on his shoulder.

"Thomas, should I say you're getting taller, smarter, or better-looking?"

Thomas replied, "How about all three, but I can't get any better-looking."

Lucas smiled and said, "Yes, sir."

Ari hugged Thomas and kissed him on the cheek.

A Secret Service agent went over to Tsirch and whispered to him.

Tsirch said, "Okay, it's time to go."

They gathered their collective composures and exited out to the garden area.

CHAPTER 55

Change of Plans

The Hat Creek gathering sat at café tables watching a large monitor on the wall. The SETI crew was at their workstations, watching data streams and the feeds from other sites and news feeds.

Michael was at his workstation, feverishly typing on his COM. Sal noticed Michael's urgency and went to his side.

"What's up, Michael, you look stressed?"

Michael replied, "I just got a notice that there was an explosion at the JC in Johannesburg. I can't reach Cory and Jo."

Sal took a breath. "Let me see if Richard can get some more information."

Sal started to walk away when he heard Michael exclaim, "Yes!"

He turned back toward Michael and asked, "What happened?"

Sal saw Jo on the monitor. Michael spoke to her, "Jo, I was worried. I heard about the explosion, and I couldn't make contact."

Jo asserted, "Yes, there was an explosion. Someone tried to sabotage the power grid. But fortunately, all the explosives didn't detonate. They shut down the grid as a precaution. The SA military caught the militants with the help of some alert 'civilians.' Cory found out from Silver that he couldn't confirm or deny that the alert civilians were his CIA operatives. So all is well here."

Michael sighed in relief. "Thank goodness." He paused. "Did you get to view the hologram?"

Jo nodded. "We caught the visage, but some of the translation was interrupted by the power outage. We only caught the last of the audio."

Sal was puzzled.

"Jo, this is Sal."

She said, "Hi, Sal, good to see you."

Sal replied impatiently, "Jo, good to see you, too, but you said there was audio? Did you set up a remote audio to listen from your SETI signal arrays while you were at the coordinates?"

Jo tried to explain, "Sal, yes and no. We did initially set up a remote to send the audio from inside the SETI so we could sync and hear what the hologram was saying instead of trying to read lips. We had set up the COM to document the video portion and listen in our headsets.

"But we didn't know the power grid went down just before the appearance time. When the hologram appeared, we couldn't hear the audio in our headsets. We frantically checked our connections for a disconnected component. I was exasperated and took off my headset.

"That's when I realized that I, somehow, could hear a voice, and it was closely synced with the hologram. I nudged Cory, and I took his headset off so he could hear. That's when we realized there was audio along with the visual."

Michael and Sal stalled in thought.

Michael asked, "Where was the audio coming from?"

Jo replied, "We realized the audio was coming from our COMs. It somehow was patched into them."

Sal, still in thought, said, "We have to share this with everyone."

Jo said, "Cory is getting the message out as we speak. The whole world will be able to hear the message."

Sal said, "That's great. I'll try to do the same."

Jo stopped Sal, "But, Sal…you also have to correct our mistake."

Sal asked, "What mistake."

Jo added, "The diffusion is not happening at the same time as the hologram but at midnight tonight, Greenwich Mean Time. When our event did not include the diffusion, we reached out to other SETI stations, and they registered no diffusion. I checked the data stream signals and found the confusion was in our assumption that the translation of meridian to be the same as antemeridian that Adam referenced in the conversation with Dominique. It's actually happening postmeridian."

Sal said, "Does the president know that?"

Jo said, "I told the secretary of state, and he said he would let him know. I've tried to verify the information."

Sal advised, "The vice president is here, and I'll let him know right now."

Sal walked away from the monitor and headed toward Richard.

Richard was talking to Eve when Sal touched him on the shoulder.

"Richard, there are new developments, and we have a mistake to correct."

Richard put on his serious face. "Okay, Sal, let's have it."

"First, Jo found that the diffusion was not happening during the midday event. It is happening tonight, 2400 hours GMT."

Richard thought for a moment and said, "Did Honrí say anything about it?"

Sal related, "Jo reached out to him and to other SETIs, and there was no diffusion event. Jo and Cory rechecked the data and found the error. But there is good news."

Richard perked up. "Okay?"

Sal relayed, "There is no need to protect anyone from the diffusion today, and anyone can actually hear Adam using any COM device."

Richard shook his head. "But how—" He stopped himself and said, "Okay, I'll let the president know, and I'll call the media."

Eve was listening to the exchange and offered to Richard, "I have my news feed ready to COM everyone, if you want me to do that?"

Richard said, "Do it."

Eve smiled and hurried away.

Richard retrieved his executive COM from his pocket and COMed Tsirch.

Sal peeled off to tell the others the news.

CHAPTER 56

The Good News Is

Tsirch and his guests sat on a dais, waiting for attendees and media to find their seats. Tsirch was talking on COM when the COM vibrated. He looked at the COM screen.

"Marilyn, thank you. Richard is COMing. I'll get back to you, okay?"

Tsirch spoke, "Richard, tell me something good."

Tsirch listened carefully.

"Okay and what about that audio feed?"

He methodically absorbed the message.

"Eve is going to do that?"

Tsirch took a relieved breath. "Thanks, Richard, we got this."

Tsirch closed his COM and put it away. He stood and walked to the center of his group and said, "I have to make an announcement."

Lucas's COM vibrated, and he got it out of his pocket.

Tsirch walked over to the microphone and spoke, "Hello, is this working?"

His voice echoed across the grounds.

He smiled and chuckled. "Yeah, I guess it is." He continued, "I know it's a little early for the festivities to start, but I have a few important announcements to make. I have some good news, some okay news, some good news, and some better news."

He paused. "Which do you want first?"

He looked around the garden area and asked, "What, no hecklers? Okay, here's the good news and the okay news. We made an error in our calculations. The diffusion event is not happening at noon today. It's been changed to tonight at midnight, in Greenwich Mean Time, which means at about 8:00 p.m. here."

There was a buzz among the crowd.

"Now more good news. We don't have to worry about the effects when the hologram appears."

A little applause was heard.

"Now for the better news. During the event today, we have been told that anyone with a COM will be able to hear the audio of the event. So hopefully everything goes as planned. Thank you."

Tsirch went back to his group, and they discussed the changes.

Validation

Eve was outside the SETI complex delivering the changes and messages to the worldwide media and public COMs. She finished the news feed and went back inside and joined the group.

Perry and Michael sat at their workstations, verifying data streams and COMing with other SETI stations. Amir and Dominique were enjoying the interactions with their visitors.

Sal was on a COM with Lucas.

"I asked Amir and Dom about that. They agreed that the Alphas found a way to tap into COM frequencies and sync that with the hologram at each particular coordinate."

Lucas said, "Yeah, hacking the COMs would be expected, but syncing that with all the coordinates is herculean."

Sal asked, "You heard from Brie about our hologram theory that she entered into the DOD Super-COM?"

Lucas said, "She got a level-3 result, but our basis of creating a hologram and a receiver simultaneously is non sequitur. It takes two separate signals."

Sal added, "But sending one signal, immediately following with a different type of signal, of course requires two different sources being sent to the same exact location."

Lucas replied, "Dom suggested that the generating source must have an automatic dual-mode switch. The logic was there, but the mechanical aspects are problematic. But I sent that along also."

Sal said, "Well, buddy, so much for solving the world problems. I'm gonna get back to socializing."

Lucas said, "Yeah, our visitor event is getting ready to unfold. Tsirch is about to speak. I'll let you know if ours works out."

Sal replied, "Okay, Lucas, later."

Sal rejoined the pre-event party. Amir and Dominique were talking to Richard and Johnny.

Eve and Yost were engaged in a serious conversation. She was setting up a camera at a separate table.

"Are you certain it's okay for me to record this segment?"

Steven nodded. "Sure. It is part of my soon-to-be unclassified report."

Eve took a printout out of her valise and gave it to Yost.

"Commander Yost, I know you were hesitant to divulge what you believe the hologram was saying as you read his lips. Why was that?"

Steve followed up, "Let me preface this interview with a personal declaration. I was born partially deaf and eventually had an extremely successful cochlear implant operation. I am a certified hearing-impaired translator in signing and reading lips. I am also yet a qualified Mission Commander.

"Now, Ms. Walker, as the Mission Commander, it was my responsibility to complete the mission and return all crew members home safely. My crew needs to work seamlessly to ensure that to happen. If I was to appear unstable, how could the crew trust my judgment and follow orders? So for the safety of the crew, I downplayed the event.

"Subsequently I realized that admitting to seeing an apparition, without verification of the sighting, would be problematic for my career. However, that rationalization was overshadowed when I took into account what the effect of such a sighting, if verified, would have on me personally and humanity as a whole."

He paused for a moment, and Eve smiled supportively.

"How did that affect you personally?"

He continued, "For me, I internalized the event in logical analysis. The sighting was simply an unexplained anomaly or either an alien manifestation or a religious apparition, any of which I could accept because I certainly did see the visage."

Eve observed, "I understand you did document the event, and in a classified brief, you described your word-for-word translation. What was the reason for wanting that to be classified?"

He replied, "To me that information was unusable for dissemination as it was MY interpretation and unverifiable, much like the sighting."

Eve continued, "You mentioned effects on humanity. What did you believe the effects might be?"

He explained, "If the sighting was just an unexplained anomaly, then it would fall into the category of little green men and alien abduction lore and government conspiracy. That would be that. However, if there was verification of the sighting, then the options of alien manifestation or a religious apparition would come into play, either of which lends to the need for more explanation and that may lead to doubts of personal convictions."

He paused and added, "We've already seen the anxiety, denial, turmoil, and confusion resulting from, first, the verified contact, and then the actual conversation."

Steve became introspective and deliberate of speech. "But now…now with the verification being seen by the entire world… maybe I can finally come to terms with my personal state of mind."

Eve nodded and calmly asked, "The printout you have in front of you is from the English translation of data stream. Can you verify if any of these words are what you remember from the reading of the lips?"

Steve looked down at the printout and smiled.

He asked, "If you have a pen, I'll circle the words."

Eve reached into her valise, took out a pen, and handed it to Steve.

He took the pen and smiled as he began to circle four words on the paper.

CHAPTER 58

The Words

Richard smiled at Eve as she activated the COM. They watched the entire documentation of her journey. The monitor displayed the final interview segment of Commander Yost circling the last four words in the last sentence on a printout of a data stream. The next segment was a split screen. On one side was the president in the garden, with his family, friends, watching the appearance and audio of Adam. The other side was of Dominique and Amir watching and hearing Adam's promised appearance.

The hologram and audio fell in sync in the final frames of the English version of the COM.

"We wish to share knowledge from across the universe that may help you prosper. We offer these words of purpose for your life. Whether life is a cycle or a step forward, live today as you believe."

Surely It Comes Quickly.

Eve smiled and snuggled back into Richard's arms.

ABOUT THE AUTHOR

Terol McCullar spent his first forty-two years working dozens of jobs, gaining life experience, and preparing for a career that brought him personal satisfaction as a California Correctional Officer and Sergeant Instructor known as T-Mac.

The author has acquired an insight into the passions and obstacles that forms the basis for one's self-motivation. His own motivation has been molded having lived through the changes witnessed from the 1950s and 1960s to the present. The dichotomy of witnessing both good times and turmoil was tempered by the belief in self-efficacy.

The author's passion for the law and teaching is commingled with his being a Singer/Songwriter.

This being his second published work is an incentive to pursue credibility as an author.